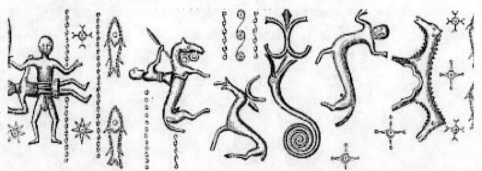

The Trickster and the Thunder God
Loki and Thor in Old Norse Myths

The Poetic Edda [Volume 2]

Maria Kvilhaug

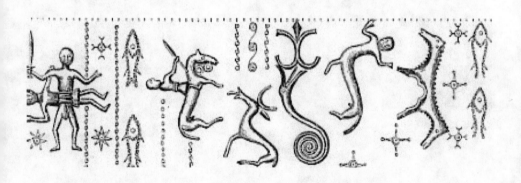

TLS

ISBN13: 978-1-959350-13-2

Set in: Symbola 10/11pt, Georgia 10/11pt, Gabriola 22/17pt
Weight: bold/italic

©The Three Little Sisters
USA/CANADA

-Footnotes have been converted to endnotes-

Contents

Forward

There are many books out there about Old Norse myths, whether they are retelling the myths in a modern fashion, or whether they are providing discussion and analysis of these myths, either on an academic or on a "Neopagan" level. I myself have published two non-fiction books about Norse myths, written on an academic level but often appreciated by an audience to whom these myths may mean something on a spiritual level; The Seed of Yggdrasill and The Maiden with the Mead. Adding to books about Norse myths, there are several available translations of the original myths, that is, the Old Norse texts written down by Icelandic and Scandinavian scholars of the 11th-14th centuries; the Edda poems, the Skaldic poems, the Prose Edda and the Saga literature. These are our written primary sources to Old Norse pagan mythology; which alongside runic inscriptions and archaeological finds may be referred to as historical sources in academic works.

I have also published one such book earlier; The Poetic Edda [Volume 1] – Six Cosmology Poems. In that book, I provided my own direct translations of six Edda poems from the Old Norse to modern English. Adding to these translations, I provided some commentary and interpretations, explaining my translations as they sometimes differ slightly from the norm insofar as I pay attention to the meaning of names and place names in a way few other translators have done. This book is a sequel to the latter work, a "Poetic Edda [volume 2]", and also consists of my own translations of several Old Norse texts. It differs from the first insofar as I have not limited myself to Edda poetry, but have also added several passages from the Prose Edda and also three Skaldic poems.

As such, this is not a book about Norse myths, and it is not a retelling of the myths in a modern language; this is a primary source in direct translation, providing the reader with the original myths as they were once written down by medieval scholars who were still familiar with the lore of old. As such, the translations provided here may be used as an additional primary source to Old Norse myths. The reader may notice that the English translations sometimes appear a little broken, that sentences could have been made in a more proper English. The reason for this is that I have chosen to translate as directly and literally as possible without losing meaning, this to give the reader a sense of the original language, as a way of better perceiving the Old Norse mindset.

I have here collected all the myths in which the characters Thor and Loki play a vital part, whether the sources belong to the Edda, Skaldic or Prose Edda category, and even added a passage from a saga known as Flateyiarbók. As to the focus on Thor and Loki, I have coupled these two gods because they often appear in the same stories and are intimately intertwined in all their endeavors. This is an attempt to show how the Aesir gods Thor and Loki appear in the whole lore of old, and by putting these stories together in a natural chronology based on how they are also presented in the original texts, I hope to show how there was indeed a red thread to these stories, even with character arcs and a build-up towards a climax, showing a larger myth containing all the smaller ones. I will leave it up to the reader to recognize this larger storyline. The only main Edda poem that I have left out here is the Allvísmál [The Song of All-Knowing], in which Thor plays the role of a father about to wed his daughter to a dwarf called All-Knowing. I have left this story out because it is one of the poems I provided in volume 1. If this poem had been a part of this book, it would have appeared at the very end.

Enjoy!

Maria Kvilhaug

CORNELIUS TACITUS: GERMANIA (80 A.D.):

"In their [the Germanic tribes´] ancient songs, their only way of remembering or recording the past, they celebrate a god born of Earth, Tuisco, and his son Mannus[1], as the origin of their people, as their founders.

To Mannus they assign three sons, from whose names, they say, the coast tribes are called Ingaevones; those of the interior, Herminones; all the rest, Istaevones.

Some, with the freedom of conjecture permitted by antiquity, assert that the god had several descendants, and the nation several appellations, as Marsi, Gambrivii, Suevi, Vandilij, and that these are nine old names.

The name Germany, on the other hand, they say is modern and newly introduced, from the fact that the tribes which first crossed the Rhine and drove out the Gauls, and are now called Tungrians, were then called Germans. Thus what was the name of a tribe, and not of a people, gradually prevailed, till all called themselves by this self-invented name of Germans, which the conquerors had first employed to inspire terror.

They say that Hercules [Thor[2]], too, once visited them; and when going into battle, they sing of him first of all heroes. They have also those songs of theirs, by the recital of which ["baritus," they call it], they rouse their courage, while from the note they augur the result of the approaching conflict. For, as their line shouts, they inspire or feel alarm. It is not so much an articulate sound, as a general cry of valor. They aim chiefly at a harsh note and a confused roar, putting their shields to their mouth, so that, by reverberation, it may swell into a fuller and deeper sound."

Introduction

How old is the Thunder god? Or, more precisely, when and where did the first people conceive of one? We may never know. I would assume that it all began when people first began to perceive spiritual entities within or behind natural phenomena; a very, very long time ago. Spirits or gods or goddesses of thunder and storm and lightning have existed in the minds of people since time immemorial. In some places, at some times, they became gods with human-like personalities, family lives and narratives of their own. Thor [Þórr], the Norse god of thunder, possesses numerous attributes and functions that are often universal, but which are in their details particularly common to the Indo-European traditions.

His name, which means "thunder" in Old Norse, may be etymologically connected to ancient, Indo-European, Anatolian thunder gods such as Luwian Tarhunzas, Hittite Tarhunt and Thracian Zibelthiurdos, names that may have been inspired by Anatolian, pre-Indo-European thunder-gods such as the Hurrian Taru, but are also related to Western European thunder-gods like Gaul Taranis, Irish Tuireann, as well as to his Anglo-Saxon alter ego Þunor, and his Estonian derivative, Taara or Tharapita. When it comes to attributes, narratives and functions, Norse Thor also shares a lot with other Indo-European thunder gods such as Slavic Perun and his Baltic alter ego, Perkūnas or Pērkons ["Oak Striker" – "Thunder"], Greek Zeus, Latin Jupiter and Vedic Indra.

Each one of these gods is a chariot driving, battle-axe (thunderbolt) wielding god of thunder and lightning who is either married to or else the son of the Earth goddess, and who usually spends a lot of time slaying monsters on behalf of the gods and of humankind. The last decade has yielded new archaeological and genetic evidence for the origins of the Indo-European languages and culture types. Let us scroll back some seven to eight thousand years. Increasingly warlike, pastoral, nomadic tribes were roaming the Pontic-Caspian steppes of West Central Asia. There were many different tribes living there, moving steadily about. Some came from as far east as the Lake Baikal, descending from East Siberian Ice Age hunters. Others descended from Ice Age hunters from Eastern Europe who had gradually moved east into Central Asia. Others descended from Ice Age hunters of the Altai Mountains.

Some of them waged war with each other; others merged together and became new tribes. Among their descendants were the tribes that finally gave birth to the Turkic, the Mongolic and the Indo-European language families. Some six to seven thousand years ago, one of these newly merged tribes had successfully settled (to the degree a nomadic culture may settle) as far west as the north of the Caucasus and the Black Sea, to the east of the river Don, which forms a natural barrier between Europe and Asia. Earlier, archaeologists such as the Lithuanian-American Marija Gimbutas referred to this culture as the Kurgans, destined to change the Neolithic cultures of Old Europe forever. While embraced by other Eastern European archaeologists who had actually been doing research in situ, her "Kurgan (versus "Old Europe") hypothesis" was nevertheless rejected in Western academia for a long time, a "debunking" based more on an insistence of a different theoretical paradigm than it was based on any actual counter-arguments.

As proven by the Swedish archaeologist Erik Rodenberg even back in 1991, those responsible for debunking her theories in the west never dared to discuss the hard evidence that she provided, but simply (and irrationally) rejected her hypothesis outright. Recently, however, further evidence, not the least evidence of genetic ancestry, has proven Gimbutas right. Her Kurgans are now called the Yamna; Ukrainian for "Pit Grave" after their burial customs. It is now also quite certain that these were the first speakers of an Indo-European language. The Yamna were obviously successful and increased their numbers rapidly. Soon enough, some of them had branched out westwards to cross the river Don, meeting up with the Tripyllia-Cucuteni, a sedentary Neolithic village culture that had existed between the Don and the Danube River for thousands of years already.

They were culturally related to the Aegean Neolithic cultures that were to finally yield a Bronze Age civilization; the Minoan, the last Pre-Indo-European outpost of Europe. Entering the Danube river valley, some of the new tribes that had emerged from the meeting between the Indo-European Yamna and the Old European Cucuteni branched out into Anatolia and southeastern Europe, becoming Thracians, Greeks, and Anatolians (such as the Hittites). Not much later, the remaining Yamna expanded northwards. Five thousand years ago, these pioneers had settled an area that reached from the river Volga in the east to the river Rhine in the west, and which included the southern parts of Scandinavia.

This Neolithic "empire" has been called the Corded Ware culture, replacing the older Megalithic-Neolithic cultures that had existed in these areas before. Bringing their Indo-European language and traditions, they still met with several strong, native Neolithic cultures of the north, and soon enough, new branches such as the Germanic and the Balto-Slavic had formed. In Jutland and Scandinavia, the merging of the newcomers with the old evolved into what is often referred to as a Battle Axe culture, ultimately resulting in the Nordic Bronze Age and the proto-Norse culture. After about five hundred years, yet new branches arose as descendants moved south and west; the merging between these people and the older European populations led to the forming of the Celtic and the Italian branches.

To the easternmost part of their "empire", yet another branch formed which was to move southwards into Iran and the Indus valley. Everywhere they went; they met with and merged with the older populations, influencing their languages and their cultures while also getting influence right back at them. As the Bronze Age emerged, the ruling Indo-European classes of Europe maintained contact with each other across the tribal and geographical barriers, mutually influencing each other even further, and they always, it appears, brought with them their version of a thunder-god. There is little doubt that the Thundergod's place in the pantheons of Indo-European peoples was prominent, often taking the High Seat as the father or king of gods, or else as the oldest son of the king.

As the son of the king, the thunder-god is often more of a warrior hero type, and the Romans often equaled the hammer-wielding, Germanic Þunor to Hercules rather than to Jupiter, king of the gods. Usually, the thunder-god is a bit of both, a ruling all-father and an adventurous son. In Old Norse myths, however, the Thundergod's aspect as adventurous son became more prominent some time before the Viking Age. When Tacitus wrote about the "Germans" near two thousand years ago, he places a god called Tuisco and his son Mannus [Thor and his son Magni] on their top pantheon and as divine ancestors.

The god Wodan-Óðinn, on the other hand, is referred to as the less prominent Roman god Mercurius [Mercury], the messenger of the gods, to whom they also compared the Celtic god Lugh. This Classical identification between Lugh, Wodan and Mercury is certain – it is an identification we also find in votive altars from this time, when Romans, Celts and Germans alike happily identified their gods with each other´s, thinking that everybody worshiped the same gods, only by different names.

The fact that their gods all carried the same Indo-European ancestral roots probably also served to cement this assumption. At some point, however, the Norse Thundergod's role as the highest lord among gods and the father of men faded in favor of Óðinn. Why that happened may be due to dynastic changes during the Iron Age, when royal dynasties who thought themselves descended from Óðinn grew to prominence. Suddenly, Thor was the son of Óðinn rather than his ancestor.

Traces of older beliefs are found, however, in Snorri´s Prologus to the Prose Edda [see chapter 1 in this book], where Snorri clearly identifies Óðinn as a king of men - descended from the thunder-god, who in turn is associated with the Thracian and Anatolian branches of the Indo-European family. Even if we cannot read that story as a literally true account, the associations presented do in fact provide elements of a more ancient, historical reality.

Thor remained central and important to his people though, even more so than the subtle, unapproachable Óðinn, but he was no longer the god associated with kings and rulers. Or, as Óðinn himself says mockingly to Thor in the Edda poem Hárbarðsljóð; "Óðinn owns the earls who fall in battle, Thor owns the throng of thralls" (See chapter 5). With this humiliating remark, Óðinn, who is, ultimately, the god of higher mysteries and wisdom paths, sets Thor on a path towards self-insight and initiation where he, the toughest and the manliest of gods, must become like a bride, like a young boy, and like a weak, unarmed, defenseless stranger in order to reclaim his true power.

DIVINE ADVERSARIES

In Old Indian Vedic mythology, Indra is the great savior of the day, protector of gods and people against violent adversaries whose primary purpose is to obstruct the happiness and enlightenment of people. One of his main adversaries is Vritra, a huge, heavenly serpent of Asura stock – another divine tribe that became the enemies of the Devas, who are beneficial to people where the Asura are not. This ancient enmity between divine tribes is common to Indo-European myths and could appear to reflect some ancient schism: In Old Iranian mythology, the Asura are called the Ahura, but here, they are the ones who are beneficial to people while the Daeva are the bad ones.

The Norse Aesir[3] may very well be etymologically related to the Asura of Vedic and the Ahura of Old Iranian texts, but the Norse tradition had no Devas or Daevas, and historically speaking, this schism may have been particular to the eastern branches. The Iranian Daeva and the Vedic Deva/Devi are etymologically linked to Indo-European names for "god/goddess", such as the Latin Deus/ Dea, the Greek Theos/ Thea, and the Norse Tív, which usually appears in the plural, Tívar, containing both genders. In the Norse tradition, however, no opposition is known between the Aesir/ Ásyniur and the Tívar – they are the same. The latter, however; Tívar, is more universal and may be used for all the divine powers, while the Aesir belong to a particular tribe of gods.

However, the theme of supernatural conflicts must be Pan-Indo-European; In Norse myths, they have Jotnir, whose name actually means "Devourers", although they are generally taken to refer to "Giants", important and often very wise and powerful primeval beings who are vital to the universe, but who are also, generally, dangerous and often act as adversaries. We also have the Vanir, who are described as very beneficial and wise, worthy of being adopted into the Aesir tribe. From the way the Vanir are described in the myths, it is easy to imagine that they originated as gods of some of the people that the Aesir-worshipers encountered on their way and whom they blended with and incorporated into their tribe.

In his Ynglinga saga, Snorri Sturluson gives an eerily accurate account of how the "Men from Asia" lived to the east of the river Don[4], just like the historical, Proto-Indo-European Yamna people did five thousand years ago. According to Snorri, these "Asians" finally crossed the Don and found the "Vanir" living there, just like the historical Yamna met with the Tripyllia-Cucuteni once they crossed the river Don into Europe.

While Snorri´s other ancestral story (the one found in his Prologue to the Prose Edda and which is rendered in translation in chapter 1) may be preposterous in its claim to a Trojan/Thracian ancestry, his Ynglinga saga version, where the Aesir represent people who migrated into northern Europe from the east of the Don river, is so correct in so many details that one may seriously wonder if elements from legends about these earliest ancestors may have somehow survived into the Middle Ages - a remarkable feat; If it is true that the Norse Aesir are directly related to the Indian Asura and the Iranian Ahura, then the concept of Asura/ Ahura/ Aesir as a tribe of gods must be at least five thousand years old.

Incidentally, that would roughly be the time when a cultural separation between the European and the Asian branches of the Indo-European culture actually took place. Little less than four thousand five hundred years ago, the westernmost parts of the Corded Ware culture mentioned earlier began to branch into Germanic and Balto-Slavic, Celtic and Italic Copper Age cultures, a result of their merging with several different, ancient European cultures, while to the southeast of their "empire," the same culture branched into an Indo-Iranian culture.

This was the culture that finally experienced a schism; the Vedic-Indian branch brought the divine tribe of the Devas with them into the Indus Valley, banishing the Asura, while the Iranian cultures favored the Ahura and banished the Daeva. It is probable that the schism was particular to this eastern branch: In Norse myths we simply do not find the same clear schism, at least not so evident. Unlike the Asian branches, we find no concept of absolute evil on one side and absolute good on the other - although the core to conflict with otherworldly creatures certainly is there too.

In Norse myths, all the diverse powers are and remain essential to the creation of the universe, even to its continuance, whether they be gods, giants, elves or dwarfs; each of the cosmic-spiritual powers is acknowledged rather than judged. The often conflicting tribes of gods and giants often keep truce, and while having peace, they keep visiting each other, seeking knowledge from each other, marrying each other, befriending, adopting and having children with one another.

If mythology reflects ancient social realities - and in view of the latest archaeological and genetic discoveries, they do - then this was the reality that the people who brought the Aesir to the north lived with, and their descendants. While war and battle was an integral part of life, conflict leading to truce and alliances would usually be preferable to outright war, and no enemy had as yet been so hated that they became symbols of absolute evil; even the darkest and most mischievous of powers were still honored in poetry and myth, often as sources of valuable knowledge and power.

THE TRICKSTER

The myth of Thor and the Middle World Serpent has a very old root, one that must have existed before the separation between the eastern and the western branches of Indo-European traditions. According to the Rig Veda, the snake Vritra ["The One Who Surrounds"] kept the waters of the world captive until he was killed by Indra, liberating the imprisoned rivers.

Before the battle, which took place as soon as Indra was born, he had drunk a huge amount of the sacred drink, Soma, in order to become sufficiently empowered before using his thunderbolt to win the battle. The Soma [Haoma in Iranian tradition] was a sacred drink that was directly related to the Old Norse concept of a precious mead of poetry, inspiration, wisdom, memory and immortality, a concept also found in many other Indo-European traditions. As we shall see, Thor tackles both the en-girdling serpent and a large kettle of mead for the gods in chapter 11 of this book.

In the Vedas, Indra´s thunderbolt weapon was fashioned by a god of artisanry, Tvaṣṭr, and given to Indra in order to destroy Vritra - despite the fact that the same god, Tvaṣṭr, was also the father of the serpent Vritra. This ambivalence is also seen in the Norse god Loki, who is father to the Middle World Serpent and who often provides the Aesir with great gifts and solutions to the problems he has also caused in the first place. This theme of ambivalence in certain very creative kinds of gods or spirits is quite common and widespread and well-known from many shamanic mythologies as well. Nobody has ever been able to agree on the meaning of Loki´s name.

The closest word in the Norse language itself would be loka – "to close", or logi – "flame" – and in the myths he is also referred to as Loptr, which literally translates as "Air". However, the uncertainty regarding his name means that it is possible that his name derives from some earlier or foreign source – there have been attempts to link him to the Celtic god Lugh, who is often pictured with mistletoe and who was otherwise identified with Wodan by people who worshiped either of these gods.

That Loki may be a shady aspect of Óðinn is by no means improbable, but the exact origins of the Loki character is, it must be concluded, unknown: even if we may find similarities here and there, suggesting some very ancient, shared root themes, such as with Tvaṣṭr, it appears that Norse Loki long since took on a life of his own in Old Norse mythology. There is no evidence at all that Loki was a worshiped god, even if he may have descended from one. He is, after all, father to Death [Hel] herself, and mother to inter-dimensional travel (Sleipnir), also he is the father of the power that separates the worlds of the cosmos (the Middle World Serpent), and to the great wolf of Greed who is intended to swallow Óðinn.

He is associated also with a stock of wolves who set the heavenly bodies in motion by chasing them, and which eventually will swallow them too. He is grandfather to Night, the dark goddess who birthed the Earth goddess, mother of Thor, and brother to Wind Lightning – Byleistr – a name for Óðinn, the highest god of creation. When he is bound beneath the earth, he creates earthquakes. His Cosmic, larger, alter ego is Outer World Loki (chapter 5), who creates great illusions for gods and men.

As such, Loki is ultimately a great, ancient, cosmic creator god of immense power, on par with Óðinn and the giant stock too. However, his function in the myths has fared the way of Thor; while Óðinn sits smugly in his High Seat, both Loki and Thor have devolved into younger gods who, like young warriors and aspiring shamans need to explore the world by traveling, and who - often together - set out in order to achieve whatever knowledge the gods require from them.

While Thor was clearly a god who was worshiped widely by Norse pagans, Loki was not, but still played a central, vital core part to almost every mythical narrative there is to find in Old Norse sources. One of the skalds even refers to him as the very catalyzer of the stories: Sagna Hrærir – the Stirrer of the Stories.

In many ways, Loki represents the core conflict of the human condition; our amazing creativity, clever solutions and incredible daring combined with the many unexpected consequences of our actions and our need to fix the problems we created. There is also soreness to his story. The many myths concerning him and Thor (they usually appear together) have been left to us in a conspicuously logical order, a sort of intentional, but hidden chronology.

When Snorri Sturluson wrote his Prose Edda, he divided it into three parts. The ones that, thematically speaking, concern us here, and which have been translated and presented in this book, are from the first and the second part, the Gylfaginning and the Skaldskaparmál. The Skaldskaparmál, the second part, fits into the middle of the Gylfaginning like a hidden pearl within the oyster, and when using the latter as the framework [beginning and end], the former functions as the middle of the story, also providing the oldest and most enigmatic of our primary sources, the Skaldic poems.

Likewise, the Edda poems that Snorri refers to and quotes from are also presented in a sensible chronology in the original leather Codex, and are also referred to in due order in the Prose Edda. By following this clue to chronology, I have in this book presented all the primary sources (original, Old Norse written sources on mythology) concerning Thor and Loki in a particular order that makes sense as a whole, as if all the different stories were intended to tell one long story: It begins with Loki being a true friend and companion to the gods, serving them in every way, solving the problems that he is always blamed for and punished for - even when other characters could actually have taken similar responsibility.

His many gifts to the gods are never recognized – all praise goes to the one who is blameless and pure. One day, he has had enough and turns on them all. Jealousy overcomes him, and he finally commits the ultimate crime – using his high intelligence to trick a disabled person into committing murder. His role as the enemy of the gods that he once was a part of is cemented.

Detail from the Gosforth cross, Cumbria, an area settled by Norse peoples between the 9th and 10th centuries and which, despite being a cross, contained numerous scenes from Norse myths.

The cross dates to about 950 AD. This is a detail showing the bound Fenrir wolf [above], and Thor who goes fishing with Hymir and pulls up the Middle World Serpent.

THE PRIMARY SOURCES

FLATEYJARBÓK (CHAPTER 9 IN THIS BOOK): The latest (youngest) source in which Loki is described, this formidable work was written down between 1387-1394, consisting of several long sagas about kings and heroes as well as a number of short stories, most dating back to the Viking Age, however the late date of the writing means that it is more heavily colored by medieval, Christian thought than the other sources applied in this book.

PROSE EDDA BY SNORRI STURLUSON (ALL CHAPTERS): The Prose Edda was written by Snorri (1179-1241) around 1225 A.D. It was intended as a treatise and explanation of Edda and Skaldic poetry, especially meant to explain all the allegories, metaphors, kenningar and heiti in such poetry. The book consists of three parts, the first being Gylfaginning, in which Edda poetry is explained, the second being Skaldskaparmál, in which Skaldic poetry is explained. The third, Háttatal, is not represented in this translation, where I have picked out and presented all the chapters featuring Loki and/or Thor.

EDDA POETRY: The Poetic Edda or Elder Edda is a collection of Pre-Christian poetry about gods and heroes, first written down sometime during the 11th-12th centuries but probably dating, in the form they were remembered at the time of writing, to the late Viking Age [9th-10th centuries]. The poems in which Thor and/or Loki feature prominently are:
- Hárbarðsljóð (Chapter 5)
- Þrymskvíða eða Hamarsheimt (Chapter 5)
- Hymiskvíða (Chapter 11)
- Vegtamskvíða (Chapter 12)
- Lokasenna (Chapter 12)
- Allvismál (See The Poetic Edda [Volume 1] – Six Cosmology Poems)

SKALDIC POETRY: Skaldic poetry ranks among the oldest and most uncorrupted known sources to Pre-Christian poetry and mythology and is unique because the individual authors are named and often mentioned in saga sources. In his Skaldskaparmál, Snorri quotes stanzas from several poems (see chapter 1). The skaldic poems that are preserved in more than one verse and which deal directly with Thor and/or Loki are:

- Haustlǫng by Thióðolf af Kvinir , ca. 900 A.D.(Chapter 4 & 6
- Þorsdrápa by Eilifr Goðrúnarson, ca 1000 A.D. (Chapter 7\
- Húsdrápa by Ulfr Uggason, ca 965 A.D. (Chapter 9)

About the Authors

Not all of our written Old Norse sources have known authors, and many of them were probably written down by a whole redaction of chroniclers and scholars, some of whom were monks – and almost all the chroniclers and scribes were Icelanders of the 11th-14th centuries. Iceland of this High Medieval era saw a blossoming of literature and education, embracing the new art of writing Latin letters onto leather and make them into books.

By the year 1000 AD, many Icelanders had become Christian, and at the All-Parliament of that year, 50 % of the adult male landowners – those who had the right to vote - voted for Christianity to become Iceland's new official religion. In other Scandinavian countries, the conversion did not go as smoothly.

Norway, we know, saw civil wars and centuries of conflict before the death of Ólaf the Holy in 1030 AD. Despite this Christian king losing his final battle of Stiklestad, the decades that followed actually led to the country finally accepting Christianity after a long and hard opposition from devoted Heathens. From Sweden, our sources to historical details in this era are few, but it would appear that the conversion happened even later; only in 1080 AD was the great pagan center at Uppsala destroyed and replaced by a church. In Iceland, the conversion happened by democratic vote.

This democratic mindset - not the least this pagan mindset - may have played its part in the fact that the winning, Christian fraction at the parliament acknowledged each person's right to believe and worship as they wanted, the way it had always been among Norsemen before, for as long as the great public cult was sponsored annually in some way.

Now, that cult was Christian rather than pagan, but the 50 % of people who still believed in the old ways were allowed to believe as they wanted for another hundred years before the more totalitarian attitudes of the Medieval Church finally started to sink in. In Iceland, however, the benefits of the Medieval Church started to sink in a lot earlier than any deeper understanding of the Christian faith or the tenets and decrees of Rome among the general population.

Icelanders descended from exiles, mostly Norwegians who had seen no other place for them to settle after being on the losing sides of civil wars, or as my own grandfather humorously and admiringly used to say; "Icelanders descend from the Norwegians who refused to bend the knee to a central king."

Being "exiled" and uprooted may, in my experience and observation, often lead to a keener interest in one's roots than the people who actually live closer to these, geographically speaking. In any case, Icelanders soon revealed themselves to be the foremost among chroniclers and storytellers and preservers of their own ancestral lore.

As soon as the art of writing books became available to them, they began writing down and documenting their own history, their best poetry and their myths and legends. What makes some of these works so valuable to us who study the Pre-Christian cultures of Scandinavia is just how close in time and culture these chroniclers actually were to the pagan ancestors that they were describing or quoting from.

The art of writing came to Iceland with Christianity, by the year 1000 AD. Paganism was not outlawed before a hundred years later. Paganism still existed in other Norse countries that these Icelanders dealt with, in Norway until the 1050s, in Sweden until 1080. The earliest Icelandic chroniclers still lived among real life pagans whose cultural roots were thousands of years old, and who had never known the results of thousand years of religious oppression and oblivion.

If, say, paganism was dead by the year 1100, there would still be a lot of older people who remembered, and it usually takes a few generations before people stop remembering the tales of old – particularly in such a storytelling culture as the Norse was. When Snorri Sturluson wrote his most famous works during the 1220s, he explained the need for a Prose Edda – a treatise on how to make poetry – by pointing out that young people nowadays (in the 1220s) no longer seemed to understand the poetical references to pagan mythology.

He seems to be speaking to the older population, his peers, who may have started to notice this lack of comprehension in younger people much the way we who remember a time before the mobile phones will look at younger people now, wondering who was better off.

Few of these very earliest written works have survived, apart from a few fragments. But we know that they existed because of the references in later works and copies. Fortunately, medieval scribes kept copying older works, and for centuries on end, Icelanders copied numerous books from these earliest chroniclers.

Even as late as 1387, a group of Icelandic chroniclers set out to document the history of their ancestral Norway, a country which had recently been bereft of its literate class during the Black Death some decades earlier.

In their great work Flateyjarbók, they copied (and probably edited) not only older works on Norwegian history, but also histories of the settling of Iceland alongside late medieval versions of pagan myths, as well as an Edda poem that had otherwise been lost to us, the Hyndluljóð. Had it not been for this late redaction, we would only have known about this important Edda poem from fragments and references in other works, and we would not have heard of how Freyia got her necklace either.

THE POETIC EDDA

The Edda[5] poems were probably first written down during the late 11th century. This was that century where some half of the population was still pagan. It is very likely that many of the poems were composed much earlier, during the pagan era, and that any minor Christian influence that is detectable may be due to that influence on those who would write the poems down later.

It has been suggested, by analysis of the traces of dialect in these poems, that many of them may have been composed in their present form by skalds at the court of Hlaðir in Trøndelag, Norway, during the religious wars of the early 11th century. Hlaðir was a pagan stronghold in firm opposition to Ólaf the Holy until the very end. However, we do not know who composed the Edda poems and when, although many of the myths must be a lot older than the actual poems we know.

Neither do we know who wrote them down the first time; although there has been a tradition of assuming that the Edda poems were first written down by one Sæmundr Fróði (Sæmund the Wise) Sígfusson, who lived between 1056–1133, a priest and a scholar. He was one of the first to write a History of the Norwegian Kings in the Norse language, a work that has been lost to us, but which we know was one of the main sources to Snorri Sturluson's Ynglinga saga and Heimskringla.

According to Icelandic folklore, Sæmund learned the dark arts and made a pact with the Devil so that he is brought safely back to Iceland from Europe on the back of a seal. Fortunately for Sæmund, a bible popped up on the beach before him when he reached his home shores and used the holy book to beat the seal to death, and thus conquered the Devil.

This folklore about a great scholar who lived during the long century of conversion is clearly a blend of pagan and Christian perceptions, mixing shamanic narratives of supernatural, shape-changing travel with the negative reactions of a Christian audience, perhaps one of the many originally pagan themes that were being re-shaped in order to make their audience forget the purpose of the pagan lore and teach them how to think more like Christians, perpetually condemning the pagan elements of the story as devilish and bad, no matter how life-saving benevolent that seal-shaped devil had actually been.

Whether Sæmund the Wise was the one who wrote down the Edda poems first or not, we cannot know for certain. But the first manuscript was copied several times, and we have fragments from several different copies in addition to one surviving manuscript, probably copied during the early 13th century, a little before Snorri wrote his other works. This manuscript, the only one which survived, was mysteriously hidden away and believed lost for centuries. It did not surface until 1647, when some farmer gave it over to the Icelandic bishop, who recognized the ancestral treasure and made sure it was preserved, copied and translated.

We know that the Medieval Church would often persecute books
that were deemed dangerous to their tenets, and many of these
earliest chroniclers may have had very blurred boundaries between
the pagan mindsets of their parents and grandparents and the newer
ideas from abroad. I think it is entirely possible that persecution of
books was the reason why so many early books vanished or only
survived in fragments or revised copies, and may be a reason why
"The Poetic Edda" as a whole manuscript was hidden away by
people who had obviously also taken care to preserve and protect it
– from the Church authorities.

Thanks to the efforts of people who saw the need to preserve this
part of history even when it was illegal, we have access to a body of
mythical, poetical lore that is closer in culture to the original pagan
form than most other European works on ancestral lore. In most
other places, ancestral lore was usually written down centuries after
the Christian conversion of these countries. Even if lore kept being
orally transmitted, centuries and centuries of Christian perception
of what is being told will inevitably alter the pagan stories quite
radically before they are finally written down, what we may also see
in Icelandic sagas of the 14th century in particular.

Even when dealing exclusively with the oldest of legends, these
late works display a much heavier Christian influence on both events
and how the characters of the stories are being perceived than what
we see in earlier works that were closer in time to the pagan past.
While the Edda poems keep dealing with deeply pagan subjects
such as sacrifice, death-journeys and initiation, testifying to having
been written down earlier when there was still a higher tolerance for
these things, it is clear that by the time of Snorri Sturluson, caution
is exerted.

THE PROSE EDDA

Snorri Sturluson was an Icelandic chief and scholar who lived between 1179 and 1241 AD. During the 1220s, he wrote several important works such as the Sagas of the Norwegian Kings (Heimskringla), with its invaluable Ynglinga saga, an important source to pagan mythology and ancestral lore, especially as it also quotes the Skaldic poem Ynglingatál – a source reaching back to the early 10th century – during deep Heathen times.

He also wrote the work that has become known as the Prose Edda, which is essentially a treatise on Old Norse poetry and how to understand the metaphors applied in Edda and Skaldic poetry, metaphors that were alluding to pagan myths and concepts. Incidentally (or not), Snorri wrote a masterpiece on pagan mythology that may be used as a key to understanding older, deeply pagan poetry as well as a key to understanding pagan myths in themselves.

We know that many copies of Edda poetry were lost to us, and that the only surviving one was hidden from the Church authorities for centuries, so it should come as no surprise that Snorri made an effort to tone down the pagan elements in a way we do not see in Edda or Skaldic poetry. However, his understanding of these metaphors and these myths are profound, as is his mastery of the art of telling without telling.

While careful about not offending the Christian authorities, adapting to a (relatively) Christian audience, Snorri still manages to either tell the stories in full, or else leave enough clues for us to fill in the gaps by studying the poetry he is referring to, or by studying comparative mythology and historical sources. As such, Snorri's Prose Edda is invaluable as a source to pagan myth; and it is the very key to understand the other sources.

In the Ynglinga saga, Snorri Sturluson mentions that his most important teacher and written source was Ari hinn Fróði Þorgilsson (Ari the Wise Thorgil's son), an Icelandic chronicler who lived between 1067–1148, growing up in an era when actual pagans still existed around him, being a fully grown man before paganism was finally outlawed. According to Snorri, Ari "learned a lot from Þuríð (Thurid), the daughter of Snorri góði." Góði referred to a pagan priest and lawman.

According to Snorri, Thurid was very knowledgeable ("hon var spök at viti"), she remembered her father, the pagan priest and lawman, and he had been thirty years old before Christianity came to Iceland (in the year 1000 AD), he had lived to hear about the death of Ólaf the Holy (in 1029), and only died the year after.

As such, her father personally knew both the old and the new times, and as a pagan priest had been educated in the knowledge of the past religion and its laws. In Snorri's time, Thurid was probably still a weighty source, for by mentioning her and her father as the original oral sources to his own most important written source, Snorri Sturluson could confidently declare that with a formidable teacher such as Thurid Snorradóttir, it was not strange at all that "Ari (his source) was truly wise and knew a lot of ancient tidings" ("Ari væri sannfróðr at fornum tíðindum"), for he had known old people who had been wise and knowledgeable of the old ways.

It is indeed true that the first Icelandic chroniclers had access to people who still remembered the tales of their parents and grandparents who had been pagan. However, Snorri Sturluson finally concludes, the most accurate historical accounts are to be found in skaldic poetry, for these were composed in the times of the events they describe, and even when they praise a king, all the listeners would know if the poet lied, since they had all been there. As such, the most accurate and truthful sources are the poems, "if they are correctly recited and wisely perceived" (En kvæðin þykkja mér sízt or stað færð, ef þau eru rétt kveðin ok skynsamliga upp tekin.)

THE SKALDS

While most of our sources were chronicled by Icelanders, many of the poets behind the Skaldic poetry that was recorded into sagas and other works by the early scribes were actually Norwegian. The poem Haustlǫng was composed by the Norwegian skald Þióðolfr ór Hvini – "Thióðolf from Kvina[6]". He was also called Þióðolfr hin Fróði – Thióðolf the Wise.

We have no exact dates for his birth and death or just how old he became, but he must have lived sometime between 850 and 950, for he was a skald at the court of Harald Hárfagri (850-930) and of more or less the same generation of this first king to unite all the tribes of Norway. As such, his works may be taken for the works of a pagan who actually still lived in deep pagan times, during the middle of the Viking Age in Norway, when even the concept of a central king to rule all the independent tribes was still considered new and novel. He would also have lived exactly during the era of the first Icelandic settlers.

Thióðolf the Wise composed the famous masterpiece Ynglingatál (the Counting of the Ynglings) around the year 900 AD as a way of honoring the Vestfold king Ragnvald Heiðumhæri of the Ynglinga lineage, a petty king who was still alive to hear this poem about his ancestors, an account going back from Ragnvald thirty generations through the father line. The fact that this poem was composed for a powerful king who still lived and who had a very active relationship to his own royal, dynastic lineage means that the poem accurately describes how a late 9th/ early 10th century Scandinavian petty king would, in all seriousness, count his lineage in detail from named father to named son for thirty generations –what would account for at least a thousand years or more–a lineage that was counted all the way back to the gods, their divine ancestors.[7]

The Haustlǫng was composed around the year 900 AD as well, and it was offered as a way of thanking a man called Thorleif for having given to Thióðolf a beautiful, painted shield. On the shield were illustrations from known myths at the time; such as the story of how Loki had to rescue the goddess of immortality in order to save to gods from aging and dying, and the story of how Thor battled with the giant Hrungnir. In order to thank and pay for the gift, Thióðolf composed the poem Haustlǫng, describing the illustrations and the symbols and the background myths themselves through poetry and metaphors. As such, this poem is one of our oldest sources to pagan myths, made by a pagan poet in actual pagan times.

Another Skaldic poem of importance to those of us who study mythology is the Húsdrápa by the 10th Icelandic poet Ulfr Uggason ("Ulf son of Uggi"). We are only left with fragments of this poem, sadly, but at least thanks to Snorri Sturluson, who preserved a few verses of it in his Skaldskaparmál (Prose Edda), we know a little more about Viking Age mythology. We have not been left with the remaining verses, but we do have an account describing how, when and where the poem was composed.

It was year 985 AD, and the account is given in an Icelandic regional history chronicle, the Laxdæla saga: "To this wedding came a multitude of guests, for now the new guest house was ready. Present at this wedding was Úlfr Uggason; he had composed a poem about Ólaf Hoskuldsson and about the stories that had been painted in the guest house. He recited his poem there at the wedding. This poem has been called Húsdrápa [The House Song] and is very well composed. Ólaf paid him well for the poem."

Again, a mythical poem is composed in response to images presented to the poet, in this case, a new – and newly painted – hall, walls covered in mythical imagery to which a poet has been invited. The skald is well paid for his service, the new house somehow being served or sanctified by being given a poem worthy of the skills of the artist. The very last surviving skaldic poem honoring a pagan god is the Þórsdrápa - The Song of Thunder - by Eilífr Goðrúnarson ("Eilif son of Gudrun"), a Norwegian skald who proudly carried the name of his mother only, and who served at the court of Hákon jarl inn ríki (Earl Hákon the Powerful). This earl of Norway practically functioned as the sole king of all Norway from about 970 until his death in 995 AD. Earl Hákon descended from the royal lineages of Hálógaland in northern Norway, with their seat now at Hlaðir in Trøndelag.

His grandson (the junior) by the same name and title was to become the leader of the Heathen opposition towards the end of the pagan era, the one who was to fervently combat Ólaf the Holy, and their court was the last political and religious stronghold of those who were against the forced conversion and who tried to promote the old ways. It was likely the primary seat of a Heathen cultural resistance against the new religion, where pagan poetry such as the Edda poems (as we know them), may have been composed on the basis of older tales, perhaps as a way of countering the new ideas.

At the court of Hákon Earl (the senior), Eilífr lived and worked, composing his poetry and serving in his lord's army. He was probably of the same generation of the king, but we know very little about him and his life. His Song of Thunder [Þórsdrápa][8] is the latest pagan source to a pagan poem celebrating a pagan god, composed as late as the year 1000 AD.

Some years later, Eilífr let himself be baptized, and enthusiastically - albeit in complete conceptual confusion - composed the Song of Christ [Kristusdrápa]. It was composed in good faith but with both feet firmly planted in pagan soil, happily announcing that Christ, the "southern king", was now residing by the Urðarbrunnr – the Well of Origin – in the southern realm of the norns, a fitting description of Heaven as far as Eilífr was concerned.[9]

Other skalds whose verses have survived in Snorri's Prose Edda and whose verses have been rendered in this book (chapter 1) due to being about Thor or Loki are the following;

Bragi hinn gamli Boddason (Bragi the Old, son of Boddi). Norwegian. Lived between 800 – 850 AD. His poems are our oldest sources to Skaldic poetry, and his work was evidently recorded and often referred to, although we are left with only fragments. He is sometimes referred to as Bragi Skald, or as Gamli ("the old"). He is credited with a Skaldic poem about Ragnarr Lóðbrok, the Ragnarsdrápa, of which fragments only have survived, but which was once used as a source to the people who wrote sagas and accounts about this legendary, possibly historical, Danish king.Ölvir Hnúfa Kárason (Ölvir Cut-Nose son of Kári) was a Norwegian lord and a skald who lived during the late 9th and early 10th centuries, a contemporary to (and known to) Thióðolf the Wise. He is mentioned in several sources, and plays a significant role in Egill's saga Skallagrimssonar as a friend and ally to Kveldulf and Skallagrim before these had to flee from Norway to Iceland. Ölvir served both as a warrior and as a poet at the court of Harald Hárfagri alongside other famous court skalds.

Eysteinn Valdason Gamli (Eysteinn son of Valdi the Old) was a 10th century Icelandic skald, fragments of whose poems have been preserved in other works such as Snorri's. Little else is known about this person.

Þorbjörn Dísarskáld (Thorbjörn Bard-of-the Goddess) was
an Icelandic skald who lived towards the end of the pagan era
and who probably got converted in the end. His nickname may
mean that he was devoted to Freyia, or that he had composed
a famous poem to the Dís (Freyia), but in that case, the poem
is lost to us. There is sadly little more that is known about
Thorbjörn.

1: SNORRI INTRODUCES THE GODS

FRÁ TRJÓUMÖNNUM-ABOUT THE MEN FROM TROY
[PROLOGUS 3, PROSE EDDA]

3: Near the middle of the world there were built houses and
inns that have been the most famous, that which was called Troy
and we call Turk-land.[10] That city was built much larger than
others, and with greater art in many ways, with much wealth
and resources that existed there. There were twelve kingdoms
and one High King, and there were lots of tribal lands beneath
each kingdom. There were twelve chiefs there in the fortress.
These chiefs were greater than all other men who have ever
existed in the world when it comes to manliness in all deeds.[11]

There was a king there, named Munon or Mennon. He was
married to the daughter of the High King Priamus, and she
was named Tróan. They had a son, his name was Tror, the one
we call Thor. He was bred in Thrace by a certain duke whose
name was Lórikus, and when he was ten winters old he took his
father´s weapons. He was so beautiful of appearance when he
came among other men, like ivory inlaid in oak wood; his hair
was brighter than gold.

When he was twelve years old he had the full strength of a
man, he lifted from the ground ten bear hides at once. Then
he also killed duke Lórikus, his foster-father, and his wife,
Hlóra[12] or Glora, and seized the realm of Thrace, what we call
Thrúðheim [Power World][13].

Later he traveled widely and became acquainted with all the parts of the world, and won all by himself every contest against berserkers and giants and a large dragon and many beasts. In the northern part of the world there was an oracle called Sibylla, the one we call Síf [Kinswoman], and he had her for a wife. Her lineage I do not know. She was unusually fair, her hair was like gold.

Their son was Hlórriði [Loud/Glow Rider][14] and he was like his father. His son was Einríði [Sole Rider], his son was Vingeþórr [Friend Making Thor][15], his son was Móði [Rage],[16] his son Magi, his son Seskef, his son Beðvíg, his son Athra, the one we call Ánnan, his son was Itrmann, his son Heremóð, his son Skjaldun, the one we call Skjöld [Shield],[17] his son Bjáf, the one we call Bjár, his son Ját, his son Guðólfr [Divine Wolf], his son Finn, his son Fríallaf, the one we call Friðleif [Divine Heritage].

He had that son who is called Vóden. That is the one we call Óðinn. He was renowned for his wisdom and skill. His wife was Frígida, the one we call Frigg.

***

Translator´s note: None of the above should be taken as part of the original pagan, Pre-Christian Norse mythology, but rather as a Medieval interpretation attempting to place the history of Norsemen into a comprehensible and "universally known" setting (as it was then). However, this anecdote does echo some very ancient, prehistoric connections between the Norse thunder-god and other Indo-European traditions, and follows up by explaining how the Aesir, called "Asians", descended from the Thundergod of Anatolia and Thrace, arrived in Scandinavia a long time ago. It also contains many elements of actual myth and legend.

While this version, where the Aesir descend from Thor, part Thracian, part Trojan, fits into a fanciful Medieval European tradition of assuming descent from some famous Classical culture, there is another version that places the origin of the Aesir (or the people who worshiped them) in a place that would simply not fit into this fanciful Medieval tradition, and which is, besides, eerily accurate, historically speaking: In another version of this story, the Ynglinga saga, Snorri places the original Aesir to the north of the Black Sea rather than Anatolia, as a tribe living to the east of the river Don ("Tanais" or "Tanakvisl"). They crossed the river to the west and blended with the Vanir before they moved into Russia ("Garðaríki"), then to Saxland and then into Denmark, Sweden and finally Norway.

This is also the take of the authors of the Flateyjarbók, as you will see in chapter 9. Incidentally, the area described in the Ynglinga saga and the Flateyjarbók was exactly where the proto-Indo-European Yamna people originated before they crossed the Don and entered Europe, blending with the Tripyllia-Cucuteni culture, before some of them moved south into Thrace and Anatolia while others moved north into Russia and from there into the southern parts of Scandinavia, where they introduced the Indo-European language form.]

FRÁ ÁSA-ÞÓR–ABOUT THOR OF THE AESIR
[GYLFAGINNING, 21, PROSE EDDA]

21: Then spoke Wandering Learner:[18] "What are the names of the other Aesir, or what are they doing, or what sort of great deeds have they accomplished?"

The High One[19] says: "Thor is the foremost among them, he who is called Ása-Thor or Sliding Thor.[20] He is the strongest of all gods and men. He owns that realm which is called Power Fields,[21] and his hall is called Swift Passing Moment of Shining.[22] In that hall there are five hundred floors and forty more. That house is the largest that men know about. As it is said in Grímnismál:[23]

Five hundred floors	Fimm hvndrvþ golfa
And forty more	oc vm fiorom togom,
I think there is at the wide-stretched	sva hygg ec Bilscirni meþ bvgom;
Swift Moment of Shine:	ranna þeirra,
Of all the halls	er ec rept vita,
That I know have risen	míns veit ec mest magar.
My son owns the largest.	

Thor owns two rams, they are so called: Teeth-Grinder and Teeth-Barer,[24] and a chariot that he drives, and the rams draw his chariot; this is why he is called Sliding/Driving Thor.

He also owns three treasures:

• One is the hammer Miöllnir [Grinder], the one that the Frost-Thurses and the Mountain Giants[25] know when he comes whirling through the air, and it is not so strange, for this hammer has crushed many a skull on their fathers and relatives.

• Next, he owns the most formidable treasure, the best; the Power Belt,[26] and when he buckles this belt around himself, then his Divine Might[27] doubles. A third thing that he owns, and which is particularly precious to him, is a pair of Iron Gloves.[28] He needs these gloves in order to be able to hold the hammer shaft.

• But there is none so wise, that he could tell of all his great deeds, yet still I can tell you so much about him that time would run out before I could tell everything I know."

Þórskenningar-Metaphors for Thor
[Skaldskaparmál 11, Prose Edda]

11: How shall we know Thor? By calling him son of Óðinn and Earth;[29]
Father of Greatness, Rage and Power;[30]
Husband to the Kinswoman;[31]
Step-father of Ullr;[32]
Ruler and Owner of the Grinder and the Power Belt and the Swift Passing Moment of Shine;[33]
the Protector of Ásgarð and Miðgarð;[34]
Enemy and Bane of Giants and Troll Women;[35]
Bane of Hrungnir, Red-Spear and Rules-Three;[36]
Lord of Binding Together and Maturing;[37]
Enemy of the Middle World Serpent;[38]
Fosterling of Friend-Maker and Listener/Heat.[39]

Thus spoke Bragi the Skald:[40]

42. The fishing line of Viðri's [Óðinn's] heir [=Thor] was not at all slack, when, by the Island Raiser's Ski [the boat], Great Magic [Middle World Serpent] uncoiled from the sand.	Svá kvað Bragi skáld: 42. Vaðr lá Viðris Arfa vilgi slakr, er rakðisk, á Eynæfis öndri, Jörmungandr at sandi.

Thus spoke Ölvir Hnufa:

43. The One Who Girdles
All Lands
[=Middle World Serpent]
and the Son of Earth
[Thor] raged.
Thus spoke Eilífr:

Svá kvað Ölvir Hnúfa:
43. Æstisk Allra Landa
Umbgjörð ok Sonr Jarðar.

44. Enraged stood Matur-
ing's Brother[41]
when the Father of Great-
ness [Thor]
struck the victory blow:
Neither Thor's nor Binding
Together's
stones [hearts[42]] trembled
from terror.

Svá kvað Eilífr:
44. Vreiðr stóð Vrösku
bróðir,
vá gagn faðir Magna;
skelfra Þórs né Þjalfa
þróttar steinn við ótta.

And as spoke Eysteinn Valdason:

45. Looking with piercing
eyes at
the Steep Path's Ring
[Middle World Serpent]
until the Fish-Dwelling
[sea] flowed
over the boat – was the
Father of Power [Thor].

Ok sem kvað Eysteinn
Valdason:
45. Leit á Brattrar Brautar
Baug hvassligum augum,
æstisk áðr at flausti
Öggs Búð, Faðir Þrúðar.

Eysteinn also said:
46. Kinswoman's Be-
loved [Thor] quickly
brought out his fishing
gear with the man:
So that we may stir
the Blend of the Frost
Covered One
[=the precious mead].

Enn kvað Eysteinn:
46. Sín bjó Sifjar Rúni
snarla fram með karli,
hornstraum ge-
tum Hrímnis Hræra,
veiðarfæri.

And he also said:
47. Thus violently re-
sponded
the Earth's Coal-Fish
[Middle World Serpent]
that Ull's Kinsman
[Thor] struck his fists
against the gunwale,
pushing broad planks
out.

Ok enn kvað hann:
47. Svá brá viðr, at,
Sýjur,
Seiðr, renndu fram
breiðar,
Jarðar, út af borði
Ulls Mágs hnefar skullu.

Thus spoke Bragi:
48. The hammer he lift-
ed with his right hand
when he, Strong-Axe's
Terrorizer[43] [Thor],
recognized the Coal-
Fish
Binding All Lands [Mid-
dle World Serpent]

Svá kvað Bragi:
48. Hamri fórsk í hægri
hönd, þá er Allra Landa,
Ægir Öflugbarða,
Endiseiðs of kenndi.

Thus spoke Gamli:
49. The one who never
nurtured betrayal
in his heart, the Lord of
Swift Moment of Shin-
ing,
[Thor] quickly destroyed
the
Fish of The Sea-Bed
[Middle World Serpent]
with the Bane of the
Mountain Whale[44]
[the hammer].

Svá kvað Gamli:
49. Þá er Gramr, hinn er
svik samðit,
snart Bilskirrnis hjarta,
Grundar Fisk með
grandi
Gljúfrskeljungs nam
rjúfa.

Thus spoke Thorbjörn Bard-of-the Goddess:

50. Thor has, with Ygg's
[Óðinn's] retinue [=the
Aesir]
defended Ásgarð with
great power.

Svá kvað Þorbjörn
Dísarskáld:
50. Þórr hefir Yggs með
árum
Ásgarð af þrek varðan.

Thus spoke Bragi:

51. And the Road of
the Side-Oar Ship's [the
ocean's]
Ugly Ring [=Middle
World Serpent]
stared defiantly up at
Hrungnir's Skull-Splitter
[Thor].

Svá kvað Bragi:
51. Ok Borðróins Barða
Brautar Hringr inn Ljóti
á Haussprengi Hrungnis
harðgeðr neðan starði.

And Bragi said:

52. Well have you held
back your steeds,
Tearer Apart of the Nine
Heads of Rules Three
[=Thor][45] with the infa-
mous drinking feast.

Enn kvað Bragi:
52. Vel hafið yðrum
eykjum
aftr, Þrívalda, haldit
simbli sumbls of
mærum,
Sundrkljúfr Níu Höfða.

Thus said Eilífr:

53. The Crusher of the
Relatives of the
Women who Run in the
Night [=Thor]
gaped with his arm-
mouth [banged with his
fist]
against the heavy, red
tool-grass [iron][46]

Svá kvað Eilífr:
53. Þröngvir gein við
þungum
þangs rauðbita tangar
Kveldrunninna Kvinna
kunnleggs alinmunni.

Thus said Ulf Uggason:

54. The Thick-Grown
Stocky One [Hymir]
was extremely terrified
by the
Goat-Owner's [Thor's]
heavy catch.

Svá kvað Úlfr Uggason:
54. Þjokkvöxnum
kvaðsk þykkja
þikling firinmikla
hafra njóts at höfgum
hætting megindrætti.

And also this:

55. The Powerful Bane of the Mountain-Man [Thor] let his fist ram into the ear of the Resident [giant] of the Bone of Reed Beds [rock]. A great damage it was. [...]	Ok enn þetta: 55. Fullöflugr lét fellir fjall-Gauts hnefa skjalla, rammt mein var þat, reyni reyrar leggs við eyra. [...]

And Thorbjörn Bard-of-the-Goddess said:

58. The crown of the Gorge[47] gave a clang The Caretaker[48] you broke completely. Before that you killed Bent Back and Disliked One[49], You made Large Ears[50] bleed; You stopped Hanging Gaping Mouth,[51] Fire-Spinner[52] died before; Still was the darkening life of Shamed Goddess[53] taken earlier.	Ok svá kvað Þorbjörn dísarskáld: 58. Ball í Keilu kolli, Kjallandi brauzt þú alla, áðr draptu Lút ok Leiða, léztu dreyra Búseyru; heftir þú Hengjankjöftu, Hyrrokkin dó fyrri; þó var snemr in sáma Svívör numin lífi.

Frá Loka Laufeyjarsyni-About Loki Laufey's son
[Gylfaginning 33, Prose Edda]

33: "Among the Aesir is counted the one whom some call the Slanderer among the Gods, and he is the origin of all treason, and a shame to gods and men. His name is Loki or Loftr[Airy], the son of Dangerous Hitter, the giant.[54] His mother is called Leaf Island or Needle.[55] His brothers are Wind Lightning[56] and Death Blinder[57].

Loki is beautiful and fair to look at, but evil of character and fickle in his behavior. More than other men he had that quality called cunning, sly tricks for every purpose. Often he led the Aesir into great trouble, and often he solved these troubles with his cunning advice. His wife is Sígyn[Victory Woman], and their son is Nári or Narfi[Corpse]."

***

Translator´s note: In Gylfaginning 10, we read: "Nörfi or Narfi was that giant called who built in the Giant World. He had a daughter whose name was Night. She was black and dark as her lineage. She was married to the man who is called Naglfari [Nail Traveler]. Their son was Abundance. After that she was married to the one called Ánarr [Ancestor]. Their daughter was Earth. Finally she was married to Dellingr [Shining/Famous One], and he was of divine lineage. Their son was Dagr [Day]." As Earth´s son, Thor is by this lineage actually a great, great grandson of Loki.

FRÁ BÖRNUM LOKA OK BUNDINN FENRISÚLFR-ABOUT LOKI'S CHILDREN AND THE BINDING OF THE GREED WOLF-
[GYLFAGINNING, 34, PROSE EDDA]

34: "Loki also had more children. Anger-Bidder[58] was the name of a giantess[59] in the Giant World.[60] By her, Loki had three children. One was the Greed-wolf.[61] Another was Great Magic, that is the Middle World Serpent.[62] The third is Hel [=Death].[63]

When the gods knew that these siblings were being brought up in the Giant World, and they considered the prophecies, that these siblings may cause misfortune; on the mother´s side they had a very bad legacy, and it was even worse on the father´s side, then All-Father [Óðinn] sent the Aesir on their way to claim the children and lead them to him.

[Great Magic – the Middle World Serpent:] And when they came to him, he threw the serpent out into the deep ocean that surrounds all lands, and the serpent grew so that it lies in the middle of the sea around all lands and bites its own tail.

[Death:] He threw Hel into Misty World[64] and gave her the power to rule nine worlds, so that she could lead away all those who were sent to her, the ones who die from illness and old age. She has great estates and halls there, and around them there is a fearsome high fence and an enormous gate. Her hall is called Dampened By Rain, her table Hunger, her knife Starvation, her slave Slow Walk, and her slave girl Slow Walk, her doorstep is called Falling Danger, her bed Sickly, her bed covers Shining Accident.[65] She is blue [black, dark] on one side, but has an ordinary complexion on the other side, so that she is easily recognized, somber and scary as she is.

[Greed:] The Aesir fed the wolf at home, and Týr alone had the courage to go and feed him" (...)

LOKAKENNINGAR-METAPHORS FOR LOKI
[SKALDSKAPARMÁL 23, PROSE EDDA]

• How shall we know Loki? By calling him the Son of Dangerous Hitter and Leaf Island, and Needle; [66]
• Brother of Wind Lightening and Death Blinder;[67]
• Father of the Hope-River´s[68] Demons; they are the Greed-wolf and Great Magic, that is the Middle World Serpent, and
• Death [Hel] and Nári [Corpse] and Choice;[69]
• Kinsman and Uncle and Comrade and Seat Companion to Óðinn and the Aesir;[70]
• Red-Spear´s Guest and Casket-Decoration;[71]
• Thief of the Giants, the Goat and the Fiery necklace and Iðunn´s Apples;[72]
• Kinsman to Sleipnir;[73] and Husband to Sígyn;[74]
• Enemy of the Gods;[75] and Harmer of the Kinswoman´s Hair;[76]
• Mischief-Smith;[77]
• The Sly God;[78]
• Slanderer and Tricker of the Gods;[79]
• The Counsel-Bane of Balder;[80]
• The Bound God;[81]
• The Great Enemy of Heimdall and Skaði[82]

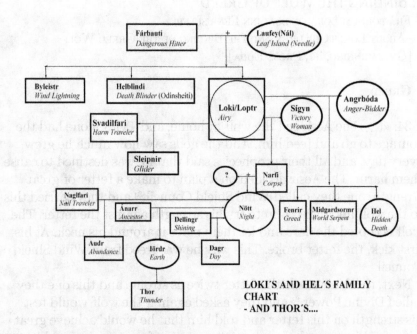

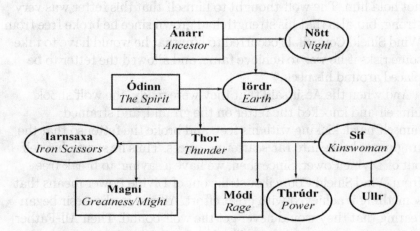

LOKI'S AND HEL'S FAMILY
CHART
- AND THOR'S....

2: BINDING THE WOLF OF GREED
FRÁ BÖRNUM LOKA OK BUNDINN FENRISÚLFR
-ABOUT LOKI'S CHILDREN AND THE BINDING OF THE GREED WOLF-
[GYLFAGINNING, 34, PROSE EDDA]-

GREED

34: «(...)The Aesir fed the wolf at home, and Týr [83] alone had the courage to go and feed him. And the gods saw how much he grew every day, and all their prophecies said that he was destined to cause them harm. The Aesir decided on a plan to make a fetter of great strength, one they called Wind Shield Council,[84] and they carried this to the wolf and dared him to try his strength against the fetter. The wolf accepted the dare and let them place it around his neck. At his first kick, the fetter broke. This way he was freed from Wind Shield Council.

Next, the Aesir made the fetter twice as strong, and this one they called Divine Power,[85] and they asked again if the wolf would test his strength on this fetter and told him that he would achieve great fame for his strength if such mighty pieces of engineering could not hold him. The wolf thought to himself that this fetter was very strong, but also that his strength had grown since he broke free from Wind Shield Council. It occurred to him that he would have to take some risks if he was to achieve fame, and allowed the fetter to be placed around his neck.

And when the Aesir said that they were ready, the wolf shook himself and knocked the fetter on the ground, and strained himself hard, kicking with his feet, and broke the fetter so that the fragments broke into far-scattering pieces. Thus he struck himself out of Divine Power. Since then, we have a saying: to break free from Wind Shield Council or strike out of Divine Power means that something is achieved with great effort. After this, the Aesir began fearing that they would never get the wolf bound. Then All-Father (Óðinn) sent someone named Shining One[86], Freyr's messenger, down into the World of the Black Elves,[87] where he met some dwarfs and let them make that fetter which is called Opening One.[88]

It was made out of six ingredients: The sound of a cat's steps, a woman's beard, the mountain's roots, the bear's sinews and the fish's breath and the bird's spittle. And even if you did not know these tidings before, you can now discover true proofs that you are not being deceived in the following: You must have seen that a woman has no beard, and there is no noise from a cat's running and there are no roots beneath a mountain, and I declare now by my faith that everything I have told you is just as true even if there are some things that you cannot test.

Then spoke Wandering Learner: "This I can see is true, as is spoken. I can understand the things you have given me as proofs, but what was the fetter made like?"

The High One says: "I can easily tell you that. The fetter was smooth and soft like a silk ribbon, and yet so firm and strong as you shall hear now: When the fetter was brought to the Aesir, they thanked the messenger heartily for carrying out their errand.

Then the Aesir went out on a lake they called Black Darkener[89] on that islet called Shrine Covered by Heather,[90] and summoned the wolf to them, showing him the silky band and asked him to tear it and declared that it was rather firmer than seemed probably judging from its thickness, and passed it to each other and tried it by pulling at it with their hands, and it did not tear; yet the wolf, they said, would be able to tear it.

Then the wolf replied: "It looks to me, concerning this ribbon, that I will not gain any fame from it if I do tear apart such a slender thread, but if it is made with deceit and trickery, then even if it looks thin, I am not having it around my legs."

Then said the Aesir that he would surely be able to break such a soft silky band when he had before broken great iron fetters, "however if you cannot break it, then you cannot possibly be a threat to us, and then we will free you."

The wolf says: "If you bind me so that I may not break loose, then I am sure you will stand by and leave me to wait for a long time before you help me out. I am not willing to have this bond put on me. But rather than that you question my courage, let one of you put his hand inside my mouth as a pledge that this is done in good faith."

Each one of the Aesir looked to the other and thought this was a great dilemma, and all refused to offer their hand, until Týr put forth his right hand and put it in the wolf's mouth. And the wolf struggled and kicked, but the more he struggled, the stronger the bond hardened around him, and the harder he fought, the tougher the band. Then all the gods laughed except Týr; he lost his hand.

When the Aesir saw that the wolf was bound completely, they took the cord that was hanging from the fetter, which is called Post[91] and fastened it deep down inside the Earth, and pulled her through a large protruding rock/stone slab – it is called Bellowing[92]. And they took a huge rock and shoved it even further down into the Earth, that is called Batterer,[93] and used this rock as an anchoring peg.

The wolf stretched its jaws enormously and reacted violently and tried to bite them. They thrust into its mouth a certain sword; the hilt touches his lower gums and the point his upper ones. This is his gum-prop. He howls horribly and saliva runs from his mouth. This (saliva) forms the river called Ván [Hope]. There he lies until Ragnarök.

Then spoke Wandering Learner: "Terrible children had Loki, and all these siblings are very important! But why did the Aesir not kill the wolf if they have such ill hopes for him?"

The High One replies: "So greatly did the gods respect their sanctuaries and their places of Truce[94] that they did not want to defile them with the wolf's blood even though the prophecies say that he will be the bane of Óðinn."

Image depicts all four Torslunda Plates. Plate Two, Upper Right Corner: Eight century representation of Tyr binding the Fenrir-wolf, Sweden

Photograph of one of the Torslunda Plates. Photographer: Knut Stjerna (1874–1909) - Knut Stjerna, "Hjälmar och svärd i Beovulf" (1903). [Common Domain]

3: The Birth of Sleipnir-Æsir rufu eiða sína á borgar-smiðnum

-The Aesir Break their Oaths to the Fortress-Smith-
[Gylfaginning, chapter 42, Prose Edda]

42: Then spoke Wandering Learner: «Who owns the horse, Sleipnir [Glider], and what is there to say about him?"

The High One says: "You do not know what there is to share about Sleipnir, and you do not know how he was conceived, and you shall soon learn that it is worth your while to talk about him.

It was early in the beginning-times that the gods had established Middle World[95] and made Valhalla,[96] then a certain smith came and offered to build them a fortress in less than a year and a half, a rock wall so strong it would easily withstand attacks from mountain giants and frost thurses, if they were to try and come into Middle World.

For salary, he wanted Freyia, and Sun and Moon as well. Then the Aesir gathered for Parliament and that deal was made with the building master that he should have what he demanded if he could build the wall within one winter's time. But if there was even one rock missing on the first day of summer, then he should have no salary at all. And he could not bring any man with him to work.

When they set forth these terms, he asked if he could use the help of his horse, Harm Traveler,[97] and Loki made them agree to that. On the first day of winter, he started building the wall, and in the nights he brought rocks with the horse. The Aesir thought it was quite incredible how large pieces of rock that stallion could pull, indeed the horse did twice as much work as the building master.

But the deal had been made with many witnesses and many oaths, for the giants did not dare to be together with the Aesir without such security, just in case Thor was to return home. But he had traveled east to destroy trolls. As winter passed, little lacked to complete the fortress wall, and she was so strong at nobody could possibly succeed in attacking it. And when there was only three days left before the first summer day, then the wall was almost finished even to the gates.

Then the gods gathered in their seats of judgment and asked each other who had been so foolish as to promise Freyia away to the giant world, and to darken the heavens and the air by promising away Sun and Moon to the giants.

Then all of them decided that this was the fault of Loki Leaf Island's son. And they said that he was worthy of a painful death if he could not find a way to stop the building master from finishing his work, and they attacked Loki this way.

Then Loki was frightened, and swore that he would ensure that the building master lost his claim, no matter how much he appeared to be winning it.

The same night, when the wall-builder drove away with the stallion Harm Traveler to get more rocks, then a mare ran out from the forest and started to flirt with and whinny to the stallion.

As the horse sensed the mare he became horny, broke through his ropes and ran after the mare into the forest, and the stonemason after to get his horse back.

Image of Óðinn riding Sleipnir, the eight-legged horse, Gotland 7th century

But the horse couple ran the whole night, and he was not able to do enough on his own, and the next day, the building did not run as smoothly as before.

And when the building master saw that he could not manage to finish his work in time, then the giant rage[98] came above him.

And when the Aesir now saw that here was a true mountain giant, they no longer felt they needed to keep their oaths. Then they call for Thor, and he came at once. And now the hammer Grinder hurled through the air.

Then he was given salary for his work, but not with Sun or Moon. He (Thor) did not even let him live in the Giant Worlds, for with the first thrust he crushed his skull into small pieces and sent him down into Misty World.[99] But the intercourse that Loki had with Harm Traveler made him pregnant, and after some time he bore a foal.[100] It was gray and had eight feet. And this horse is the best among the Aesir and among men.

It is said in the Vǫluspá: [101]
Then all the powers went
to the High Chairs of Fate,
the sacrosanct gods to discuss this:
Who had blended the air all with harm
or to the Devourer´s kind
given Poetry´s Maiden?

> Þá gengu regin öll
> á rökstóla
> ginnheilög goð, ok um þat gættusk,
> hverr hefði loft allt
> lævi blandit
> eða ætt jötuns
> Óðs mey gefna.

Oaths were broken then
words and promises
all the powerful words
that had passed between them.
Thor was then the only one striking
seized by rage;
He seldom sits
when he hears such things.

> Á gengusk eiðar,
> orð ok særi,
> mál öll meginlig,
> er á meðal fóru;
> Þórr einn þar vá
> þrunginn móði,
> hann sjaldan sitr,
> er hann slíkt of fregn.

4: Iðunn's Abduction-Ægir sækir heim Æsi.

Aegir Invites the Aesir Home [Skaldskaparmál 1, Prose Edda]

1: A man has been called Aegir [Terrifying One][102] or Wind
[Death]-Shielded.[103] He lives on that island which is now called Wind
[Death]-Shielded Island.[104]

He was very knowledgeable/versed in magic. He made a journey
to Ásgarð, and the Aesir could foresee his journey, and he was well
received even though many of the things they did to entertain him
were mere illusions.[105]

And when evening came and they were to drink, then Óðinn let
carry into the hall swords that were so bright that they shone, and
other light than this they had not while they were seated at the
drinking banquet.

The Aesir came to the banquet, and the twelve who were to sit
as judges sat down in their high seats, and they were the following
gods: Thor, Njǫrðr, Freyr, Týr, Heimdallr, Bragi, Víðarr, Váli, Ullr,
Hænir, Forseti, Loki.

The goddesses came to their seats just like the gods: Frigg, Freyja,
Gefiun, Iðunn, Gerðr, Sígyn, Fulla, Nanna.

Aegir thought it was all very splendid-looking. All the walls were
decorated with beautifully adorned shields. There was a lot of strong
mead there, and a lot was drunk.

Next to Aegir sat Bragi. The two of them drank together and
spoke, and Bragi told Aegir about many things that had happened
to the Aesir, and he started thus.

Þjazi jötunn rænti Iðunni

when Slave-Binder the Devourer Stole Iðunn
[Skaldskaparmál 2, Prose Edda]

2: Bragi said:

This here is the story about how three Aesir left home; Óðinn,
Loki and Hænir[106], and they traveled across mountains and
wilderness, and there was very little to eat. And as they came
into a certain valley, they saw a huge flock of oxen, and they took
one ox and put it to the earth-oven. And so they thought that
they would soon eat and that the meat must have cooked, but
when they opened up the earth-oven they saw that the meat was
as raw as before.

Images are taken from a medieval publication of The Prose Edda

-SÁM 66 (Stofnun Árna Magnússonar á Íslandi). 18th-century manuscript. Public Domain-

After a while more, they checked again. But the meat was not cooked now either, and they asked themselves how this could be possible.

Then they heard speech from the oak above them, and they agreed that the one seated up there was guilty of obstructing the cooking.

They looked up, and there sat an eagle, and he was not tiny.[107]

Then the eagle spoke: "If you will give me a good piece of your meat, then it shall soon be cooked." They agree to that. Then the eagle descended from the tree, sat down on the fireplace and swiftly gathered both the legs and the torso.

➤Then Loki was angry, grabbed a huge wand, lifted it with all his might and struck it against the eagle's body. The eagle bolted and flew upwards, and the wand stayed as glued onto his back, and Loki's hands were as glued to the wand.

The eagle did not fly higher than that Loki's feet were still touching on rocks and rock piles and the roots of fallen trees, and he felt as if his arms were being pulled off his shoulders. He cried and begged the eagle to let him go free.

Images are taken from a medieval publication of The Prose Edda

-SÁM 66 (Stofnun Árna Magnússonar á Íslandi). 18th-century manuscript. Public Domain-

➡ And the eagle said that he would never go free unless he swore that he should lure Iðunn with her apples out of Ásgarð, and Loki promised this.

He was let free and went to his traveling companions. And nothing more is told about this journey until they returned home.

At the agreed time, Loki lured Iðunn out of Ásgarð into a certain forest and said that he had found some apples there that he thought she would think particularly valuable and asked her to bring her own apples in order to compare them with the others.

Then came the giant/devourer Slave-Binder[108] in eagle's hide,[109] and he took Iðunn and flew away with her to his homestead in Thrymheim [The World of Drumming].[110]"

Loki náði Iðunni ok dráp Þjaza
Lóki Saves Idunn and Kills the Slave Binder
[Skaldskaparmál 3, Prose Edda]

3: "The Aesir went sick when Iðunn was gone, and they were soon getting grey and old.[111] Then they held Parliament and asked each other whatever each of them knew about the disappearance of Iðunn, and it was soon discovered that she was last seen when she left Ásgarð in Loki's company. Then Loki was seized and led out to stand before the Parliament, there they threatened to torture and kill him. He was frightened then, and said that he would search for Iðunn in the Giant Worlds,[112] if only Freyia would lend him the falcon hide[113] that she owned.

And when he got the falcon hide, he flew north into the Giant Worlds and came one day to the devourer, Slave Binder. He had rowed out to the sea, and Iðunn was at home. Loki transformed her into the shape of a nut and held her in his claws as he flew the fastest he could. And when Slave Binder returned home and discovered that Iðunn was missing, he took his eagle hide and flew after Loki, and his wings were eagle-blown [wind in his wings].[114]

And when the Aesir saw that the falcon came flying with a nut in his claws, and the eagle after, they went out beneath the wall that encircles Ásgarð, carrying huge piles of wooden splinters.[115] The falcon flew in above the wall and let himself fall down by the rock wall. Then the Aesir set fire to the splinters.

Images are taken from a medieval publication of The Prose Edda

-SÁM 66 (Stofnun Árna Magnússonar á Íslandi). 18th-century manuscript. Public Domain-

➥The eagle could not manage to halt his speed when the falcon escaped him, and then the fire reached his feathers so that he could no longer fly.

The Aesir were now close, and killed Slave Binder the Devourer inside of the Divine Gate [Ásgrindr]; that slaughter is widely famous.

But Skaði [Injury], the daughter of Slave Binder the giant, took helmet and byrnie and all sorts of army-weapons and went to Ásgarð to avenge her father. And the Aesir invited her to sit and offered her compensation and truce, and the first thing she should have for compensation was to choose for herself a husband among the Aesir. But she could only choose him by the feet, more she could not see.

Then she saw a pair of man-feet that were unusually beautiful, and she said; "I choose this one. Few things are ugly on Balder." But it was Njǫrðr from Ship's Harbor.[116]

In her truce terms, she had also demanded that the Aesir should manage something she was certain they would never be able to; and that was to make her laugh. Then Loki had an idea. He tied a rope to the beard of a goat, and the other end to his own genitalia. And they took turn pulling and yielding, and both of them were screaming loudly. Finally Loki rolled over and fell right into the lap of Injury [Skaði], and then she laughed. Then there was agreement between her and the Aesir."

AF ÆTT ÞJAZA-OF THE SLAVE-BINDER´S LINEAGE
[SKALDSKAPARMÁL 4, PROSE EDDA]

Design on purse lid from Sutton Hoo, Suffolk, 7th century AD – hawk chased by an eagle?

4: "It is also said that Óðinn offered to her the added compensation of taking Slave Binder´s eyes and hurled them up to heaven, and made two stars out of them."

Then said Aegir: "Great it seems to me that the Slave Binder must have been. Do you know more of his lineage?"

Bragi said: "Ale Ruler[117] was his father named, and about him I can tell you something that you might think worthy of mention: He was particularly rich in gold. When he died, and the sons were to shift the inheritance among them, then they used that for a measure cup; if each should get his equal share of the gold, then each of them should swallow an equal number of mouthfuls of it. Slave-Binder was the first among the brothers, the second was Returns to Source,[118] the third was Wanderer.[119]

And now we apply this saying amongst ourselves, that we call gold "the Mouth-Speech" of these giants. And in runes or poetry we hide the word "gold" in that way that we call it the "language" or the "words" or the "speech" of these giants."

Aegir said: "I think that is cunningly hidden in symbols [runes].[120]"

HAUSTLǪNG I-THE LONG AUTUMN
A SKALDIC POEM BY THIÓÐOLF AF KVINIR [850-930 A.D.]

2. The Eloquent Woman's
[Iðunn's]
Wolf [abductor = Þiazi][121]
Flew with loud-sounding
wing-flapping for a non-
short time ago [a very long
time ago] to The Tellers of
the Stories[122] [the Aesir/gods]
wearing the ancient shape
of the Year-Old [young
bird=Eagle]

The Eagle settled in the
beginning (of time) where
the Aesir carried food to the
earth-oven
The Fortress-Animal the
Mountains [giant] of the
Provideress [giantess][=Þi-
azi][123] was no lowly coward.

3. Partly Unblended Treason
[Þiazi]
was late to begin the cook-
ing for the gods*
The Helmet Clad Giver
[Óðinn]
of Wisdom to the Chains
[gods]
claimed that someone was
behind this
The Very Wise
Corpse-Thrower of
Wave Guts Seagull [=Eagle]
[=Þiazi]
spoke from the Age-Old
Tree [=Yggdrasill]
Hænir's Friend[=Loki] was
not fond of him

2. Segjǫndum fló Sagna
Snótar Ulfr at móti
í gemlis ham gǫmlum
glammi ó fyr skǫmmu;
settisk ǫrn, þars æsir,
ár (Gefnar) mat bǫru
(vasa byrgi-Týr bjarga
bleyði vændr) á seyði.

3. Tormiðluðr vas tívum
tálhreinn meðal beina;
hvat kvað Hapta Snytrir
Hjalmfaldinn því valda;
Margspakr of nam mæla
mór Valkastar bǫru
(vasat Hœnis Vinr hǫ-
num
hollr) af fornum þolli.

4. The Mountain Howler
[wolf =Þiazi] asked Armor
Step [Hænir] to share with
him a part of the sacred
meal,
The Friend of the Raven
God[Óðinn][=Loki] had to
blow the fire
The Battle-Hungry Ruler
of the Wagon of Friendship
[Þiazi] let himself descend
from above to where the
Loyal Protectors of Gods
[=the three Aesir]had
arrived.

5. The Decent King of the
Earth [=Óðinn] quickly
told the Son of Farbauti
[=Loki] to share the Whale
of the Spring of the Roaring
Belt [=the bull] with the
Servant Man [=Þiazi]
And the Cunning-Clever
Defyer of Gods [=Loki]
now parted the bull in four
up from the broad table
[=altar]

6. And the Hungry
Father of Giantesses [=Þi-
azi] then ate greedily the
Yoke-Bear [=bull] on the
oak-roots [=oak=ash=-
roots of Yggdrasill]-
This was a long time ago
- before the Deep-of-Soul
Hiding Beast [=Loki]
battered the War-Trophy
[=Þiazi] with a staff: [he
hit] the Powerful Enemy of
Earth[=Þiazi] from above
between the shoulders.

4. Fjallgylðir bað fyllar
fet-Meila sér deila
(hlaut) af helgum skutli
(Hrafnásar Vinr blása);
Ving-rǫgnir lét vagna
vígfrekr ofan sígask,
þars vélsparir vóru
varnendr goða farnir.

5. Fljótt bað Foldar Dróttinn
Fárbauta mǫg Várar
þekkiligr með þegnum
þrymseilar hval deila,
en af breiðu bjóði
bragðvíss at þat lagði
ósvífrandi ása
upp þjórhluti fjóra.

6. Ok slíðrliga síðan
svangr (vas þat fyr
lǫngu)
át af eikirótum
okbjǫrn faðir Marnar,
áðr djúphugaðr dræpi
dolg ballastan vallar
hirði-Týr meðal herða
herfangs ofan stǫngu.

7. Then was The Burden
of Sígyn's Arms [=Loki],
whom all gods perceive in
chains,
tied to The Educator
[=Þiazi]of the Ski-Dei-
ty[=Skaði]
The staff was glued to the
Ghost of the Giant Worlds
[=Þiazi]and the hands of
Hænir's Faithful Friend
[=Loki]were glued to the
staff.

8. The Vulture of the
Flock [=Þiazi], happy
with the catch, flew a long
way with the Clever God
[=Loki] so that the Wolf's
Father [=Loki] was about
to be torn apart
Then Thor's Friend
[=Loki] had to beg
for mercy from Gi-
ant-Child[=Þiazi]
Despite all his power the
heavy Air [=Loki] was
about to break.

9. The Lineage-Tree of
Hymir [=Þiazi]
asked the Stirrer of Stories
[=Loki],
mad with pain,
to bring to him The Maid-
en Who Knows
the Age-Cure of the Aesir
[=Iðunn]
The Belt-Thief of the
Fiery Gods[=Loki]
Then lured The Goddess
of the Benches
of the Watersource-Field
to the world of the
Rock-Ruler [=Þiazi]

7. Þá varð fastr við fóstra
farmr Sigvinjar arma,
sás ǫll regin eygja,
ǫndurgoðs, í bǫndum;
loddi rǫ́ við ramman
reimuð Jǫtunheima,
en holls vinar Hœnis
hendr við stangar enda.

8. Fló með fróðgum tíví
fangsæll of veg langan
sveita nagr, svát slitna
sundr ulfs faðir mundi;
þá varð Þórs of-rúni
(þungr vas Loptr of
sprunginn)
mólunaut, hvat's mátti,
miðjungs friðar biðja.

9. Sér bað Sagna Hrœri
sorgœran Mey fœra,
þás Ellilyf Ása,
Áttrunnr Hymis, kunni;
Brunnakrs of kom bekkjar
Brísings Goða Dísi
Girðiþjófr í Garða
Grjót-Níðaðar síðan.

10. The Residents of the
Steep Mountains
[=The Giants]
were then not sad (=were
then very happy)
that Iðunn had come
from the South [=Ásgarðr]
to the giants
All the clans of Yn-
gvi-Freyr [=gods and
men]
ageing and grey-haired
went to the Parliament
The Kings [=The gods]
were rather ugly of hide.

10. Urðut brattra barða
byggvendr at þat hrygg-
vir;
þá vas Ið með jǫtnum
unnr nýkomin sunnan;
gættusk allar áttir
Ingvifreys at þingi
(vóru heldr) ok hárar
(hamljót regin) gamlar.

11. Until they found
the Blood-Hound of
the Flowing Corpse Sea
[=wolf=thief=Loki] of the
Ale-Provider[=Iðunn],
and bound the thief,
the Tree of Treason
[=Loki], who had led
the Ale-Provider [=Iðunn]
astray.
"You shall suffer terribly,
Loki,"
thus spoke the angry one;
"until you return with
the Wonderful Maiden
Who
Increases the Joy of the
Chains [gods]
[divine joy] [=Iðunn]."

11. Unz hrynsæva hræva
hund ǫlgefnar fundu
leiðiþirr ok læva
lund ǫlgefnar bundu;
þú skalt véltr, nema,
vélum,
- vreiðr mælti svá - leiðir
mun stœrandi mæra
mey aptr, Loki, hapta.

12. I have heard this
that Hænir's Intent-Tester
[=Loki]
later tricked back the
Lover of the Aesir
[=Iðunn]
he flew away in the shape
of a hawk
and the Father of the Gi-
antess [=Þiazi]
that Swift Wing-Flapping
King-Tricker [=Þiazi]
followed the Child of the
Hawk [=Loki]
with Eagle-Wind
[=death].

13. The wood began to
burn
that the Sacred Powers
[=gods]
had made into fuel
and the Son of the Grasp-
ing One's[=giantess's]
Lover [=Þiazi] burnt:
In suddenness his journey
ended…

12. Heyrðak svá, þat (síðan
sveik opt ǫsu leikum)
hugreynandi Hœnis
hauks fló bjalfa aukinn,
ok lómhugaðr lagði
leikblaðs reginn fjaðrar
ern at ǫglis barni
arnsúg faðir Marnar.

13. Hófu skjótt, en skófu,
skǫpt, ginnregin, brinna,
en sonr biðils sviðnar
(sveipr varð í fǫr) Greipar.
Þat's of fátt á fjalla
Finns ilja brú minni…

5: TRIALS AND HUMILIATIONS IN THE OUTER WORLD-
ÞÓRR HÓF FÖR SÍNA TIL ÚTGARÐA-LOKA.
-THOR TRAVELS TO OUTER WORLD LOKI-[GYLFAGINNING, 44, PROSE EDDA]

44: Then spoke Wandering Learner: "… Has it never happened that Thor has met something so mighty and powerful that he has come out as the lesser man in terms of power or great cunning?"

Then spoke The High One: "There are not many, I think, who can tell you about something like that – but even he has met some whom he found hard to tackle. And if it should have happened that something has been so formidable and powerful that not even Thor has been able to deal with it, and then one should still not talk about it; for there are many examples of how Thor is the strongest, and all are obliged to believe that."

Wandering Learner: "It seems to me that I have now asked something that no one is capable of answering.[124]"

Just-as-High[125] spoke then: "We have heard spoken of events that we think cannot possibly be true. But here beside me there is one who may give true testimony; and you may trust that he will not start lying now, he who has never lied before."

Wandering Learner: "Here I shall stand and listen, waiting to hear a solution to this case; and if there is none, then I shall say that you have been defeated, since you cannot answer to what I ask."

Then spoke Third: [126] "It is seen in abundance, now, that he wants to know these tidings even if it is not deemed fair for us to speak of them.

This is the origin of these tales, that Sliding Thor drove with his rams and rode also with that Áss [god] who is called Loki. In the evening they came to a farmer and got there a night-place. And in the evening, Thor took his rams and killed them both. After that they were flayed and carried to the kettles. And when they were cooked, then Thor and his companion sat down for the night-meal. Thor offered to share the meal with the farmer and his wife and their children.

The son of the farmer was Binding Together [Þiálfi],[127] and the daughter was called Maturing [Rǫskva].[128]

Then Thor took the pieces of ram out of the fire and said that the farmer and his home-people needed to leave the bones from the rams unbroken. Binding Together, the son of the farmer, held the thigh leg of the ram and with his knife cut into the bone to reach the marrow.

Thor slept there for the night. And in the morning before day, he got up and dressed himself, took the hammer Grinder and with it he sanctified the pieces of ram.[129] The rams were revived and alive as before, and this was when he saw that one of the rams was lame in one hind leg. Thor noticed this and said that the farmer or his people had not acted properly with the rams' bones. He could feel that the hind leg was broken.

Needless are words to describe how terrified the farmer was when he saw Thor frowning with his brows down above his eyes, everybody can know that. And even as little as he saw of those eyes, he thought he was going to fall to the ground just from that sight.

Thor clenched his hands on the shaft of the hammer so hard that his knuckles went white, and the peasant did as one might expect, and his entire household too, they started to cry and begged for mercy and offered him everything they owned. And when he realized their terror, the rage left him, and he calmed down and accepted as compensation their children, Binding Together and Maturing. They were made his bondspeople, and steadily followed him since.

FRÁ SKIPTUM ÞÓRS OK SKRÝMIS-FROM THE WORKS OF THUNDER AND LOUD SPEAKER
[GYLFAGINNING, 45, PROSE EDDA]

45: He left the rams behind there and started his journey east into the Giant Worlds and all the way to the ocean, and then he traveled across the deep sea. And when he came to land, he went up and with him came Loki, Binding Together and Maturing.

When they had walked for a while, they came to a large forest. They walked the whole day until dark. Binding Together was of all men the swiftest of foot. He carried Thor's food-bag, but as to a good resting place, there were small hopes.

When it was dark, they searched for a night-place and found for themselves an enormous house. In one end, there was a door as broad as the house itself. Well inside they made a night-hive for themselves. And in the middle of the night, there was a great earthquake. The ground beneath them trembled, and the house shook.

Then Thor got up and called for his companions, and they crawled forth and found a side-room to the right, in the middle of the long wall, and went inside there. Thor sat down in the door-opening with the others behind him.

They were frightened, but Thor held his hammer shaft and was ready to defend his own. Then they heard a strong rumbling sound and a groaning too.

As day arrived, Thor went out and saw a man in the forest not far from there, and he was not tiny.[130] He slept and snored loudly. Then Thor understood what sorts of sounds they had been hearing in the night. He bucked up the Power Belt, and thereby his divine power increased.

Just at the same time, the man woke up and got up quickly to stand. And it is said that even Thor hesitated to strike with his hammer then.

He asked him what he was called. He said that his name was Loud Speaker:[131] "But I do not have to ask your name," he said, "I understand that you are Thor of the Aesir. But tell me; have you pulled away my glove?"

And with these words, Loud Speaker bent down to pick up his glove. Thor saw that his man's glove that they had used for a house in the night, and that the side room was the thumb of the glove.

Loud Speaker asked if Thor wanted to add him to his traveling herd, and Thor accepted this. Then Loud Speaker took out his food bag to eat his day meal, and Thor and his companions sat elsewhere and did the same.

Then Loud Speaker said that they should keep the same food company. Thor agreed to that. And then Loud Speaker collected all the food – his own and theirs – into one bag, tied it up and placed it on his back. He walked before them the whole day and took large steps.

Late in the evening, Loud Speaker looked for a night-place for them and found one beneath an enormous oak.

Loud Speaker told Thor that he wanted to lie down to sleep, "but you can take the food bag and eat your evening meal." Thereafter, Loud Speaker fell asleep and snored so loudly that the world rumbled.

Thor took the food bag and tried to open it, and it is said, even as incredible as it sounds, that he could not undo one single knot, and not pull out a single piece of rope so that it was less tight than before.

When Thor could not get anywhere with his effort, he became angry, clasped the hammer grinder with both hands, and moved forth with one foot towards where Loud Speaker was sleeping, and struck hard into his head.

Loud Speaker woke up and asked if a leaf had fallen down from the oak onto his head, and if they had eaten and were ready for bed.

Thor replied that they were going to sleep, and they went to lie beneath another oak. But you will understand that theirs was not a fearless sleep.

In the middle of the night, Thor heard that Loud Speaker snored and slept deeply, so that the forest shook like waves. Then he stood up and went up to him, swung his hammer hard and fast, and struck down into the center of his crown. He felt the face of the hammer sink deep into his head. And at that moment, Loud Speaker woke and said: "What now? Have some acorns fallen onto my head, or what is up with you, Thor?"

But Thor backed away fast and replied that he had just woken up, but that it was just midnight and still more time to sleep. Then Thor decided that if he could only strike a third blow, then the man would never open his eyes again, so he laid waiting for Loud Speaker to fall asleep. And a little before dawn he could hear that Loud Speaker was sleeping, and he got up again, ran towards him, and throve his hammer with all his might against his temple, and the hammer sank in up to the handle.

Loud Speaker sat up and stroked his cheek, saying: "Are there perhaps some birds sitting in the tree above me? I am sure as I woke up, that some rubbish from the branches fell on my head. Are you awake, Thor? It is time to get up and get dressed. And you do not have very far to go on to the castle called Outer World.[132] I have heard you whisper amongst yourselves, that I am not small of growth.

But when you come to Outer World, you are going to see people who are even larger. And now I must counsel you well: Don't try to act like you are great men there. Not will the army-men of Outer World Loki take well to bragging from little boys like you. If you do not heed this counsel, you ought rather turn around and go home, I think that might be safer for you. But if you want to keep going, then take the eastern path. My path goes north, to the mountains you see there."[133]

The Loud Speaker takes his food bag, throws it across his shoulders, and walks away from them into the forest. And it is not said that the Aesir wished him back.

FRÁ ÍÞRÓTTUM ÞÓRS OK FÉLAGA HANS-ABOUT THE SPORTS OF THOR AND
HIS COMPANIONS
[GYLFAGINNING 46, PROSE EDDA]

46: Thor and his companions moved on, and walked until midday.
Then they saw a fortress wall standing on open ground and had to
turn their necks back to their spines in order to look up at it. Thor
tried to open the gate, but it was impossible. If they were to enter,
they had to sneak through between the planks.

That they did, and came inside. There was a large hall there, and
they went there. The door was open, and they went inside. There
they saw many men seated on two benches, and most of them were
over the top large.

Then they went to stand before the king, Outer World Loki,[134] and
greeted him. It took a while before he let his gaze see them. Then he
grinned and said; "It takes a long time to take notice when there is a
long distance between us, but am I amiss if that little boy over there
is Sliding Thor?

But maybe there is more to you than what it seems like to me?
What sorts of manly sports do you companions consider yourselves
good at? Nobody shall stay here with us, unless he has some sort of
cunning above the average."

Then said the one who is called Loki; "I know that sport that I am
bid to show; that there is nobody inside here that is able to eat their
food faster than I am."

Then replied Outer World Loki: "That is a sport, if you are good at
it, and we shall try that sport." And he called for one seated further
out on the benches, one called Flame [Logi],[135] that he should come
forth on the floor and try himself against Loki.

They brought out a large tray and place it on the hall floor, and
it was filled with meat. Loki sat down at one end, and Flame sat
down at the other end. Both ate as fast as they could and met at the
middle of the tray.

Then Loki had eaten all the meat off the bones. Flame had also
eaten all his meat, but also the bones and the tray too. And it was
clear that Loki had lost that contest.

Then asked Outer World Loki what sorts of sports the young man could play, and Binding Together said that he could try to run faster than anyone that Outer World Loki names. Then said Outer World Loki that this was a good sport, and that he must be unusually swift of feet if he was to win this contest; surely they should be able to find out.

Outer World Loki then stood up and walked out. And there, on the flat field, there was a great running court. Outer World Loki called to him a small boy named Intent [Húgi][136] and asked him to run a race with Binding Together. They took the first race. And Intent came so far before him that he could turn around to see him by the goal.

Then said Outer World Loki: "You need to put yourself more forward, Binding Together, if you are to win this contest – even if I can say truly that there has never before come anyone else faster of legs than you."

They took another race. And as Intent reached the goal and turned around, there was still an arrow shot's distance to Binding Together.

Then said Outer World Loki: "I cannot deny that Binding Together runs fast, but I don't think he wins this game. But we shall see at the third race." Then they race yet again. But as Intent has reached the goal and turns around, Binding Together had not even reached halfway to the goal. Everybody present said that the results are clear.

Now Outer World Loki asked Thor what sports could be the ones that he would show them as there had been many tidings of his great deeds. Then Thor said that he would prefer to compete at drinking with someone.

Outer World Loki said that this would be fine and went inside the hall to call for his pouring lad, and asked him to take the Correction Horn,[137] the one that his warriors were accustomed to drinking from. Next thing, the pouring lad comes with the horn and offered it into Thor's hand.

Then spoke Outer World Loki: "Of this horn it is well drunk if you can empty it in one draught. Some men need two draughts, but none is so little of a drinking man that he cannot drain it on the third draught."

Thor looked at the horn. He did not think it was very broad, but it was weirdly long. But he was very thirsty, and started drinking, and took enormous draughts, and thought that he was not going to have to bend down over the horn more than this one time. But as he could no longer hold his breath and lifted his head up from the horn to see what was left of the drink, he saw that it was only slightly lower in the horn than before.

Then spoke Outer World Loki: "It is well drunk if not so much. I would not have believed it, if somebody told me that Thor of the Aesir did not drink a bigger draught. But I am sure you are going to empty the horn next."

Thor replied nothing, set the horn to his mouth and thought now that he should drink more than before, and he kept drinking so long as he could hold his breath. But now too he saw that the end of the horn would not lift from the ground as high as he expected it to. And he took the horn from his mouth and looked into it, and did not see that the content was particularly less than before. But still there was now some more room for spilling.

Then said Outer World Loki: "What now, Thor, are you keeping back for one more drink that you will find easy to manage? It seems to me that if you are going to drain this horn on the third draught, then you must have left the most for last.

But here among us you shall not be counted for such a big man as those Aesir are calling you, unless you give a better impression of yourself in other contests than it appears to me that you are going to give in this one."

Then Thor was angry, set the horn to his mouth and drank as hard as he could and struggled for a long time with his drink. And when he looked into the horn, this was the draught that had made most difference. And then he handed back the horn and would drink no more.

Then said Outer World Loki: "It is abundantly seen, now, that your might is not so great as we believed, but maybe you will try some more games, for it is easily seen now that you cannot win this one."

Thor replied: "I may well try some other game. But it would be a strange thing if draughts like these were considered so small among the Aesir at home. What sort of sport do you want to invite me to now?"

Then said Outer World Loki: "Around here, young boys sometimes try at something we do not deem as a great deed. That would be to lift my cat up from the ground. I would never have thought to mention this to Thor of the Aesir, unless I had already seen for myself that you are somewhat less of a man than I thought before."

Just then, a cat ran out onto the floor of the hall, gray and rather big. Thor went forth and held its belly and began lifting. But the cat bent and bent as Thor was straightening out his arm. And when Thor had stretched his arms as high as he could, then the cat had to lift one of his paws from the ground. Further than that, Thor could not get with this contest.

Then said Outer World Loki: "It happened with this game as I had suspected. The cat is rather big, and Thor is short and tiny compared to the men who live here."

Then said Thor: "As tiny as you call me, now I want to fight whoever you let compete with me, now I am angry."

Outer World Loki replied as he gazed down at the benches: "I cannot see anyone in here who will not deem it too small of a feat to fight with you – but let us see," he added, "Invite here that old wench, my foster mother, Old Age,[138] , and let Thor fight with her if he wants to. She has thrown men to the floor that did not seem weaker to me than Thor is."

Next, an old wench came into the hall, and Outer World Loki bid her to wrestle with Thor of the Aesir. There is no need for many words here. In that fight, it happened so that the harder Thor tried to squeeze, the more firmly she stood. But then the wench began to use tricks, and soon Thor was wavering on his feet. And now there was a wild pulling and throwing, and soon enough Thor fell to his knee with one leg. Then Outer World Loki went forth and asked them to stop their wrestling and said that Thor did not need to invite more of his warriors to a wrestling contest. By then it was night. Outer World Loki showed Thor and his companions to their seats, and they stayed there the whole night and were well treated.

SKILNAÐR ÞÓRS OK ÚTGARÐA-LOKA-THE PARTING OF THOR AND OUTER
WORLD LOKI
[GYLFAGINNING, 47, PROSE EDDA]

47: In the morning at dawn, Thor and his companions got up, got
dressed and made ready for the home journey. Then Outer World
Loki came there and set a table for them. There was no lack of food
and drink, and they were well treated. When they were fed, they
commenced their journey home. Outer World Loki followed them
out and walked with them as far as to the outsides of the wall. And
as they were to separate, he asked Thor what he thought of his
journey, and if he had ever met a mightier man than him.

Thor said that he could not deny that he had harvested great
shame in being together with him. "I know that you hold me for a
weak poor thing, and it is shameful to think about."

Then said Outer World Loki: "Now I shall tell you the truth, now
that you have come outside of the wall. For as long as I live and can
rule it, you shall never again get inside of it.

And I tell you this; that you would never have entered here if I had
before believed that there was such power in you. You had nearly
caused us great misfortune. I have made great illusions[139] for you.

First time, in the forest, I was the one who came to you. You tried
to open the food bag, but I had bound it with a sorcerer's band[140]
that you could not move.

After that, you struck me three times with your hammer. The first
was the least, and yet it was so hard that it would have killed me if it
had actually reached me.

But did you not see a flat mountain by my hall? And did you
not see three square valleys in it, and that one was deeper than the
others?

Those were the marks of your hammer strikes; that mountain I
moved forth to receive the strikes, but you could not see that.

Likewise it was with the contests that you had with my warriors.
The first was the one Loki dared. He was very hungry and ate fast.
But the one whose name was Flame; that was in fact the wild fire,
and he burned up both the tray and the meat.

And then Binding Together was supposed to run race with Intent.
But that was my thought,[141] and it is not to be expected that anyone
could surpass that in speed.

And when you drank from the horn and thought that it was slow to decrease in content, yes believe me in this; that then a great miracle happened that I would never have believed. The other end of the horn was far outside in the ocean, but you could not see that.

And now, when you arrive at the ocean, then you will see how much of the sea you have drunk and how much lower it now is, it is now what we call the tides."

And he continued: "No less of a great deed I thought it was when you lifted the cat. Yes, in truth, all who saw it were frightened when they saw that you lifted the cat so as to lift one paw from the ground. For that cat was not what you thought. It was the Middle World Serpent that lies around all lands, and it was hardly so that its length was enough, for his head and his tail to stay on the ground.

And so far did you reach up that you were not far from the sky. And another wonder was this; that you hardly even fell to one knee when you wrestled with Old Age. For never has there ever been a man, and will never be either, who is not thrown to the ground by Old Age – if he lives so long as to reach her.

But now it is truly spoken that we must separate, and it will be the best for both parts that you never again come here and try to find me; all-knowingly I shall protect my fortress with illusion arts of the same or other kinds, so that you shall never conquer me."

When Thor heard these words, he clasped his hammer and swings it through the air, but as he is to strike, he cannot see Outer World Loki anywhere. Then he turned and raced towards the fortress in order to break its walls, but by then he saw only fair fields and no fortress. Then he turned again, and traveled until he reached home to Power Fields.

But I shall say this about it; that he had already decided then that he should have another meeting with the Middle Earth serpent, and that actually happened too. Now I think nobody can give you further tidings about this journey of Thor."

The Path from Earth to Heaven
Gylfaginning 13-15 (Prose Edda) & Grímnismál 29 (Poetic Edda):

> 29: Wandering Learner said: "What path leads from Earth to Heaven?
>
> The High One replied, and laughed then; "That was not a clever question. Have you not heard that the gods built a bridge from Earth to heaven, the one called Shivering Voice[142]? You must have seen it; but it is possible that you call her Rainbow. She has three colors; one is very strong, and made with greater art and wisdom than any other work. But even as strong as she is, she will break when the sons of Muspell[143] come to ride her. [...]

The third root of the Ash[144] stands in Heaven and beneath that root there is a well that is particularly holy, and which is called the Well of Origin,[145] there the Aesir keep their Parliament. Every day, the Aesir ride up there across the Shivering Voice, which is also called the Bridge of the Gods.[146] [...] Thor walks on foot to the Parliament, and he wades across some rivers to get there; and they are called:

Protecting and Diverting[147] and the two Kettle Baths[148] these must Thor wade every day, when he goes to be a court judge by the Ash Yggdrasill; For the Divine Bridge stands all in flames glowing hot are holy waters."	Karmt oc Avrmt oc Kerlaugar tvꝫr, þꝫr scal Þorr vaða dag hvern, er hann dꝍma ferr at Asci Yggdrasils; þviat Asbru brenn all loga, heilog votn hlóa.

The Song of Long Beard-[Hárbarðsljóð, Poetic Edda]

Thor travelled the eastern paths and came to a certain inlet; on the other side of the inlet was the Ferryman with his ship.	Þorr for or avstrvegi oc kom at svndi ꝫino; avdrom megom svndzins var Feriokarlinn meþ scipit.

1 Thor called:
"Who is that lad of lads
standing across the inlet
there?"

2 The Ferryman replied:
"Who is that peasant of
peasants,
who is calling across the
gulf?"

3 Thor said:
"Ferry me across the inlet!
I shall feed you in the
morning;
I have a knapsack on my
back
No food could be better.
I ate in calm before I left
home,
herring and oat, I have
eaten my fill."

4 The Ferryman said:
"Of your morning's activ-
ities
you appear to be proud.
You don't know
what stands before you
that your kinfolks are sad;
Dead, your mother[149]
seems to me."

5 Thor said:
«What you are saying now
is what anyone would
want to know the most;
That my mother is dead.»

1 Þorr callaþi:
"Hverr er sa sveinn sveina,
er stendr fyr svndit han-
dan?"

2 Feriokarlinn svaraþi:
"Hverr er sa karl karla,
er callar vm vaginn?"

3 Þorr qvaþ:
"Ferþv mic vm svndit!
feþi ec þic a morgon:
meis hefi ec a baki,
verþra matrinn betri.
Át ec i hvíld, aþr ec heiman for,
silldr oc hafra, saþr em ec
enn þess."

4 Feriokarlinn qvaþ:
"Árligom verkom hrosar
þv verþinom,
veitzatv fyr gorla,
daᴘr ero þin heimkynni,
daᴘþ hygg ec at þin moþir
se."

5 Þorr qvaþ:
"Þat segir þv nv,
er hveriom þiccir
mest at vita,
at mín moþir dauþ se."

6 The Ferryman said:
«You do not seem like one
who owns three good
estates,
barefoot you stand
and you carry the gear of
the beggar
you don't even have any
breeches."

7 Thor said:
"Steer over here that oak-
en boat
I will direct you to the
port;
And who owns the ship.
that you are keeping by
the bank?"

8 The Ferryman said:
 "Battle Wolf[150] he is called
the one who bade me keep
it,
rich in wise counsel -
and lives at Council Island
Inlet;
He bade me not to ferry
robbers,
or horse thiefs,
only the good men
and those whom I easily
recognize.
Say you your name if you
want to cross the water."

6 Feriokarlinn qvaþ:
"Þeygi er sem þv
þriv bv́ góð eigir,
berbeinn þv stendr
oc hefir braᴸtinga gervi,
þatki at þv hafir brøkr
þinar."

7 Þorr qvaþ:
"Styrþv hingat eikionni!
ec mvn þer staᴸþna kenna;
eþa hverr a scipit,
er þv heldr viþ landit?"

8 Feriokarlinn qvaþ:
"Hildolfr sa heitir,
er mic halda baþ,
reccr inn rádsvinni,
er bv́r i Raþseyiarsvndi;
baþat hann hlennimenn
flytia
eþa hrossa þiófa,
goða eina
oc þa er ec gerva kvnna;
segðv til nafns þíns,
ef þv vill vm svndit fara."

9 Thor said:
"I shall say my name
even if I were an outlaw,
and all my lineage;
I am Óðinn's son
brother of the Lovely
One[151]
and father of Greatness,[152]
Powerful leader of the
gods;
With Thor you are speak-
ing here,
and now I want to ask
what you are called?"

10 The Ferryman said:
«Long Beard I am called
and I rarely conceal my
name.»

11 Thor said:
«Why would you conceal
your name,
unless you have cases
unsolved?"

12 Long Beard said:
"Even if I had no cases
unsolved
I would defend my life
against people like you,
unless I was already
doomed."

13 Thor said:
"It seems to me unpleas-
ant work
wading across the waves
to you
and wet my balls;
I will pay you back,
you nursery babe,
for your taunting words
if I can cross the inlet."

9 Þorr qvaþ:
"Segia mvn ec til nafns
mins,
þótt ec secr siac,
oc til allz aþliss:
ec em Oþins sonr,
Meila broþir,
enn Magna faþir,
þrvðvaldr goða,
viþ Þór knattv her dǫma.
Hins vil ec nv spyria,
hvat þv heitir."

10 Feriokarlinn qvaþ:
"Hárbardr ec heiti,
hylc vm nafn sialdan."

11 Þorr qvaþ:
"Hvat scaltv of nafn hylia,
nema þv sakar eigir?"

12 Hárbarðr qvaþ:
"Enn þot ec sakar eiga,
þa mvn ec forþa
fiorvi mino fyr slicom sem
þv ert,
nema ec feigr se."

13 Þorr qvaþ:
"Harm liotan mer þiccir i
þvi at vaþa vm vaginn til
þin
oc vęta † argvr minn;
scylda ec larna cargorsveini
þinom kanginyrþi,
ef ec kǫmvmc yfir svndit."

14 Long Beard said:
"Here I shall stand
and wait for you
you have not encountered
sterner foe
since the death of Hrung-
nir.[153]

14 Hárbarðr qvaþ:
"Her mvn ec standa
oc þin hedan biþa;
fanntaþv mann inn harda-
ra
at Hrvngni daðan."

15 Thor said:
"This is what you are
getting at,
that I contested with
Hrungnir
that giant of great intent
and of stone his head was
made

Yet I let him fall and killed
him
what were you doing
meanwhile,
Long Beard?"

15 Þorr qvaþ:
"Hins viltv nv geta,
er vid Hrvngnir deildom,
sa inn stórvþgi iotvnn,
er or steini var hofvþit a;
þo let ec hann falla oc fyr
hniga.
Hvat vantv þa meþan,
Hárbarðr?"

16 Long Beard said:
«I was with Great Guard-
ian[154]
for five whole winters
on that island
which is called All Green;
We fought there
and fell the chosen
much to try out
many a girl to seduce."

16 Hárbarðr qvaþ:
"Var ec meþ Fiolvari
fimm vetr alla
i ey þeirre,
er Algrøn heitir;
vega ver þar knattom
oc val fella,
margs at freista,
mans at kosta."

17 Thor said:
"How were they to you,
your women?"

17 Þorr qvaþ:
"Hverso snv́nvþo yþr
konor ydrar?"

18 Long Beard said:
 "Full of life-sparks were
the women
had they only been com-
pliant with us!
Very wise were the women
had they only been true
to us!
From the sand they
wound ropes
From the deep valleys
they dug out the ground;
I was the one who man-
aged
to rule them all;
I rested with the Seven
Sisters
and had all their love and
pleasure.
What did you do mean-
while, Thor?"

Thor said:
19 "I killed the Slave
Binder[155]
that giant of powerful
mind
I threw up the eyes of
the All-Ruler´s[156] son
into the bright open heav-
en:
That may be the best sign
of my deeds
that all men can see ever
after.
What did you do mean-
while,
Long Beard?"

18 Hárbarðr qvaþ:
"Sparkar atto ver konor,
ef oss at sparkom yrði;
horscar atto ver konor,
ef oss hollar veri;
þer or sandi síma vndo
oc or dali divpom
grvnd vm grofo;
varþ ec þeim einn allom
efri at raþom,
hvilda ec hia þeim systrom
siav
oc hafða ec geþ þeirra allt
oc gaman. Hvaþ vanntv
þa meþan, Þorr?"

19 Þorr qvaþ:
"Ec drap Þiaza
enn þrvðmoþga iotvn,
vpp ec varp argom
Allvalda sonar
a þann inn heiða himin;
þav ero merki
mest minna verca,
þar er allir menn siþan vm
se.
Hvat vanntv meþan,
Hárbarðr?"

Long Beard said:
20 "Great spells of desire
I had with the Dark Rid-
ers;[157]
those whom I seduced
from their men;
A hardened giant/devour-
er
I found Wind Shield
Beard[158] to be.
He gave me a magic wand
and I bewitched him from
his wits."

Thor said:
21 "With a bad intent did
you repay him
for his good gifts."

Long Beard said:
22 "One oak will thrive
that brings down another;
each for himself in such
matters.
What did you do then,
Thor?"

Thor said:
23 "I was in the east
I fought against devourers
and brides versed in mal-
ice,
they who roamed the
mountains;
Great would the lineage of
devourers
have been if they all lived
little would be mankind
within Middle World.
What did you do mean-
while, Long Beard?"

20 Hárbarðr qvaþ:
„Miclar manvelar
ec hafða viþ Myrcriþor,
þa er ec velta þer fra
verom;
harþan iotvn
ec hvgða Hlebarð vera,
gaf hann mer gambantein,
en ec velta hann or viti."

21 Þorr qvaþ:
„Illom hvga laˌnaþir þv þa
goþar giafar."

22 Hárbarðr qvaþ:
„Þat hefir eik,
er af annarri scefr;
vm sic er hverr i slico.
Hvat vanntv [þá] meþan,
Þorr?"

23 Þorr qvaþ:
„Ec var aˌstr
oc iotna bardag
brvþir baˌlvisar,
er til biargs gengo;
micil mvndi ett iotna,
ef allir lifði,
vetr mvndi manna
vndir Miþgarþi.
Hvat vanntv meþan, Hár-
barðr?"

Long Beard said:
24 "I was in the Land of
the Chosen[159]
And I waged war
I created conflict between
princes
that may never be solved
Óðinn has the earls
who fall in battle
and Thor owns the breed
of slaves."

Thor said:
25 «Unevenly did you shift
people between the Aesir,
if you had as much power
as you say."

Long Beard said:
26 "Thor has much
strength
but no heart;
out of terror and bland of
intent
you hid in the glove[160]
and you seemed not like
Thor then;
you were so paralyzed
by your own terror
you dared not fart nor
cough,
in case the Observer[161]
heard you."

Thor said:
27 "Long Beard, you
shameful one!
I would strike you into Hel
if I could sail across this
inlet!"

24 Hárbarðr qvaþ:
„Var ec a Vallandi
oc vigom fylgdag,
atta ec iofrom
enn aldri sęttac.
Oþinn a iarla
þa er i val falla,
enn Þorr a þręla kyn."

25 Þorr qvaþ:
„Oiafnt scipta er þv
mvndir
meþ asom liþi,
ef þv ęttir vilgi micils
vald."

26 Hárbarðr qvaþ:
„Þorr a afl ǫrit,
enn ecci hiarta;
af hrǫzlo oc hvgbleyþi
þer var i hannzca troþit,
oc þottisca þv þa Þorr
vera:
hvarki þv þa þorþir
fyr hrǫzlo þinni
físa ne hniosa,
sva at Fialarr heyrþi."

27 Þorr qvaþ:
„Hárbarþr inn ragi!
ec mvnda þic i Hel drepa,
ef ec mętta seilaz vm
svnd."

Long Beard said:
28 "Why should you sail
across the inlet,
When we have no quarrel?
What were you doing
then, Thor?"

Thor said:
29 «I was to the east
and I was guarding the
river
when I was assaulted
by the sons of An-
ger-Witch;[162]
They threw stones at me
but they won little from
this
before me they had to beg
for peace.
What were you doing
then,
Long Beard?"

Long Beard said:
30 "I was to the east
and judged between some-
one
I laid with the Linen
Bright
and had with her a Secret
Parliament[163]
I made the Golden Bright
happy,
she granted me pleasure."

Thor said:
31 "Good were the maid-
en-folks
with you then."

Long-Beard said:
32 "Your help I could have
needed,
Thor! Then I might have
been able to
keep onto that linen bright
maiden."

28 Hárbarðr qvaþ:
Hvat scyldir þv vm svnd
seilaz, er sakir 'ro alls
ongar?
Hvat vanntv þa, Þorr?"

29 Þorr qvaþ:
„Ec var aˈstr
oc ána varþac,
þa er mic sotto
þeir Svárangs synir;
grioti þeir mic baˈrþo,
gagni vrþo þeir þo litt
fegnir,
þo vrþo þeir mic fyrri
friþar at biþia.
Hvat vanntv þa meþan,
Hárbarðr?"

30 Hárbarðr qvaþ:
„Ec var aˈstr
oc viþ einhveria dǫmþac,
lęc ec viþ ena Línhvito
oc Leynþing háþac,
gladdac ena gvllbiorto,
gamni męr vnði."

31 Þorr qvaþ:
„Goð atto þeir mankynni
þar þa."

32 Hárbarðr qvaþ:
„Liþs þins var ec þa þvrfi,
Þorr!
at ec helda þeirri enni
linhvito mey."

Thor said:
33 "If I had known about that
I would have come to you."[164]

Long Beard said:
34 «I would have believed you,
if you had not betrayed my trust."

Thor said:
35 "I do not bite the heel like an old leather shoe in the spring."

Long Beard said:
36 "What were you doing then, Thor?

Thor said:
37 "Berserker brides did I wrestle at Wind-Shield Island,[165]
they were the worst of the worst
they felled all people."

Long Beard said:
38 "Shame did you win, then, Thor,
when you beat up women."

Thor said:
39 "She-Wargs they were not at all women;
they battered my ship, the one I had just made;
they threatened with iron sticks
and they chased Connector.[166]
What were you doing meanwhile,
Long Beard?"

33 Þorr qvaþ:
„Ec mvnda þer þa þat veita,
ef ec viðr of kǫmomc."

34 Hárbarðr qvaþ:
„Ec mvnda þer þa trva,
nema þv mic i trygð vęltir."

35 Þorr qvaþ:
„Emkat ec sa hęlbítr,
sem hvǫscór forn a vár."

36 Hárbarðr qvaþ:
„Hvat vanntv [þá] meþan, Þorr?"

37 Þorr qvaþ:
„Brvþir berserkia barþac i Hléseyio,
þer hofðo verst vnnit,
velta þioþ alla."

38 Hárbarðr qvaþ:
„Klęki vantv þa, Þorr!
er þv a konom barþir."

39 Þorr qvaþ:
„Vargynior þat varo,
enn varla konor;
sceldo scip mitt,
er ec scorþat hafdac;
ǫgðo mer iarnlvrki,
enn elto Þialfa.
Hvat vanntv meþan, Hárbarðr?"

Long Beard said:
40 "I was in the army
the one coming our way
with a swaying war-ban-
ner
to make red the spears."[167]

Thor said:
41 "This you want to bring
up now
that you led enemies to-
wards us."

Long Beard said:
42 "Compensation you
shall have
it should be the Ring,
in the manner of legal
judges
when they want to settle
an agreement."

Thor said:
43 "Where did you find
these hurtful words,
I have never heard any-
thing
more wounding."

Long Beard said:
44 "I got them from the
men
they who are ancient,
they who live in the
burial mounds of the
world."

Thor said:
45 "You give
good names to the cairns
when you call them
the burial mounds of the
world."

Long Beard said:
46 "That is how I judge
in these matters."

40 Hárbarðr qvaþ:
„Ec varc i hernom,
er hingat gorðiz
gnefa gvnnfana
geír at rioþa."

41 Þorr qvaþ:
„Þess viltv nv geta,
er þv fórt oss olivfan at
bioþa."

42 Hárbarðr qvaþ:
„Beta scal þer þat þa
mvnda Baugi,
sem iafnendr vnno
þeir er ocr vilia sætta."

43 Þorr qvaþ:
„Hvar namtv þessi
in hnofiligo orþ,
er ec heyrþa aldri
in hnofiligri?"

44 Hárbarðr qvaþ:
„Nam ec at monnom
þeim enom aldronom,
er bva i
heimis haugom."

45 Þorr qvaþ:
„Þo gefr þv
gott nafn dysiom,
er þv kallar þer heimis
hauga."

46 Hárbarðr qvaþ:
„Sva domi ec
vm slict far."

Thor said:
47 "Your word-circles
will turn out badly for
you,
if I can manage to wade
into the wave;
Higher than the wolf
I think that you shall howl
If you get a beat of the
hammer."

Long Beard said:
48 "Síf has a secret lover
at home
him you would love to
meet,
That sort of work you can
manage,
it is more appropriate for
you."

Thor said:
49 "You speak as your
mouth rules,
so that it seems to me the
worst
cowardly and frightened
you are,
I think that you are lying."

Long Beard said:
50 "Truth I think myself
saying
and you are late for yours
far you could have gone
already, Thor,
if you could have led the
boat."

Thor said:
51 "Long Beard the
Shamed!
You are the one who has
withheld me!"

47 Þorr qvaþ:
„Orðkringi þín
mvn þer illa coma,
ef ec reþ a vag at vaþa;
vlfi hœra
hygg ec þic œpa mvno,
ef þv hlytr af hamri
hœgg."

48 Hárbarðr qvaþ:
„Sif a hó heima,
hans mvndo fvnd vilia,
þann mvntv þrec drygia,
þat er þer scyldara."

49 Þorr qvaþ:
„Mœlir þv at mvnns ráþi,
sva at mer scyldi verst
þiccia,
halr enn hvgblaþi!
hygg ec, at þv liѵgir."

50 Hárbarðr qvaþ:
„Satt hygg ec mic segia,
seinn ertv at for þinni,
langt mvndir þv nv com-
inn, Þorr!
ef þv litvm fœrir."

51 Þorr qvaþ:
„Hárbarþr enn ragi!
heldr hefir þv nv mic
dvalþan."

Long Beard said:
52 "Thor of the Aesir
I had never believed that
you
could be held up thus by a
shepherd!"

Thor said:
53 "Advice I shall tell you
now;
Row here the boat
Let us stop the threats,
And you shall see the
Father
of Greatness!"

Long Beard said:
54 "Travel around the
inlet!
You shall not cross."

Thor said:
55 "Show me the way now,
since you will not let me
cross
through the wave."

56 Long Beard said:
"Little there is to show
a long way it is to travel:
A while to the stick
another to the stone;
Keep to the left-hand path
until you find the Land of
Men.
There may Life Struggle
[Earth]
find Thor, her son,
and she may show him the
Path of the Ancestors
to the lands of Óðinn."

Thor said:

57 "May I reach there
today?"

52   Hárbarðr qvaþ:
„Asaþórs hvgða ec
aldregi mvndo
glepia fehirði farar."

53   Þorr qvaþ:
„Raþ mvn ec þer nv raþa:
ró þv hingat batinom,
hettom hetingi,
hittv farþvr
Magna!"

54   Hárbarðr qvaþ:
„Farþv firr svndi!
þer scal fars synia."

55   Þorr qvaþ:
„Visa þv mer nv leiþina,
allz þv vill mic eigi vm
vaginn feria!"

56 Hárbarðr qvaþ:
«Litiþ er at synia,
langt er at fara:
stvnd er til stocsins,
annor til steinsins,
haltv sva til vinstra veg-
sins,
vnz þv hittir Verland.
Þar mvn Fiorgyn
hitta Þór son sinn,
oc mvn hon kenna hanom
attvnga brautir
til Oþins landa."

57   Þorr qvaþ:
„Mvn ec taca þangat i
dag?"

Long Beard said:
58 "Consider toil and
obstacles
by the rising of the Sun,
when it is thawing, I
think."

Thor said:
59 "Short will our speaking
now be
Since you answer me only
with insults;
I shall reward your disser-
vice
if we meet again.

Long Beard said:
60 "Go you now
where the enemies can
have you!"

58 Hárbarðr qvaþ:
„Taca viþ víl oc erfiþi:
at uprennandi solo
er ec get þána."

59 Þorr qvaþ:
„Scamt mvn nv mál occat,
allz þv mer scǫtingo einni
svarar;
laⁿna mvn ec þer farsyn-
ion,
ef viþ finnomc i sinn an-
nat."

60 Hárbarðr qvaþ:
„Farþv nv þars
þic hafi allan gramir!"

The Song of the Drummer or the Hammer-Retrieval
Þrymskvíða eða Hamarsheimt (Poetic Edda)

1. Wrath was Friendly
Thor
when he awoke
and his hammer
he missed;
His beard was shaking,
his hair stood up
The Son of Earth
began searching.

2. And he was the very
first
to speak these words;
"Hear me now, Loki,
What I am saying now
is something unknown
to anyone on Earth
nor in the higher heaven;
the hammer has been
stolen
from the God!"

3. They went to the beau-
tiful
court of Freyia
and he was the very first
to speak these words;
"May you, for me, Freyia,
lend out your feather hide,
so that I may find
my hammer?"

4. Freyia said:
"That, I would have given
to you
even if it was made of
gold,
and even if it were made
of silver!"

1. Reiðr var þa Vingþórr,
er hann vacnaþi
oc sins hamars
vm sacnaði;
scegg nam at hrista,
scǫr nam at dyia,
reþ Iarþar bvrr
vm at þreifaz.

2. Oc hann þat orða
allz fyrst vm qvaþ:
„Heyrðv nv, Loci!
hvat ec nv męli,
er eigi veit
iarðar hvergi
ne vphimins:
áss er stolinn hamri".

3. Gengo þeir fagra
Freyio tvna,
oc hann þat orða
allz fyrst vm qvaþ:
„Mvntv mer, Freyia!
fiaþrhams liá,
ef ec minn hamar
męttac hitta?".

4. Freyia qvaþ:
„Þo mvnda ec gefa þer,
þott or gvlli vęri,
oc þo selia
at vęri or silfri."

Loki flew then
the feather hide whis-
tled
until he came outside
the divine settlements
and into the giant
worlds.

6. The Drummer[168] sat
on the burial mound
the lord of thurses
spinning golden ropes
for his she-wolves
an trimming the manes
of his mares.

7. The Drummer said:
"How is it with the
Aesir?
How is it with the elves?
Why have you alone
arrived
in the giant world?"

Loki said:
"Bad it is for the Aesir
Bad it is for the elves
Have you hidden the
hammer
of the Loud/Glow Rider?

8. The Drummer said:
"I have hidden the
hammer
of the Loud/Glow Rider
eight leagues
beneath the Earth;
No man shall find him
unless he brings to me
Freyia for my woman."

5. Fló þa Loci,
fiaðrhamr dvnþi,
vnz fyr vtan com asa
garða
oc fyr innan com iotna
heima.

6. Þrymr sat a hǫrgi,
þvrsa drottinn,
greyiom sinom
gvllbǫnd snǫri
oc mǫrom sinom
mǫn iafnaði.

7. Þrymr qvaþ:
„Hvat er meþ asom?
hvat er meþ alfom?
hví ertv einn kominn
í iotvnheima?"

Loci qvaþ:
„Ilt er meþ asom,
ilt er meþ alfom;
hefir þv Hloriþa
hamar vm folginn?"

8. Þrymr qvaþ:
„Ec hefi Hlorriþa
hamar vm folginn
átta rǫstom
fyr iorþ neþan;
hann engi maþr
aptr um heimtir,
nema fǿri mer
Freyio at qvǫn."

9. Loki flew then
the feather hide whis-
tled
until he came
out of the worlds of the
giants
and into the settlements
of the gods;
He met Thor
in the middle of the
settlement
and he was the very
first
to speak these words:

10. Thor said:
"Have you your errand
successfully accom-
plished?
Tell me from the air
the tidings in full;
Often, when seated
the stories fail
and lying down
lies are being barked."

Loki said:
"I have successfully
accomplished my er-
rand;
The Drummer has your
hammer,
the lord of thurses,
no man may take
it back again
unless he gives him
Freyia for a woman."

9. Fló þa Loci,
fiadrhamr dvnþi,
vnz fyr vtan com
iotna heima
oc fyr innan com
asa garða;
mętti hann Þór
miðra garða,
oc hann þat orda
allz fyrst vm qvad:

10.„Hefir þv erendi
sem erfiði?
segðv a lopti
long tiþindi:
opt sitianda
sǫgvr vm fallaz,
oc liggiandi
lygi vm bellir."

11.Loci qvaþ:
„Hefi ec erfidi
oc orindi;
Þrymr hefir þinn hamar,
þvrsa drottinn;
hann engi maþr
aptr vm heimtir,
nema hanom fǫri
Freyio at qván."

They walked then to
find
the beautiful Freyia,
and he was the first
to speak these words:
"Make ready, Freyia,
don the bridal linen,
we two shall travel
together
to the World of the
Giants."

Wrath was Freyia
and scoffed so hard
that the entire court of
the Aesir
began to tremble,
and ruptured did the
mighty
Gem of Flames;
"You must think me
desperate for a man
if I went with you
to the Giant Worlds!"

Then all the Aesir came
to hold Parliament
and the goddesses
all to have their say;
and to speak about this,
the powerful rulers,
how they should re-
trieve
the hammer of the Loud
Rider.

12.Ganga þeir fagra
Freyio at hitta,
oc hann þat orda
allz fyrst vm qvað:
„Bittv þic, Freyia!
brvþar líni,
viþ scolom aka tvaʼ
i Iotunheima.“

13.Reið varð þa Freyia
oc fnasaþi,
allr ása salr
vndir bifðiz,
starcc þat iþ micla
Men Brisinga:
„Mic veiztv verþa
vergiarnasta,
ef ec ek meþ þer
i Iotvnheima.“

14.Senn varo æsir
allir a þingi
oc asynior
allar a mali,
oc vm þat reþo
rikir tifar,
hve þeir Hloriþa
hamar vm sętti.

Then said Great World
[Heimdallr]
the brightest of the
gods,
He knew well the fu-
ture
like all the Vanir –
"Bind around Thor
the bridal linen
Let him carry the
mighty
Gem of Flames!

Let him carry
the jingling keys
and women's skirts
fall down his knees
and on his chest
broad stones place
and an appropriate veil
to be hiding his head!"

Then said Thor,
the powerful/manly
god:
"Me should the Aesir
call disgraced,
if I let bind around me
the bridal linen."

Then said Loki,
Leaf Island's son:
"Be silent, Thor!
Such words
must not be spoken;
The Devourers may
settle in Ásgarð
unless you fetch
your hammer back."

15. Þa qvaþ þat Heimdallr,
hvitastr ása,
— vissi hann vel fram
sem vanir aþrir —:
„Bindo ver Þor þa
brvþar lini,
hafi hann iþ micla
Men Brisinga!

16. Latom vnd hanom
hrynia lvcla
oc kvennvaþir
vm kne falla,
en a briosti
breiþa steína
oc hagliga
vm ha'fvþ typpom!"

17. Þa qvaþ þat Þorr,
þrvðugr ass:
„Mic mvno ęsir
argan kalla,
ef ec bindaz lęt
brvþar líni."

18. Þa qvaþ þat Loci,
La'feyiar sonr:
„Þegi þv, Þorr!
þeirra orþa;
þegar mvno iotnar
Asgarð bva,
nema þv þinn hamar
þer vm heimtir."

They bound around
Thor
the bridal linen
and the mighty
Gem of Flames,
let him carry
the jingling keys
and women's skirts
fell down his knees
and on his chest
broad stones
and the appropriate
head-veil.

Then said Loki
Leaf Island's son:
"I shall come with you
and be your maidser-
vant
We two shall travel
together
to the Giant Worlds."

Then were the rams
driven home
They hurried into the
harness
They were bound to run
well;
Mountains burst,
the Earth burned with
flames,
Óðinn's son traveled
In the Giant Worlds.

19.Bvndo þeir Þór þa
brvþar líni
oc eno micla
Meni Brisinga,
leto vnd hanom
hrynia lvcla
oc kvennvaþir
vm kne falla,
enn a briosti
breiþa steina,
oc hagliga
vm ha̋fvþ typþo.

20.Þa qvaþ Loci,
La̋feyiar sonr:
„Mvn ec oc meþ þer
ambót vera,
vid scolom aka tvęr
i iotvnheima."

21.Senn varo hafrar
heim vm reknir,
scyndir at sca̋clom,
scyldo vel renna;
biorg brotnoþo,
brann iorþ loga,
ók Oþins sonr
í iotvnheima.

25

Then said the Drummer,
lord of thurses:
"Stand up, giants!
Put straw on the bench-
es;
now they are leading to
me
Freyia for my woman,
the daughter of Njǫrðr
of Ship's Harbor!"

Here in the settlement
golden-horned cattle
walk
all-black oxen
for the pleasure of the
giants;
Many treasures do I
own
many gems do I own
only Freyia
I was missing."

It was evening when
they came together
and before the giants
ale was carried;
alone he [Thor] ate the
oxen
eight salmons
and all the sweetmeat
that was reserved for
the women;
Sífs husband
drank three caskets of
mead.

22. Þa qvaþ þat Þrymr,
þvrsa drottinn:
„Standit vp, iotnar!
oc straiþ becci;
nv foriþ mer
Freyio at qvan,
Niarþar dottvr
or Noatvnom!

23. Ganga her at gardi
gvllhyrnþar kýr,
oxn alsvartir
iotni at gamni;
fiolþ a ec meiþma,
fiolþ a ec menia,
einnar mer Freýio
avant þiccir."

24. Var þar at qveldi
vm comiþ snimma,
oc fyr iotna
aˡl fram borit;
einn át oxa,
átta laxa,
krasir allar
þer er konor scyldo,
dracc Sifiar verr
sáld þriv miaþar.

Then said the Drummer,
lord of thurses:
"Where did you see a
bride
bite sharper?
I have never seen
a bride bite broader,
nor did I see more mead
drunk by a maiden!"

There sat the all-elo-
quent
Maidservant before
him,
And words she found
To counter the speech of
the giant:
"Freyia ate nothing
for eight nights,
such was her yearning
for the Giant Worlds."

He looked beneath her
veil
eager to kiss her,
and he bolted back-
wards
to the other end of the
hall;
"Why are the eyes of
Freyia
so terrifying?
It seems to me that her
eyes
are burning with fire."

25. Þa qvaþ þat Þrymr,
þvrsa drottinn:
„Hvar sattv brvþir
bíta hvassara?
saca ec brvþir
bíta breiðara,
ne inn meira mioþ
mey vm drecca. "

26. Sat in alsnotra
ambót fyr,
er orð vm fann
við iotvns máli:
„Át vętr Freyia
átta nottom,
sva var hon oþfýs
í iotvnheima. "

27. Láʼt vnd líno,
lysti at cyssa,
enn hann vtan staʼcc
endlangan sal:
„Hvi ero aʼndótt
aʼgo Freyio?
þicci mer or aʼgvm
[eldr of] brenna. "

Sat there the all-elo-
quent
maidservant before
him,
and she found words
to counter the giant's
speech:
"Freyia did not sleep
for eight nights,
thus was her yearning
for the Giant Worlds!"

In came the wretched
sister of the giant,
she alone dared to ask
for the bride's gift;
"Let me take from your
hands
the red rings,
if you want to merit
my friendliness,
my friendliness
and all my favor!"

Then said the Drummer,
lord of thurses;
"Bring here the hammer
To wed the bride,
Place the Grinder
[Miöllnir]
in the maiden's lap,
we shall wed us together
by the hands of Aware-
ness!"[169]

28. Sat in alsnotra
ambót fyr,
er orð vm fann
við iotvns máli:
„Svaf vetr Freyia
átta nottom,
sva var hon oþfvs
i iotvnheima. "

29. Inn com in arma
iotna systir,
hin er brv́þfiár
biþia þorði:
„Lattv þer af handom
hringa ráða,
ef þv aþlaz vill
astir minar,
astir minar,
alla hylli! "

30. Þa qvaþ þat Þrymr,
þvrsa drottinn:
„Beriþ inn hamar
brv́þi at vígia,
leggit Miollni
i meyiar kne,
vígit ocr saman
Várar hendi! "

Then laughed the heart
In the Loud Rider's
chest;
And, hard of intent,
He clasped the hammer;
First he struck the
Drummer,
lord of thurses,
and the lineage of De-
vourers
he battered them all.

He struck then the an-
cient
sister of the giant,[170]
she who had asked
for a bridal gift;
She got a trashing
for shillings
and hammer-strikes
instead of many rings
Thus Óðinn's son
got his hammer back.

31.Hló Hlorriþa
hvgr i briosti,
er harðhvgaþr
hamar vm þecþi;
Þrym drap hann fyrstan,
þvrsa drottin,
oc ętt iotvns
alla lamþi.

32.Drap hann ina ałdno
iotna systvr,
hin er brvþfiár
of beþit hafði;
hon skell vm hlát
fyr scillinga,
enn hągg hamars
fyr hringa fiolþ.
Sva com Oþins sonr
endr at hamri

Bronze Age rock carving from Sweden, Bohuslän, Tanum, Vitlycke rock carvings, showing a couple probably being sanctified by Thor´s Bronze Age predecessor, the "axe god". Norse sources suggest that Thor´s hammer was used to sanctify marriages, such as stanza 30 in this poem suggests; "Place Miöllnir in the maiden´s lap, we shall wed..."

6: Thor and Hrungnir-Frá Hrungni jötni.
About Roarer the Giant
[Skaldskaparmál 24, Prose Edda]

24: Now it shall be told more about the underlying stories behind the metaphors[171] that we have now listed and their origins, those whose origins have not yet been told, as Bragi told them to Aegir, that Thor had traveled the eastern paths to beat trolls.

Óðinn rode Glider [Sleipnir] into the Giant Worlds[172] and came to the giant/devourer who has been called Roarer [Hrungnir[173]]. Then Roarer wondered who the man with the golden helmet was, who rode both high and low,[174] and said that he owned a formidable horse.

Óðinn said that he would wager his own head that there would not be a horse equal to his in the entire Giant World. Roarer said that the horse was certainly good, but that he had a horse with even greater legs, and his name was Golden Mane.[175] Roarer had gotten angry, and now he leaped up to sit on his horse, galloping after Óðinn, wanting to reward him for his preposterous boasts.[176]

Óðinn rode so fast that he that he kept a whole league ahead, and Roarer possessed so much giant rage[177] that he was unable to halt until he had passed the Divine Gate.[178]

And as he came to the doors of the hall, the Aesir invited him to drink. He went into the hall and asked for a drink. The vessels that Thor was used to drinking from were brought before him, and Roarer emptied each one of them.

And as he became drunk, he did not lack for boastful words.[179] He claimed that he would lift all Valhalla and take her[180] to the Giant Worlds, and he would cause Ásgarð to sink, and kill all the gods except Freyia and Síf, whom he wanted to take home with him. And only Freyia still dared to serve him drink, and he said he would drink all the Divine Ale.[181]

When now the Aesir had tired of his boasts, they named Thor.[182]

Next, Thor appeared in the hall and he had lifted his hammer high and was fully enraged, and asked who was responsible for allowing dog-wise giants to drink, or who had given Roarer an invitation to Valhalla, and why Freyia was serving him – as if it was a divine banquet.

Then Roarer replied and looked not with friendly eyes on Thor, and said that Óðinn had invited him to drink and that he was owed truce. Then spoke Thor and said that Roarer would regret the invitation before leaving the hall. Roarer said that Thor of the Aesir would have little honor[183] by killing him when he was unarmed. It would be a greater deed of courage if he dared to fight him by the borders of the Rock-Court-Farms.[184] "And it was very thoughtless of me to leave my shield and my armor at home, for if I had my weapons, we should already have tried each other at holmgang,[185] but if you now kill me while I am unarmed, then I shall accuse you of being cowardly/dishonorable.[186]"

Thor would not at any cost avoid a man-to-man combat[187], when he was now invited to a holmgang; nobody had ever tried that with him before.

Then Roarer went away from there and rode powerfully until he reached the Giant Worlds, and this journey was widely known among the giants, and also that a challenge had been made between them and Thor. The giants knew that who won would have a lot of impact on them. They had bad hopes in waiting from Thor if Roarer lost, for Roarer was the strongest among them. Then the giants made a man out of clay there in Rock-Court-Farms. He was nine leagues tall, and three leagues broad between his arms. But a heart so large that it would fit him, they could not find, before they took one from a certain mare, but the heart did not stay calm when Thor arrived.

Roarer owned a heart that is famous, of hard stone and spikey with three corners. Of stone was his head also. His shield was a broad and thick rock, and he held it before him when he stood in Rock-Court-Farms awaiting Thor. For a weapon he had a whetstone that he kept laying on his shoulders, and he did not look like a nice man to fight with. Next to him stood the clay giant, who was called Dirt Calf,[188] and he was all fear.[189] It is said that he pissed himself when he saw Thor.

Thor went to the reef-contest[190] and with him was Binding Together.[191]

Then, Binding Together ran forth to where Roarer was standing, and said to him; "You stand unaware, devourer, you hold the shield before you, but Thor has seen you, and now he has descended into Earth and is coming to get you from beneath!" Then Roarer thrust his shield to the ground beneath his feet and stood on top of it, and held his whetstone with both hands. Next, he saw fires and heard great roars of thunder. Then he saw Thor in his Divine Rage.[192] He came at great speed and swung his hammer and hurled it from afar against Roarer.

Roarer lifted his whetstone with both hands and hurled right back. It met the hammer in the air and broke. One piece fell to Earth, and from this piece descends all honing/whetting mountains.[193] The other part broke into Thor's head so that he fell forwards to the Earth. And the hammer Grinder [Miöllnir] struck right into Roarer's head and left his skull in tiny pieces, and he fell down before Thor, so that his foot fell down to lie across Thor's throat. Binding Together attacked Dirt Calf, and he fell with few good words [little honor]. Then Binds Together went over to Thor and wanted to lift the foot of Roarer from him, but he could not lift it. When the Aesir heard that Thor had fallen, they arrived all together and tried to move the foot, but to no avail.

Then came Greatness/Might [Magni], son of Thor and Iron Scissors.[194] He was only three days old. He moved the foot of Roarer away from Thor and said; "It was bad, father, that I came so late. I think I would have killed this giant with my bare fist if I had met him." Thor now got up and bid his son welcome, and said that he was going to become quite the man. "I want," he said, "give you the horse Golden Mane, that Roarer once owned."

Then Óðinn spoke and said that Thor made a mistake by giving that good horse to the son of a giantess[195] instead of to his own father [Óðinn].[196]

FRÁ GRÓU VÖLU-ABOUT GROWTH THE WAND-WITCH
[SKALDSKAPARMÁL 25, PROSE EDDA]

25: Thor returned home to Power Fields[197] and the whetstone was still stuck in his head. Then came that Wand-Witch [vǫlva] who is called Growth [Gróa],[198] wife of Aurvandill[199] the Famed. She sang her spell songs [galdr] over Thor[200] until the whetstone loosened.

And when Thor felt that and realized that there was good hope for her being able to remove the whetstone piece completely, he wanted to reward Growth for her healing by doing something that would give her happiness, and told her the tidings, that he had been north above the Age-Waves[201] and had carried, in a knapsack on his back, Aurvandill away from the Giant Worlds. And as evidence he mentioned that one of his toes had been sticking out of the knapsack and frozen, and then he had broken her off and thrown her up into the sky, and made her into a star that is called the Toe/Beam of Aurvandill.[202]

Thor said that it would not be long until Aurvandill could come home, and Growth was so happy that she no longer managed to sing her spell songs, and the whetstone did not loosen more, and still stands in Thor's head.

And it is now said that people should be careful about throwing a whetstone straight across the floor, for if they do that, then the piece of rock in Thor's head moved.

Thióðolf of Kvínir has composed about this saga in Haustlǫng."

Bronze Age rock carving from Vitlycke, Bohuslän, showing the "axe god" (Thor's Bronze Age predecessor) and another warrior carrying a shield - or a "whetstone" - aboard a ship, which may represent the journey of the soul.

HAUSTLǪNG II–THE LONG AUTUMN
A SKALDIC POEM BY THIÓÐOLF OF HVÍNIR (850-930 AD)

13. The wood began to burn,
- the ones that the Sacred Powers
made into fuel [203] -
But the Son of Grasper´s Wooer[204]
[=Slave Binder] was burned:
In suddenness his journey ended.
It is painted on my Mountain-Finn´s[205]
Bridge of the Sole [shield]
that ring [shield], inlaid with colors[206] -
that I received from Thorleif.

13. Hófu skjótt, en skófu,
skǫpt, Ginnregin, brinna,
en Sonr Biðils sviðnar
(sveipr varð í fǫr) Greipar.
Þat's of fátt á fjalla

Finns ilja brú minni.
Baugs þák bifum fáða
bifkleif at Þórleifi.

14. Furthermore one may see, on the ring [=shield],
Tree [man] of the Cave of Flames [gold][207] -
that the Terror of Giants [=Thor]
visited the Mound[208] of the Rock-Courts.
Earths Son [=Thor] drove to the
Iron Game [=the battle/ combat]
and the Path of Moon [=heaven]
resounded beneath him;
Rage increased in the brother of Meili[209] [=Thor]

14. Eðr of sér, es Jǫtna
Ótti lét of sóttan
Hellis baur á hyrjar,
Haug Grjótúna, baugi;
ók at Ísarnleiki
Jarðar Sunr, en dunði,
móðr svall Meila blóða,
Mána Vegr und hǫnum.

15. The whole Shrine
of the Sacred Descendants
[=the air]²¹⁰
burned for Ull's Stepfather
[=Thor]
and the utterly low ground
was battered with hail
as the rams pulled the
chariot
of the Lord of the Temple
[=Thor]
up to the meeting with
Hrungnir;
The Widow of Svölnir
[=Earth]
was sundered.

16. Balder's Brother
[=Thor] did not spare
that gluttonous Enemy of
Humans [Hrungnir];
Mountains shook and
rocks broke;
Heaven above burned.

I have heard that The
Watcher
of the Dark Bone of the
Land
of Haki's Chariots
[=Hrungnir]²¹¹
moved into great resis-
tance
when he saw his
war-minded bane.

15. Knǫttu ǫll, en, Ullar
endilǫg, fyr mági,
grund vas grápi hrundin,
Ginnunga Vé brinna,
þás hafregin hafrar
hógreiðar framm drógu
(seðr gekk Svǫlnis ekkja
sundr) at Hrungnis fundi.

16. Þyrmðit Baldrs of
barmi,
berg, solgnum þar Dolgi,
hristusk bjǫrg ok brustu,
brann Upphiminn, Manna;

mjǫk frák móti hrøkkva
myrkbeins Haka reinar,
þás vígligan, vagna
vátt, sinn bana þátti.

17. Fast flew the pale
shield beneath
the Rock-Shepherd's
[Hrungnir's] feet;
the Bonds [gods] caused
that;
the Battle-Goddesses
[valkyriur] wanted that;

The Rock-Lad [Hrungnir],
after that, did not need to
wait long
for a swift blow from the
hard smashing
Friend of Trolls' Retinues.
[=Miöllnir].

18. The Destroyer of the
Lives
of Bellower's Harmful
Troops [Thor][212]
made the Roaring Storm's
Bear's
Hiding Place [Hrungnir]
fall on the Reef of Shields;
there, the Earth's
Gorge's[Mountain's] Lord
[Hrungnir]
fell before the sharp hammer
and the Mountain-Dane's
Breaker [Thor]
defeated the Great Enemy
[Hrungnir]

17. Brátt fló bjarga gæti
- Bǫnd ollu því - randa
(ímun) fǫlr und iljar
íss (vildu svá Dísir);

varðat hǫggs frá hǫrðum
Hraundrengr þaðan lengi
Trjónu Trolls of-Rúna
tíðs fjǫllama at bíða.

18. Fjǫrspillir lét falla
fjalfrs ólágra gjalfra
bǫlverðungar Belja
bolm á randar holmi;
þar hné grundar gilja
gramr fyr skǫrpum hamri,
en Berg-Dana bægði
brjótr við Jǫrmunþrjóti.

19. And the hard splinter
of whetstone
of the lord [Hrungnir] who
visited
Vingnir's [Óðinn's] Wom-
an [Freyia]
hurled whistling at the
Earth's Son [Thor]
into his brain-ridge
so that the steel [whet-
stone]
was stuck in Óðinn's Boy's
[Thor's] skull
(who) stood there, splat-
tered
with the blood of the Soli-
tary Rider [Thor].

20. Until the Ale-Provider
[Gróa][213]
sang the Red Rust's Hid-
den Hurt
[the whetstone] out of the
slopes of the hair of the
Wound-Giving God [Thor]
[214]

On the ring of the moving
cliff [the shield]
that I received from Thorleif
I can clearly see these
events.[215]

19. Ok hǫrð brotin herju
heimþingaðar Vingnis
hvein í hjarna mœni
hein at Grundar sveini,
þar svát, eðr í Óðins
ólaus burar hausi,
stála vikr of stokkin
stóð Einriða blóði.

20. Áðr ór hneigihlíðum
hárs ǫl-Gefjun sára
Reiði-Týs et rauða
ryðs hœlibǫl gœli.
Gǫrla lítk á Geitis
garði þær of farðir.

Baugs þák bifum fáða
bifkleif at Þórleifi.

7: THOR TRAVELS TO RED SPEAR-FÖR ÞÓRS TIL GEIRRÖÐAR-GARÐA.

THOR TRAVELED TO THE HOMESTEADS OF RED SPEAR-[SKALDSKAPARMÁL 26, POETIC EDDA]

26: Then said Aegir: "Great to me seems Roarer to be. Did Thor win any more deeds while he dealt with trolls?"

Then answered Bragi: "Great stories are told of how Thor traveled to the homesteads of Red Spear.[216] This time, he had neither his hammer Grinder [Miöllnir], nor his Power Belt, nor his Iron Gloves, [217] and this was Loki´s fault; he traveled with him.

Sometime before this, it had so happened that Loki for the sake of pleasure had flown wearing Frigg´s falcon hide,[218] and in curiosity he flew to the homesteads of Red Spear. There he saw a huge hall. He sat down and looked into the hall through a hole in the wall. And Red Spear set his eyes on him and bade someone to take the bird and lead it to him. But the errand-man had a hard time getting that high up on the hall-wall, he was so high. Loki thought this was funny, to watch the man struggle so to reach him, that he did not want to fly away before the man had painstakingly reached all the way up to him. When the man was about to clasp him, he lifted his wings and thrust away with his feet. But he feet were stuck. Loki was taken and led to Red Spear the Devourer/Giant. And when he saw his eyes, he became suspicious, thinking that this bird may be a man.

He asked him to answer, but Loki remained silent. Then Red Spear put Loki down into a casket[219] and starved him for three months. When Red-Spear took him out again and bade him speak, Loki said who he was. And in order to save his life, Loki swore that oath to Red Spear that he should get Thor to come into the homesteads of Red Spear without bringing his hammer or his Power Belt.

On the journey, Thor [and Loki] came to this giantess[220] who is called Truce [Gríðr]. She is mother to Víðarr the Silent.[221] She taught Thor the truth of Red Spear; that he was a dog-wise[222] [sly, cunning] giant and a difficult associate. She lent him her own Power Belt and Iron Gloves that she owned, as well as her staff, which is called the Wand of Truce [Gríðarvölr].[223] Then Thor went to this river that is called Vibrating One[224] and is the largest of all.

Then he fastened the Power Belt around himself, and thrust the Wand of Truce into the bottom of the stream beneath him. Loki held onto his belt. Then Thor said this:

"Do not grow, Vibrating One,
for I want to vade you
into the settlements of the giants;
Know, that if you grow,
then my Divine Power grows
as high as heaven."

> Vax-at-tu nú, Vimur,
> alls mik þik vaða tíðir
> jötna garða í;
> veiztu, ef þú, vex,
> at þá vex mér Ásmegin
> jafnhátt upp sem himinn.

Then Thor looked up into a mountain pass and saw that Howler,[225] Red-Spear's daughter, stood spreading her legs to either side of the river and was the cause of the increase of the river flow. Then Thor took a large rock and threw at her and said this; "By the source shall the river be halted." He did not miss when is threw the stone. Right that moment, the stream led him to the other shore, and he managed to hold onto the Experience [rowan tree][226] and in this way he was able to get out of the river. From this comes the saying that "Experience is Thor's Salvation."[227]

And when Thor came to Red Spear, then he and his companion [Loki] were first given sleeping quarters in a goat-stable. To sit, they only received one chair, and there Thor sat himself down. But now he noticed that the chair began to rise beneath him and up towards the roof. Then he set the Wand of Truce up against the ceiling and forced the chair back down. A loud snap and a scream were heard. The daughters of Red Spear, Howler and Grasper,[228] had been beneath the chair, and now he had broken the backs of them both.

Afterwards, Red Spear let Thor call into the hall for a contest. There were large fires there alongside the walls of the entire hall. When Thor came to stand before Red Spear, the giant took a glowing piece of iron with a tong, and threw it at Thor. But he clasped it with the iron gloves and held it up in the air.

Then Red Spear ran to hide behind an iron pillar. Thor threw the piece of iron right through the pillar and through Red Spear and through the wall so that it did not stop before it was in the ground outside. This saga has Eilífr Goðrúnarson composed about in his poem, Þórsdrápa."

Bronze Age rock carvings

ÞÓRSDRÁPA-THE SONG OF THUNDER
EILÍFR GOÐRÚNARSON [CA. 1000]

1.The Father of the Ocean Rope[229] [Loki] commenced to urge from his home the Bane [Thor]of the Fate-Web [life] of the Gods of the Sheer Cliffs [the giants]. Loptr [Air =Loki] was great at being a liar, not at all loyal: The Challenger of the Wits [Loki] of the War-Thunder Man [Thor] said that green, safe roads led towards where Red Spear's Walls' Horse [house] is.	1.Flugstalla réð Felli Fjörnets Goða at hvetja, Drjúgr var Loptr at ljúga, Lögseims Faðir heiman. Geðreynir kvað grænar Gauts Herþrumu brautir vilgi tryggr til Veggjar Viggs Geirröðar liggja.

2.Hard-headed Thor did
not let
the Vulture-Path [Loki]
ask many times
for him to make the jour-
ney;
They were eager to test
the Descendants
of Thorn[230] [giants], when
the Tamer [Thor]
of Magic Bay's Girdle
[Middle World Serpent],
more powerful than the
Scots [giants]
of Iði's[231] Settlement [of
the Ocean],
again set out from the
realm of
the Third[232] [Óðinn's realm
= Ásgarð]
towards Ymsi's[233] kindred
[giants].

3. Deceitful, the Burden
[Loki] of the Arms
of the Fetter [deity] of
Spell-Songs [Sígyn]
was swiftly on his way,
ready to join (Thor) sooner
than
the Lord of the Stories
[Þiálfi].[234]
I recite the Lip-Streams
of The Masked One
[Óðinn][=poetry][235]
The Trapper of the Halls
of the Shrill Cryer [Eagle]
[=Thor]
stretched his sole-palms
[feet]
into Endill's[236] moor
[ocean=river].

2.Geðstrangr of lét göngu
Gammleið Þórr skömmum
fýstusk þeir at þrýsta
Þorns Niðjum, sik biðja þá
er Gjarðvenjuðr görðisk
Gandvíkr, skotum ríkri,
endr til Ymsa kindar,
Iðja Setrs frá Þriðja

3.Görr, varð í för fyrri,
farmr, meinsvárans, arma,
sóknar, hapts, með svipti
Sagna, galdrs, en Rögnir.
Þyl ek granstrauma Grím-
nis:
gall- mantælir halla -ópnis
ilja gaupnum
Endils á mó spendi.

4.And those Accustomed
to the Course
of the Battle Wolf [warri-
ors] travelled;
until they reached the flowing blood [piss/water]
defiling the Heaven
Shield's [Sun goddess's]
Peace [=the river/ocean]
when Loki's Mischief-
Averter [Thor],
agile and too hasty,
wished, deed-generous,
to fight the Bride [gian-
tess] of the
Soul-Masked Kinsmen
[giants].

5.And the Honor-Lessener
[Thor]
of the Hilt's Nanna²³⁷
[wife][=giantess]
was able to cross the icy,
swelling rivers
that were hailing power-
fully
down on the Lynx's Ocean
[Earth].
Very enraged, the One
Who Disperses[Thor]
the Bandits of Rock Walls
[the giants]
greatly disturbed the
Broad Staked Path
[ocean],
where mighty rivers spe-
wed poison.

4.Ok, Gangs, -Vanir gengu
gunn-, vargs himintörgu.
Fríðar, unz til, fljóða
frumseyrir kom dreyra,
þá er bölkveitir brjóta
bragðmildr Loka vildi,
bræði vændr, á brúði
bág Sefgrímnis Mága.

5.Ok vegþverrir varra
vann fetrunnar Nönnu
hjalts af hagli oltnar
hlaupár um ver gaupu.
Mjök leið úr stað stökkvir
stikleiðar veg breiðan
urðar þrjóts, þar er eitri,
æstr, þjóðáar fnæstu.

6.There they pushed Shoo-
ting Serpents [spears]
into the Web Forest
[ocean]
against the loud Wind of
the Forest [ocean-current].
The slippery, round bones
[pebbles] did not sleep.
The Noisy Files [spears]
jangled against the
pebbles,
while the mountains' fal-
ling roar [cascade]
rushed, beaten by an ice-
storm,
along Feðja's anvil.

7.The Promoter of the
Whetstone Land [Thor]
let the mightily-swollen
ones [waves] fall over him.
The Man who benefited
from
the Girdle of Might [Þiálfi]
²³⁸,
knew no better course of
action.
The Diminisher [Thor] of
Mörn's²³⁹ children [giants]
threatened that his power
would grow
unto the Hall's Roof [hea-
ven],
unless the Gushing Blood
of Thorn's²⁴⁰
Neck [the ocean] would
diminish.

6.Þar í -mörk fyrir -mark-
ar,
málhvettan byr settu,
ne hvélvölur hálar,
háf- skotnaðra, sváfu;
Knátti, hreggi höggvin,
hlymþél við möl glymja,
en fellihryn fjalla
Feðju þaut með steðja.

7.Harðvaxnar lét herðir
halllands of sik falla;
gatat maðr, njótr, hin
neytri,
njarð-, ráð fyrir sér,
-gjarðar.
Þverrir lét, nema þyrri
þorns, barna sér mörnar,
snerriblóð, til, svíra,
salþaks megin vaxa.

8.The glorious, battle-wise warriors,
oath-sworn Vikings of Gauti's dwelling,
[Thor and Loki/Þialfi] waded hard,
while the Sword-Fen [ocean] flowed.
The Wave of the Earth's Snow-Dune [river],
blown by the tempest,
rushed forcefully against the Increaser of the Distress [Thor]
of the Home-Dwellers of the Ridge's Land [the giants].

8.Óðu fast, en, fríðir flaut, eiðsvara Gauta setrs víkingar snotrir, sverð-, runnar, -fen, gunnar.
Þurði hrönn at herði hauðrs rúmbyggva nauðar,
jarðar skafls af afli,
áss, hretviðri blásin.

9. Until Þiálfi, with Men's Helper [Thor]
jumped, by himself, into the air
onto the shield-strap [girdle]
of the Lord of Heaven [Thor]
- that was a great feat of power!-
The Widows of Mischief's Memory
[= the waves] caused a violent stream,
a grove of steel [the river tore]
the Breaker of Truce [Thor] carried
the Battle-Tree [Þiálfi] across
the uneven land of the porpoise [river].

9.Unz með ýta sinni,
aflraun var þat, skaunar
á seil himinsjóla sjálflopta kom Þjálfi.
Háðu stáli stríðan straum Hrekkmímis ekkjur;
stop- hnísu fór steypir stríðlund með -völl Gríðar.

10.The deeply set acorns
[hearts]of hostility
of the men who are
against dishonor,
did not miss a beat [were
not frightened]
by the deep mountain-
rivers furious stream.
The Brave Son of Earth
[Thor]
was not frightened by
the terror of fjord-trees
[ocean] [?]
Thor's courage-stone
[heart]
did not tremble from fear,
and neither did Þjálfi's.

11.A flock of cliff-wolves
[giants=enemies]
of the Shield of Eternal
Fire [the Sun goddess]
made the sound of the
swords´ board [shields]
[=battle]against
the ones who fastened
Gleipnir[241] [the Aesir],
before the Riders of the
Deep[242],
the Destroyers of the Low
Tide-Lands
[Thor & Þiálfi],were able
to commence
the Game of the Bowls of
the Heðinn´s
Hair-parting[243][battle]
against the
Briton´s Kinsman[244] of the
Cave [Geirröðr]

10.Ne djúp-akörn drápu
dólgs, vamms, firum,
Glamma,
stríðkviðjundum, stöðvar
stall við rastar falli;
ógn djarfan hlaut arfi
eiðs fjarðar hug meira;
skalf-a Þórs ne Þjálfa
þróttar steinn við ótta.

11.Ok sífuna síðan
sverðs lið-Hatar gerðu
hlífar borðs við herða
harð- Gleipnis dyn -barða;
áðr hylriðar hæði,
hrjóðendr fjöru þjóðar,
við skyld-Breta skytju
skálleik Heðins reikar.

12. The Wave of the
Enemy-Crowd of Svear[245]
[the giants] fled the De-
stroyer [Thor]of the
Lord of the Ness [Giant]
[=Thor]
and hurried into the temple.[246]
The Danes[247] of the Rib of
the High Tide
of the Outdoor Temple[248]
[giants]
admitted defeat, when the
Kinsmen of Jólnir's[249]
Fire-Shaker [Thor etc.]
stood securely.

13. When the warriors,
gifted with courageous
minds,
walked into the Cave of
Thorn[250],
there was a loud Sound[251]
in the Welsh[252] ring court.
The peace-delaying
reindeer-slayer of the
peak district [Þórr] was in
danger there on the
dangerous, foreboding
hood[253] of the giantess.

12. Dreif, með dróttar
kneyfi,
dólg-Svíþjóðar kólgu
sótti ferð á flótta
flesdrótt, í vé nesja;
þá er funhristis fasta,
flóðrifs Danir, stóðu,
knáttu, Jólnis Ættir,
útvés fyrir lúta.

13. Þars í þróttar hersar
þornrann hugum bornir,
hlymr varð hellis Kumra
hringbálkar, fram gingu;
Lista færðr í fasta
friðseinn var þar hreina
gnípu hlöðr á greypan
grán hött risa kvánar.

14. The High Heaven of
the Flame of the
Eyebrow of the Time
Counter[254] [Thor's head]
they [the giantesses]
forced up
against the hall beams [the
ceiling].
In return, they [the gian-
tesses] were butted
against the nuts [stones] of
the court hall
[the floor]. The Lord of the
Floating Chariot
of Thunderstorms [Thor]
crushed
the old keel of the
laughing ship
[the spines] of both cave
maidens.

15. The Son of Earth[255]
[Thor]
showed there an unusual
feat,
but the Men of the Marsh-
land of the
Fjord-Apple's Leg [the
giants]
did not divert from their
ale-joy.
The Elm-Cord's [bow's]
Aegir,[256]
the Descendant of the
Southerner[257] [Red Spear]
shot the iron morsel [iron
rod], cooked in the forge,
at the mouth of Óðinn's
Grief-Stealer [Thor].

14.Ok hám loga himni,
hall- fylvingum vallar
tráðusk þær, við tróði
-tungls brá- salar þrungu;
húfstjóri braut hváru
hreggs váfreiðar tveggja
hlátr-elliða hellis
hundfornan kjöl sprundi.

15.Fátíða nam fræði,
fjarðeplis, konr Jarðar,
mærar legs, né mýgðu
menn ölteiti, kenna;
álmtaugar laust ægir
angrþjóf sega töngu
Óðins afli soðnum,
áttruðr, í gin, Suðra.

16.The Conqueror[258]
[Thor]
of the Kinsmen [giants]
of the
Women who Run in the
Night[259] [giantesses],
that Swift Hastener of
Battle [Thor],
the old Friend of Þröng
[Freyia][260] [=Thor]
swallowed greedily the
molten iron drink
[the arrow], swiftly flying
in the air,
with the open mouth
[palm] of his hand
when the sparkling cinder
flew
from the grip's hostile[261]
chest [hand] of the
Lustful Lover of Hrím-
nir[262] Maiden [Red Spear]
towards He Who Yearns
For Power[263] [Thor].

16.Þröngvir gein við þungum
þangs rauðbita tangar
kveldrunninna kvinna
kunnleggs alinmunni.
Svá at hraðskyndir handa
hrapmunnum svalg gun-
nar
lyptisylg á lopti
langvinr síu Þröngvar,
þá er örþrasis eisa
ós Hrímnis fló drósar
til þrámóðnis Þrúðar.

17.Þrasir's[264] [the giant's]
hall trembled
when Heath Travel-
er's[265][Red Spear's]
broad head submitted
beneath
the ancient leg of the wall
of the bear of the floor-
bear [pillar].

The splendid step-father
of Ullr [Thor]
struck the harmful gem
[the iron-bolt]
most forcefully down into
the middle
of the belt of the Fishing
Line's[266]
Path's Tooth's Foe [Red
Spear].

18. The Very Angry One
[Thor] slaughtered
the descendants of Loud
Sound[267] [giants]
with his bloodied ham-
mer.[268]

The Slayer [Thor]of the
frequent visitor [Red
Spear]
of the Hall of the Stone-
goddess [cave] was victo-
rious.
The Bow-Pole [Thor] did
not lack support,
the God of the Chariot
[Thor]shortened the life-
spans
for the giant's[269] bench
companions [giants].

17.Bifðisk höll þá er höfði
Heiðreks of kom breiðu
und fletbjarnar fornan
fótlegg Þrasis veggjar;

ítr gulli laust Ullar
jótrs vegtaugar þrjóti
meina niðr í miðjan
mest bígyrðil nestu.

18.Glaums niðjum fór gör-
vagramr með dreyrgum
hamri;
of salvanið-Synjar
sigr hlaut arinbauti.

Komat tvíviðar tývi
tollur karms, sá er harmi,
brautarliðs, of beitti
bekk-, fall, jötuns -rekka.

19. The Hel-striker [Thor],
who receives sacrifice,
with the Elf [Þiálfi] slew
the forest-calves [the
giants]
of the Elf-World's Gleam's
[Sun goddess's]
underground hiding place
[cave/underworld]
with the One Who Easily
Crushes Things [Mjöllnir].
The Rogalanders[270]of the
District
of the Falcon-lair [giants]
were unable to harm
the firmly supportive
shortener[Þiálfi]
of the lifespan of the Men
of the Rock-king [giants].

19. Hel blótinn vá hneitir
hógbrotningi skógar
undirfjálfrs at álfi
álfheims bliku kálfa;
ne liðföstum Lista
látrval-Rygir máttu
aldrminnkanda aldar
Ellu steins of bella.

Detail from Gotland picture stone, 7th century AD

8: Loki Steals Síf's Hair-Af smíðum Ívaldasona ok Sindra dvergs.

Of the Forge of the Sons of the In-Ruler and Sindri the Dwarf- [Skaldskaparmál 43, Prose Edda]

43: Aegir said: "Why is gold called the Kinswoman's Hair?"[271]
Bragi said: "Loki Leaf-Island's Son had done this bad deed as to cut all the hair off of Síf [Kinswoman]. And when Thor was aware of this, he took Loki and was about to break every bone in him, until he swore this, that he should get this from the Black Elves[272]; that they should make out of gold a head of hair for Síf, that would later grow like normal hair.

After that, Loki went to those dwarfs who are called the Sons of the In-Ruler,[273] and they made the head of hair, and Skíðblaðnir [Wooden Splinters][274] and the spear that Óðinn owned, which is called Gungnir [Swaying][275]. Then Loki wagered his head with that dwarf who is called Brokk [Runner][276] about whether his brother, Sindri [Sparks][277], would be able to make equally good treasures as these others had been.

And when they came to the smithy, then Sindri put the skin of a swine into the forge and asked Runner to blow the fire with a bellow and not let go until he had taken out of the forge that which he had placed there. But as soon as he left the smithy and the other one was blowing, then a fly settled on his hand and and bit him. But he kept pulling the bellow until the blacksmith took the skin out of the forge – and then it was a boar with bristles of gold.

Thereafter, he placed gold into the forge and told Runner to blow and not stop the blowing before he returned. He went outside. And then the fly returned and settled on his neck and bit again, twice as hard as before. But he kept working the bellow until til smith pulled out of the forge the golden ring which is called Dripper [Draupnir].[278]

Then he place iron into the forge and asked him to blow and said that this work would be of no use if he failed to blow correctly. Then the fly settled between his eyes and bit so hard that blood fell into his eyes, so that he could not see, then he used both hands to snatch after it as quickly as he could while the bellow was on it's was down, and swept the fly away, and then the blacksmith returned and said that now they had come close to ruining everything in the forge. Then he pulled out of the forge a hammer.

Then he handed over all these treasures into the hands of his brother Runner and bid him to travel to Ásgarð and demand the wager. And when he and Loki produced these treasures, then the Aesir went to their judgment seats and decided that the final decision was to be made by Óðinn, Thor and Freyr.

Loki gave to Óðinn the spear Swaying [Gungnir], and to Thor the hair that Síf was to own, and to Freyr the ship, Wooden Splinters [Skíðblaðnir], and explained the features of each treasure; that the spear never stopped in its thrust, that the hair would root itself into the flesh as soon as it was placed on the Kinswoman's head, and that Wooden Splinters would get a fair wind as soon as its sails were hoisted, wherever it was meant to sail, and that it could be folded up like a cloth and put in a pocket if so desired.

Then Runner appeared with his treasures. He gave to Óðinn the ring and said that she would drip eight new gold rings of equal weight as itself every nine nights. And to Freyr he gave the boar and said that he could run across the heavens and the ocean, by night and by day, faster than any horse, and it would never get so dark, either due to it being nighttime, or else due to traveling in the dark worlds, that he [the boar] would not shine brightly enough, for that was how much light would be generated from its golden bristles.

Then he gave to Thor the hammer and said it would be able to strike as heavily as he liked, no matter the target the hammer would never fail, and if he threw it at something it would never miss, and never fly so far away that it would not find its way back to his hand; and if he wanted it so, it would be so small that he could keep it inside his shirt. But there was this defect in the handle, that it was rather short.

The gods decided that the hammer was still the best of all these treasures, because it provided the best defense against frost giants,[279] and their decree was that the dwarf had won the wager.

Then Loki offered compensation instead of his head, but the dwarf refused and said there was no chance now.

"Catch me, then," said Loki.

But when Runner tried to catch him, Loki was gone. Loki had some shoes with which he could run across the sky and sea.[280] Then the dwarf asked Thor to catch Loki, and he did. Then the dwarf was going to cut off Loki's head, but Loki said that even if the head was his, the neck was not.

Then the dwarf produced a rope and a knife, attempting to pierce holes in Loki´s lips and was going to stitch up his mouth, but the knife did not cut. Then he said that his brother´s needle would have been better, and as soon as he mentioned the needle, it was there, and it went through the lips. Thus he sewed Loki´s lips together, but Loki tore the rope out.

The rope that was used to stitch Loki´s lips shut was called Vartari [Lack of Gratitude/Bad Payment][281]

The Snaptun stone, depicting Loki with his mouth stitched together, originating in Norway or west-Sweden, now held in Århus, Denmark. It was carved around 1000 AD.

9: Loki Steals Freyia's Gem-From: Sörla þáttr eða Heðins saga ok Högna

– The Piece About Sörli – in Flateyjarbók 228-229

228: The Land east of Vanakvisl [the river Don] in Asia was called Asialand or Asiaheim, and the people who lived there were called Aesir, and their capital was Ásgarð. Óðinn is mentioned as a king there. There was a great temple for sacrifices there. Óðinn set Njǫrðr and Freyr to be sacrificial priests[282] there. Njǫrðr's daughter was Freyia. She followed Óðinn and was his concubine.[283]

There in Asia lived some men not far from the king's hall. One was called Elf Lord,[284] the other Hibernation,[285] the third Short Beam[286] and the fourth Bellower.[287] These men were so skilled that with their hands they could make everything complete. Such as these, people called dwarfs.[288] They lived inside a stone.[289] In those days they mixed more with people than they do now.

Óðinn loved Freyia very much, and she was also the most beautiful of all women in her time. She had her own estate. It was both fair and strong, and people say that if her door was closed and locked, no man could ever enter against Freyia's will.

It so happened that one day, Freyia went to the stone,[290] and it was open. The dwarfs were about to forge a golden neck-ring.[291]

Freyia thought well of the gem. The dwarfs thought well of Freyia.

She haggled with the dwarfs about the necklace, offered both gold and silver and all sorts of treasure for it. They said that treasure and money were of no use to them. Each said they would sell their part of the jewel, and no other price would they accept than that she lay one night with each of them. And whether she thought she could have gotten better or worse out of this, she bought the ring this way.

229: A man was called Dangerous Hitter.[292] He was an old man and had a wife called Leaf Island.[293] She was both thin and weak. For that reason she was called Needle.[294] Of children, they had only one son.[295] He was called Loki. He was not large of growth. He was early strong in language and quick of mind. He had before anything else that sort of wisdom called cunning. He was very sly even from a young age. Therefore, he was called Loki the Sly. He managed to get to Óðinn in Ásgarð and became his man. Óðinn followed his advice in most anything, whatever he invented.

He often got him into trouble, but he also solved these problems better than one could expect. He was also able to get knowledge about almost anything that happened. He told Óðinn everything he knew. It is said that Loki got whiff of how Freyia got her golden neck-ring, and also how she had paid for it, and he told Óðinn. And when Óðinn got to know this, he said that Loki should steal the neck-ring and give it to him. Loki said that there was little hope of managing that, for no man could enter Freyia's hall against her will. Óðinn told him to go anyway and not return until he had managed to steal the neck-ring. Loki was shouting and cursing as he went on his way. Most people were enjoying it when Loki was in trouble. He got to Freyia's hall, which was locked.

He searched about for an entrance but found none. The weather was cold, and he started to freeze. Then he transformed himself into a fly. He flew about all the locks and small gaps in the wall, but found no hole where he could enter. But all the way up by the roof beams he found a gap, not larger than that one could get a needle through it – and through this hole he entered. When he was inside, he was very alerted in his eyes and thought about whether anyone was awake, but saw that everything was sleeping in the hall. He went over to Freyia's bed and saw that she had the ring around her neck, and saw that the lock was partly open.

Then Loki made himself into a flea. He sat down on her cheek and stung hard so that Freyia woke up, but turned around and slept again. Then Loki pulled off his flea hide, lured the neck-ring off her, opened the entrance and snuck away. He gave the jewel to Óðinn. Freyia woke up in the morning and saw that the door was open, but not broken through, and the beautiful necklace was gone. She thought she knew what sort of cunning had been going on.

As soon as she was dressed, she went into the hall to stand before king Óðinn, and told him that it was really mean of him to steal her gem, and asked him to return her treasure. Óðinn said that this would never happen, as he knew how she had come to own it, "unless you make sure that the two high kings, who both have twenty kings beneath them, should become enemies and fight each other with the fate and curse that they shall get up every morning and fight again, even as they fell before, unless one Christian man would be so brave and have so much fortune and luck from his lord that he dared to enter this battle and kill these men with weapons.

Only then would the eternal war end, and what chiefs these were who were fated to release them from its slavery and the horror of all the bad things they are doing." Freyia agreed to this and got her ring-gem back.

Woman approaching
Sun disc. Bronze Age
rock carving, Norway

[Translator's note: The myth about how Freyia's necklace, the Brisingamén, was acquired and then stolen is probably old, referred to also in Snorri's Skaldskaparmál (Prose Edda) as we shall see next. However, we are left only with fragments of this story. The source above, Flateyjarbók, is a very late source, written between 1387-1394, when paganism had been more or less outlawed for almost three centuries. After telling the tale of how Óðinn made Loki steal Freyia's necklace, the editors of the Flateyjarbók move on to tell a story of how the goddess turns up in at least one disguise; as the giantess Göndul [Magician], appearing three times in a sacred grove to a young king, enticing him to perpetual war against another king, just as Óðinn had demanded. The line between original myth and medieval, Christian fiction with agendas of its own is blurred and uncertain; In Skaldspaparmál, written 150 years earlier, Snorri, referring to earlier, Pre-Christian, Skaldic poetry, offers up a different fragment to the story in which Heimdall and Loki battles over the gem in the shape of seals.]

HEIMDALLARKENNINGAR–METAPHORS FOR HEIMDALLR
[SKALDSKAPARMÁL 15, PROSE EDDA]

15: How shall Heimdall be known? So as by calling him the Son of
Nine Mothers[296] or the Guardian of the Gods,[297] such as has before
been recited, or the Bright/Light/White God,[298] Loki's Enemy, Seeker
of Freyia's Gem.[299]

Heimdall's head is called Sword.[300] It is said he was struck right
through with the head of a man. About that it is spoken in the
Spell-Song of Heimdall,[301] and ever since, "head" has been called (in
poetical metaphors) the Fate of Great World.[302]

«Sword» is called the Fate of Man.[303]

Heimdall is the Owner of Gold Top. He is also the Seeker of Waves'
Reef and the Stone of Desire/Stinginess.[304] There [at the Stone of
Desire] he competed with Loki about the Ring-Gem of Flames
[Brisingamén, Freyia's necklace]. Heimdall is also called Wind-
Shielded.[305]

Ulfr Uggason[306] composed in Húsdrápa a long time after these
events, and it is there said that they [Heimdall and Loki] had taken
the likeness of seals.[307]

LOKAKENNINGAR 308
METAPHORS FOR LOKI

[SKALDSKAPARMÁL 23, PROSE EDDA, QUOTING FROM
HÚSDRÁPA 2-3, A SKALDIC POEM BY ÚLFR UGGASON]

23: [...]As here says Úlfr
Uggason:
2. The Counsel-Wise, Fa-
mous
Guardian of the Path of the
Gods [Heimdall]
competed with The One
Blamed for Slyness,
the Son of Dangerous Hitter
[Loki]
at the Stone of Desire;[309]
The Son of Eight Mothers
And One,
of flying courage/mind
[Heimdall]
saved the Ocean-Kidney
fair [Brisingamén].
I declare this is thought
praiseworthy.

Ráðgenginn bregðr Ragna
Rein at Singasteini
frægr við firnaslægjan
Fárbauta Mög vári;
móðöflugr ræðr Mæðra
Mögr hafnýra fögru,
kynni ek, áðr Ok Einnar
Átta, mærðar þáttum.

Here is this told, that Heimdall is the son of nine mothers.[310]

3. The Moon Within shone
in the forehead of the
impressive
Friend of the Bonds[311]
The famous god shot
the Beams of Aegir/Terror
at the Gem of the Earth[312]

Innmáni skein ennis
öndótts Vinar Banda;
áss skaut Ægigeislum
orðsæll á Men Storðar,
...

10: OTTER'S COMPENSATION-AF OTRGJÖLDUM
OF THE OTTER´S COMPENSATION
[SKALDSKAPARMÁL 46, PROSE EDDA]

46: Aegir said: «What is the reason for this, that gold is called Otter's Compensation?"[313]

Bragi said: "It is said, that the Aesir traveled in order to know the world,[314] Óðinn, Loki and Hænir. Then they came to a certain river, and followed it upwards until they reached a waterfall. There sat an otter, he had taken a salmon out of the waterfall and was eating while sleeping. Then Loki took a stone and threw it at the otter, and hit him right in the head. Loki bragged about this catch; there he had managed to get both otter and salmon.

They took the salmon and the otter with them and carried them, and came to a house and went in there. And there was a farmer who is named Rage Ocean,[315] who lived there. He was very much of a man and very cunning/versed in magic.[316] They asked there for a night-place, and said they had more than enough food, and then they showed the farmer their hunting catch. And when Rage Ocean saw the otter, he called on his sons, Embracer[317] and Reginn [The Ruler], and says that Otter, their brother, has been murdered, and who had done it. Now, father and son attacked the Aesir and took them and bound them and say about the otter that he had been the son of Rage Ocean.

The Aesir asked for terms of release, as much compensation as Rage Ocean would say, and then that deal was made between them and bound with an oath. The otter was now flayed. Rage Ocean took the otter skin and said to them that they should fill it with Red Gold[318] and likewise cover it completely with it, and that should be their agreement. Then Óðinn sent Loki into Black Elf World,[319] and he came to this dwarf whose name is Spirit Alert.[320]

He was a fish in the water, and Loki took him in his hands and declared this term of release; that he must hand over all the gold he owned in his stone.[321] And when they came inside the stone, then the dwarf carried forth all the gold that he owned, and that was a formidable treasure. Then the dwarf tried to hide a little gold-ring beneath his arm. Loki saw it and asked him to show the ring.

The dwarf begged him to not take the ring from him, for with it he could produce more treasure, if only he could keep it. But Loki said he should not have a penny left, and took the ring from him and went outside, and the dwarf said that this ring should be every owner's bane. Loki did not mind that. This curse may just as well be executed, and he should let anyone who accepted the ring get to hear about the curse. With this, he left and came to Rage Ocean and showed Óðinn the gold. And when Óðinn saw the ring, then it seemed to him very fair, and he took it away from the great treasure that they were giving to Rage Ocean. Then Óðinn filled the otter skin as full as it got and covered it on the outside, and sat it up when it was full. He asked Rage Ocean to look if not the entire skin was covered.

Rage Ocean looked closely and spotted a whisker[322] sticking out and demanded that they also cover that, or their truce would come to an end. Then Óðinn took out the ring and placed it on the whisker and said that now they were released from the Otter's Debt. And when Óðinn had taken his spear, and Loki his shoes, and they no longer had anything to fear, then Loki said that he had a message from Spirit Alert; that the ring and the gold would be the bane of anyone who owned them. And so it also came to pass. Now has been told why the gold is called Otter's Payment[323] or the Need-Debt of the Aesir or the Metal of Conflict."

THE SPEECH OF THE RULER-REGINSMÁL 1-9, POETIC EDDA.

Sigurð went to Communicator's[324] stable and chose for himself that horse which has later been called Grani. Then had Reginn [The Ruler] come to Communicator's realm, the son of Rage Ocean;[325] he was more skillful than all men and a dwarf of growth; he was wise, ferocious, and very cunning/versed in magic.[326] Reginn fostered [taught] Sigurð, and educated him, and loved him very much. He told Sigurð about his parents and that tiding, that Óðinn and Hænir and Loki had come to the Spirit Alert waterfall.[327]

In that waterfall there was a lot of fish. A dwarf was called Spirit Alert,[328] and he had for a long time lived in the waterfall, taking the likeness of a pike,[329] and got his food from there. His brother was called Otter,[330] said Reginn, and often he leapt in the waterfall in the likeness of an otter.[331] He had taken a salmon and sat by the river bank, eating it with his eyes shut. Loki struck him to death with a stone, the Aesir thought this was a great fortune, and flayed the otter's skin to make a bag.

That same evening, they went as guests to Rage Ocean's, and showed him their hunting catch. Then he took them prisoners and gave them this term of release; that they fill the otter-bag with with gold within and cover it on the outside with the Red Gold.[332] They sent Loki then to produce the gold; he came to Robbery[Rán][333] and had her net, and traveled then to the waterfall of Spirit Alert and threw the net out to the pike, and she leaped into the net.

Then Loki said:
"What is that fish
which flows through the
stream
can you not be alert to
danger?
Your head you may ran-
som
out of Hel
if you find me the Flame
of the Serpent."[334]

„Hvat er þat fisca,
er renn floþi i,
kannat ser viþ viti varaz?
hofvþ þitt leystv
helio ór,
finn mer Lindar Loga!"

The Pike said:
"Spirit Alert is my name
Óinn[335] was my father,
much in the waterfall I
have fared;
A Hostile norn
decreed in the Days Be-
fore[336]
that I should wade in the
water."

Geddan qvaþ:
„Andvari ec heiti,
Oinn het minn faþir,
margan hefi ec fors vm
fariþ;
a/mlig norn
scop oss i ardaga,
at ec scylda i vatni vaþa."

Loki said:
"Say you this, Spirit Alert!
if you want to own
life in the halls of people:
What debt must they
carry
- the sons of men -
if they wound each other
with words?"

Loki qvaþ:
3.„Segðv þat, Anduari!
ef þv eiga vill
lif i lyða salom:
hver giold fa
gvmna synir,
ef þeir haggvaz orþom á?"

Spirit Alert said:
"A terrible debt must
the sons of men carry:
they must wade in Noise
of Standstill;[337]
words of untruth
and lies about others
have terribly long branches."

Andvari qvaþ:
4.„Ofrgiold fa
gvmna synir
þeir er Vadgelmi vaþa;
osadra orða,
hverr er a annan lygr,
oflengi leida limar."

Loki saw all the gold that Spirit Alert owned, and when he had produced the gold in his hands [over to Loki], then he still had one ring, and Loki took it from him. The dwarf went into the stone and said:

That gold shall
- which was owned by
Blowing Breath[338] -
be the bane
of two brothers;
and cause conflict
between eight princes:
Few may enjoy
my treasure."

„Þat scal gvll,
er Gvstr atti,
brœdrum tveim
at bana verda
oc aþlingom
atta at rógi,
mvn mins fiár
mangi niota."

The Aesir gave to Rage Ocean the treasure and spread out the Otter-skin and stretched out its legs; then the Aesir had to heap up the gold and cover it. And when that was done, Rage Ocean went forth and said that one whisker-hair could still be seen and bade them cover that too. Then Óðinn produced the ring, The Ring of Spirit Alert,[339] and hid the whisker. Then said Loki:

"The gold is now given
And you have received a great
ransom for my head;
Your sons will see
no good fortune,
and they will both be your bane."

Rage Ocean said:
"Gifts you gave -
you gave no affec-
tion-gifts,
you gave not from a whole heart;
Your lives I should have deprived from you
if I had known this be-
fore."

Loki said:
"One thing is worse
 I think I know that –
the doomed war between relatives;
Princes yet unborn
I think they are cursed towards hatefulness.

Rage Ocean said:
The Red Gold
I think I shall rule
for as long as I live;
Your threat
I do not fear at all
now go back home
across the heath.

6.„Gvll er þer nv reitt,
en þv giold hefir
micil mins ha/fvþs;
syni þinom verþra
sęla sca/pvþ,
þat verþr yccarr beggia
bani."

Hreiþmarr sagði:
7.„Giafar þv gaft,
gaftattv astgiafar,
gaftattv af heilom hvg;
fiorvi yðro scyldvt er
firþir vera,
ef ec vissa þat fár fyr."

Loki qvaþ:
8.„Enn er verra
— þat vita þicciomc —
niðia strið vm nept;
iofra oborna
hygg ec þa enn vera,
er þat er til hatrs hvgað."

Hreiþmarr qvaþ:
9.„Ra/þo gvlli
hygg ec mic raða mvno
sva lengi sem ec lifi;
hót þín
hrǫþvmc ecki lyf,
oc haldit heim heþan!"

The Embracer[340] and Reginn demanded the compensation after Otter their brother, but their father said no to this, but then the Embracer thrust the sword into Rage Ocean their father while he was sleeping...[341]

11: Thor and the Middle World Serpent-Þórr reri á sæ með Hymi.

Thor Rows Out to the Sea with Hymir [Gylfaginning, 48, Prose Edda]

48: Then spoke Wandering Learner: «Allmighty he seems to me, Outer World Loki,[342] even if he employed trickery and cunning witchcraft. That he is powerful, one may understand from having such strong warriors. Tell me, did Thor never avenge himself for this?»

The High One replied: "It is not unknown – even outside of learned circles – that Thor indeed restored his honour against this misconduct that we have now told you. He did not stay at home for a long time before he prepared for another voyage, and he was in such a hurry that he left home without his chariot and his rams, and without company too.

He went out into Middle World in the shape of a young boy. As night approached, he came to the place of a certain giant. He is called Hymir.[343] Thor stayed there as a guest. At dawn, Hymir got up and dressed himself and prepared to row out on the sea in order to fish. Thor got up quickly and was swiftly ready, and asked Hymir if he would let him row out to the sea with him. Hymir said that there would be little help from him, young and tiny as he was, "and you are going to freeze, because I lie out as far and for such a long time as I am used to."

But Thor said that he could well row far away from land, for it was not at all certain that he was going to be the first to beg for a return. He was so angry with the giant that he nearly hit him with the hammer. But then he thought better of it, for he thought it was better to try his strength against something else. He asked Hymir what they should use for a bait, and Hymir told him to get his own. Thor then went and saw a flock of oxen owned by Hymir. He took the largest ox – his name was Heaven Tearer[344] - and tore his head apart, and went down to the shore with it.

Hymir had already set out the boat. Thor embarked and sat down at the well of the boat, took two oars and began rowing, and Hymir thought that the rowing was fast progressing. Then Hymir said that they had reached the fishing ground where he usually sat catching flat fish, but Thor said he wanted to row much further, and they did another spurt of rowing. Then said Hymir that they had reached out so far that it was dangerous to go further because of the Middle World Serpent. But Thor said he would row on a bit more and did so, but Hymir was then very unhappy.

And when Thor had shipped his oars, he produced a line that was rather strong, and the hook was no smaller or less powerful looking. On to this hook Thor fastened the ox-heard and it is true to say that Thor tricked the Middle World Serpent no less than Outer World Loki had ridiculed Thor when he was lifting the serpent up with his hand. The Middle World Serpent stretched its mouth around the ox-head and the hook stuck into the roof of the serpents mouth. And when the serpent felt this, it jerked away so hard that both Thor's fists banged down on the gunwale.

Then was Thor angry, and summoned his divine power,[345] and he pushed down so hard that he forced both his feet through the boat and braced them against the sea-floor and then hauled the serpent up to the gunwale. And one must say that one does not know what a horrible sight is, who did not get to see how Thor fixed his eyes on the serpent, and the serpent stared back up at him, spitting poison.

It is said that then, the giant Hymir changed color, went pale, and panicked when he saw the serpent and how the sea flowed out and in over the boat. And just at the moment when Thor was grasping his hammer and lifting it in the air, the giant fumbled at his bait-knife and cut Thor's line from the gunwale, and the serpent sank into the sea. But Thor threw his hammer after it, and they say that he struck off its head by the sea-bed. But I think that the opposite is the truth, for I must report to you that the Middle World Serpent still lives and lies encircling the sea. But Thor swung his fist and struck at Hymir's ear so that he plunged overboard, and one could see the soles of his feet. But Thor waded ashore."

Illustration from a Medieval Prose Edda manuscript

THE SONG OF HYMIR-[HYMISKVIÐA, POETIC EDDA]

A long time ago, the gods
of choice[346]
returned from the hunt,
hungry
and in wont of drink
the carved twigs[347]
they checked for answers
and they found out
that with Aegir[348]
there was abundance [of
drink].

The Mountain-Dweller sat
like a happy child
much like the son
of the Brew-Blender[349]
Ygg´s[350] child looked him
hard in the eyes;
"You shall for the Aesir
often make drink."

For the labour that the
giant
got from the word-sharp
one
he thought about
vengeance
against the gods;
He asked Síf´s Man [Thor]
to bring before him a
cauldron[351]
"that may hold enough ale
for everyone."

But such a cauldron
the precious gods
and the sacrosanct rulers
did not know,
before the trustworthy
Týr[352] to the Loud/Glow
Rider[Thor]
a very loving advice
spoke in private;

Ar valtívar
veiþar námo
oc sumblsamir,
aþr saþir yrþi,
hristo teina
oc a hlaʀt sa,
fvndo þeir at Aegis
aʀrcost hvera.

Sat Bergbui
barnteitr fyr
mioc glicr megi
Miscorblinda;
leit i augo Yggs barn í þrá:
„Þv scalt asom
opt svmbl gora."

Avnn fecc iotni
orþbøginn halr,
hvgdi at hefnþom
hann nøst viþ goð;
bað hann Sifiar Ver
ser føra hver:
„þannz ec aʀllom ol
yðr of heita."

4.Ne þat matto
mørir tifar
oc ginnregin
of geta hvergi,
vnnz af trygðom
Tyr Hlorriþa
astraþ mikit
einom sagdi:

"There lives to the east
of the Waves of the
Ages[353]
the dog-wise Hymn
[Hymir]
at the End of Heaven;
with my father
a powerful kettle,
a bottomless cauldron
many leagues deep."

Thor said:
"Do you think he will lend
us
the Vessel of Flames?"
Týr said;
"If, my friend, we
apply some cunning!"

They traveled long
the whole day
far from Ásgarð
until they reached Egill's
home;[354]
He [Egill] took care of the
rams
the ones fair of horns
They [Thor and Týr] went
to the hall
that Hymn owned.

The Son found
Grandmother[355]
a terrifying sight;
nine hundred heads
the old one had;
but another came,
all golden, forth;
bright-browed she carried
strong drink to her son;[356]

5.„Byr fyr a'stan
Ęlivága
hvndviss Hymir
at Himins Enda;
a minn faþir
moþvgr ketil,
rvmbrvgðinn hver,
rastar divpan."

6.Þorr qvaþ:
„Veiztv ef þiggiom
þann Lögvelli?"
Tyr qvaþ:
„Ef, vinr! velar
viþ gorvom til."

7.Fóro drivgom
dag þann fram
Asgardi fra,
vnz til Egils qvomo;
hirði hann hafra
hornga'fgasta,
hvrfo at ha'llo,
er Hymir átti.

8.Ma'gr fann Ammo
mioc leiþa ser,
hafði ha'fda
hvndrvð nío;
enn a'nnvr gecc
algvllin fram
brvnhvít bera
biorveig syni:

She said:
"Descendant of Giants![357]
I would that you two,
full of intent,
shall sit beneath the
cauldron;
For my lover [Hymn]
is oftentimes
stingy with guests
and of bad temper."

Late in the evening
came the dangerous
hard-ruling Hymn
home from the hunting;
It was the farmer who
came home,
he walked through the
hall,
icicles jingling from his
frozen face-forest [beard]

The concubine said:
"Be you whole, Hymn,
and greet with good
intent;
now the Son has come to
your halls,
the one we have waited for
from long ways;
He is followed by
the Enemy of the
Quarreler [Týr],[358]
the friend of mankind (is
here);
his name is Temple Guard
[Thor].[359]

9.„Átniþr iotna!
ec viliac ycr
hvgfvlla tvá
vnd hvera setia;
er mínn frí
margo sinni
glaggr viþ gesti,
geyrr illz hvgar."

10.En vascapadr
varþ siþbvinn
harðráþr Hymir
heim af veiþom;
gecc inn i sal,
glvmþo ioclar,
var karls, er com,
kinnscogr frQrinn.

11.Frilla qvaþ:
„Verþv heill, Hymir!
i hvgom goþom,
nv er Sonr kominn til sala
þinna, sa er viþ vęttom
af vegi longom;
fylgir hánom Hroþrs-And-
scoti,
vinr verliða,
Vęorr heitir sa.

There they are seated, as
you see,
beneath the gables of the
hall!
Trying to save themselves
the pillar is before them."
The pillar broke asunder
from the mere gaze of the
giant
and the beam that
hadcarried it
broke in two.

Down from the gable
eight kettles fell;
One cauldron, hard-beaten
stood whole, out of all
(nine kettles);
They went forth
and the ancient giant
followed them with his
gaze;
saw his enemy [Thor].

He said nothing of good
will then
when he saw
the Weeping of Giantesses
[Thor]
coming out on the floor;
Soon three oxen were
taken
and the giant bid
that they be cooked.

Each of them [the oxen]
became a head shorter
and into the earth-oven
they were then carried;
Sif's Man ate,
before he went to sleep,
two of Hymn's oxen
all by himself.

12. Sé þv, hvar sitia
vnd salar gafli!
sva forþa ser,
stendr svíl fyr."
Svndr starcc svla
fyr sión iotvns,
enn aþr i tva
áss brotnaþi.

13. Stvcco atta,
en einn af þeim
hverr harðsleginn
heill, af þolli;
fram gengo þeir,
enn forn iotvnn sionom
leiddi
sinn andscota.

14. Sagðit hanom
hvgr vel þa,
er hann sa Gygiar Grọti
a golf kominn;
þar varo þiorar þrír of
teknir,
bað senn iotvnn
sioþa ganga.

5. Hvern leto þeir
harfdi scemra
oc a sæyþi
siþan báro;
át Sifiar Verr,
aþr sofa gengi,
einn meþ avllo
eyxn tva Hymis.

It seemed, to the grey-
haired
Friend of Hrungnir
[Hymir]
that the Loud Rider [Thor]
had eaten enormously;
"If we are to eat
tomorrow evening
we two must hunt for food
for the lives of us three."

16.Þótti három
Hrvngnis Spialla
verþr Hlórriða
vel fvllmicill:
„Mvnom at apni
arþrom verþa
viþ veiðimat
ver þrír lifa. "

The Temple Guard [Thor]
wanted
to row the wave [sea]
if the courageous giant
would give him a bait;
Hymn said: "Go you to the
herds
if your mind dares; you
Breaker of Moun-
tain-Danes[360] [Thor],
to seek a bait.

17.Veorr qvaz vilia
a vág róa,
ef ballr iotvnn
beítor gęfi. Hymir qvaþ:
„Hverf þv til hiarþar,
ef þv hvg trvir,
Briotr Bergdana!
beitor sǫkia.

This I expect,
that you will be able to get
a bait out of oxen
and it will be easy for
you."
The boy [Thor] shot
swiftly to the forests,
there an oxen stood
all black before him.

18.Þess vęnti ec,
at þer mynit
argn af oxa arþfeng vera. "
Sveinn sysliga
sveif til scógar,
þar er vxi stoþ
alsvartr fyr.

He broke off from the ox
the Counsel-Bane of
Thurses - [Thor] –
the high courts above
the two horns.
Hymir said:
"I think your work
is much worse,
-you ruler of the pram-
than when you sat quiet-
ly."

The Lord of Rams [Thor]
bade the
Descendant of Apes
[Hymn]
to row the Wave-Horse
[the boat][361]
further out;
But the giant said
he had little desire
to row further out

Famous Hymn, in anger,
later hauled up
two whales on his hook;
but in the stern of the ship
sat Óðinn's kins-
man[Thor],
the Temple Guard [Thor],
with cunning,
prepared his fishing line.

19. Braᴢt af þióri
þvrs ráþbani
hatᴠn ofan
horna tveggia.
Hymir qvaþ:
„Verc þiccia þin
verri myclo,
kiola valdi!
enn þv kyrr sitir."

20. Bað hlvnngota
Hafra Drottinn
Átrunn Apa
vtarr fǫra;
enn sa iotvnn sina talþi
litla fysi
at róa lengra.

21. Dró meirr Hymir
moþvgr hvali
einn a aᴠngli
vpp senn tvá;
enn aptr i scvt
Oþni sifiaþr
Veorr við velar
vað gorði ser.

He baited his hook,
the Savior of Ages [Thor],
the Sole Bane of the Ser-
pent [Thor],
with the head of the ox;
Gaped over the bait
the Enemy of Gods [Mid-
dle World Serpent]
the Circling Girdle of All
Lands,
from below.

The brave, deedstrong
Thor hauled
the poison-shiny serpent
up against the board;
the hammer struck
the mountain-peak [top]
of the hair
of the Wolf´s Terrible
Brother
from above.

The Rock Troll[362] shrieked
and the mountain howled
and the entire
ancient Earth creaked,
then later he sunk
like a fish in the sea.

Unhappy the giant
as they later rowed
so unhappy that Hymn
spoke nothing at all;
he turned the boat
rowed back to the shore.

22.Egndi a angvl
sa er Aldom Bergr
Orms Einbani
vxa hǫfdi;
geín við agni
sv er God Fiá
Umgiorþ nedan
Allra Landa.

23.Dró diarfliga
daþraccr Þorr
orm eitrfán
vpp at borði;
hamri kniþi
hafiall scarar
ofliótt ofan
Ulfs Hnitbroþvr.

24.Hreingalcn hlvmþo,
en halcn þvto,
for in forna
Fold all saman,
sacþiz siþan
sa fiscr i mar.

25.Oteitr iotvnn,
er þeir aptr réro,
sva at ár Hymir
ecci mǫlti,
veifþi hann rǫþi
veðrs annars til.

Hymn said:
"Will you share
in this toil with me,
will you carry the whales
back to the farm,
or will you pen up
our Floating-Buck
[boat?]"

The Loud Rider [Thor]
went
and clasped the prow
hauled the Bath-Stallion
[boat]
up on the shore;
and with the oars
and with the bailers
he carried then the giant's
Wave-Swine [boat] home
through a cauldron[363]
[canyon]
between forestclad hills.

Yet the giant,
ever so provocative,
wanted to argue
with Thor about strength;
He said that hard rowing
was not enough
the strong man would be
the one
who could break his Cup.

But the Loud/Glow Rider,
when (the Cup) came into
his hands,
hurled it so hard
that a pillar broke in two;
Seated, he hurled it
between the two parts:
Unbroken they carried
(the cup) to Hymn.

26.Hymir qvaþ:
„Mvndo vm vinna
verc halft viþ mic,
at þv heim hvali
haf til bøiar,
eþa Flotbrusa
festir occarn?"

27.Gecc Hlorriþi,
greip a stafni,
vatt meþ avstri
vpp Laugfáki;
einn meþ árom
oc meþ avstscoto
bar hann til bøiar
Brimsvín iotvns,
oc holtriþa hver i gegnom.

28.Oc enn iotvnn
vm afrendi
þragirni vanr
viþ Þór senti;
qvaþat mann ramman,
þott róa kynni
kravptvrligan,
nema Kálc bryti.

29.Enn Hlorriþi,
er at havndom com,
brátt lét bresta
brattstein i tvav;
slo hann sitiandi
svlor igognom,
baro þo heilan
fyr Hymi siþan

Until the fair concubine
gave him this mighty
love-counsel
that only she knew;

"Strike against Hymn´s
head;
The head is harder
on that food-tired giant
than any Cup there is."

Swiftly he got up
the Lord of Rams [Thor],
gathering all his Divine
Power;
Whole was the hel-
met-stub [head]
against the strike,
but the Wine-cup broke.

"A great treasure, unique,
I know I have lost now,
the Cup that I often
held on my knees,"
the farmer [Hymn] spoke;
"Never may I greet
the beer with these words:
"There you stand brewed!

This is your reward,
if you can manage
to carry out of my hall
the ale-ship [the caul-
dron]."

30. Vnz þat in fríþa
frilla kendi
ástráþ mikit,
eitt er vissi:

„Drep við há́s Hymiss!
hann er harðari
costmoþs iotvns
Kalci hveriom."

31. Harþr reís a kné
Hafra Drottinn,
fǫrþiz allra i Ásmegin;
heill var karli
hialmstofn ofan,
enn Vínferill valr rifnaþæ.

32. „Morg veit ec męti
mer gengin fra,
er ec Kalci se
yr kniam hrvndit;"
karl ord vm qvað:
„knacat ec segia
aptr ęvagi,
þv ert, aˈlþr! of hęitt.

33. Þat er til costar,
ef coma męttiþ
v́t or óro
ǫlkiól hofi."

Týr tried to lift it twice
but could not even move
the cauldron.

The Father of Rage [Thor]
grasped the rim
so hard that he sank
through the floor of the
hall:
high up above his head
Síf's Husband lifted it
and the rings jingled
against his heels.[364]

They had not traveled
long before
it happened that Óðinn's
son looked back;
From the east with Hymn
he saw them coming out
of the rocks:
a folk-army was traveling,
many-headed.

Off his shoulders he threw
the cauldron, standing,
he hurled Grinder against
the murderous moun-
tain-men
and he struck all
the rock-whales [trolls].

They had not traveled
long before it happened
that the Loud Rider's ram
lay half-dead;
the draught-beast was
lame
and it was the fault of the
sly Loki.[365]

Tyr leitaþi tysvar hrǫra,
stoþ at hváro
hverr kyrr fyr.

34.Fadir Móþa
fecc a þremi
oc igegnom steig
golf niþr i sal;
hóf ser a haʼfvþ vp
hver Sifiar Verr,
enn a hęlom
hringar scvllo.

35.Foro lengi, aðr líta nam
aptr Oþins sonr eino sinni;
sa hann or hreysom
meþ Hymi aʼstan
folcdrott fara fiolhaʼfdaþa.

36.Hóf hann ser af herðom
hver standanda,
veifði hann Miollni
morðgiornom fram,
oc hráʼnhvali
hann alla drap.

37.Foroð lengi, aþr liggia
nam
hafr Hlorriða halfdaʼþr
fyr;
var scirr scaʼkvls scaccr a
banni,
enn þvi inn lęvisi Loci vm
olli.

But you have heard all this already -anyone can tell you that, who understands the gods –

what Thor got for a compensation from the mountain-resident; he gave him both his children.[366]

Tiredness had escaped him when he came to the gods´ Parliament and presented the cauldron the one that Hymn had owned; and every winter they would drink well ale at Aegir´s place,[367] all the sacred ones [the gods], in delight.

38.Enn er heyrt hafið, — hverr kann vm þat godmalvgra gorr at scilia? —

hver af hrá́nbv́a hann lá́n vm fecc, er hann bęþi galt born sin fyr.

39.Þrotta⁄flvgr kom a þing goda oc hafdi hver, þannz Hymir atti; enn vear hverian vel scolo drecca a⁄lþr at Aegis eitt ha⁄rmeitiþ

12: THE DEATH OF BALDER-FRÁ BALDRI, FRÁ HEÐI, FRÁ VÁLA

ABOUT BALDER, ABOUT HÖÐR, ABOUT VÁLI [GYLFAGINNING 22, 28, 30 PROSE EDDA]

22. Then spoke Wandering Learner: "I want to ask tidings about more Aesir."

The High One said: "Another son of Óðinn is Balder,[368] and about him there are only good things to say. He is the best, and everybody adores him. He is so beautiful to look at and so bright that he shines from within, and there is a type of flower that is so white, it has been called Balder´s Brow.[369] It is the whitest/ lightest of all flowers, and from this you can understand how fair[370] he was both of hair and body. He is the wisest among the Aesir, and the one who speaks most delightfully, and he is the most fair (as in justice[371]) among the gods: And this is his nature which follows with him; that no verdict of his may stand (because he is so non-judgemental).

He lives there, where it is called Broad View.[372] That is in heaven. In that place there may be nothing unclean, as it is said:[373]

Broad View it is called
where Balder has
raised his halls
In that land I think
there is the least malice.

> Breiðablik heita,
> þar er Baldr hefir
> sér of görva sali, á því landi,
> er ek liggja veit
> fæsta feiknstafi.

28. Strife [Hǫðr] is the name of a god. He is blind. He is very strong, but the gods would have preferred to be without the need of this god, for what he did will live for a long time in the memory of gods and men. (...)

30: Sprouting[374] or Choice[375] is one called, son of Óðinn and the Rejecter.[376] He is brave in battle and a very accurate shot.

VEGTAMSKVÍÐA EÐA BALDRS DRAUMAR-THE SONG OF WAY-WONT OR THE DREAMS OF BALDER
[POETIC EDDA]

1. Later, all the Aesir gathered for Parliament and the goddesses all to have their say; and about this they spoke, the powerful gods, of why Baldr was met with ominous dreams.	1.Senn vorv æsir allir a þingi ok asynivr alla a mali, ok vm þat ræðv rikir tifar, hvi væri Balldri ballir dravmar.

2. Up stood Óðinn,
that ancient man,
and on the Glider
[Sleipnir]
he placed the saddle;
from there did he ride
down
into Misty Hel,
there he met the whelp
the one who comes out of
Hel.

3. He was bloodied around
his chest
and against the
Father of Spell-Songs
[Óðinn]
he barked for a long time.
Forth rode Óðinn,
the earth-path resounded,
until he came to
the High Hall of Hel

4. Then rode Óðinn
to the east of the door,
there he knew
of a Wand-Witch's grave.
For the wise one
he sung death-spell-
songs,[377]
and reluctantly she rose
and spoke corpse's words:

5. "What sort of man are
you
to me unknown,
who has caused me
this painful path?
I was covered with snow,
and beaten by rain,
and driven by dew,
long was I dead."

2.Vpp ræis Oðinn,
alldinn gꜹtr,
ok hann a Slæipni
sꝺðvl vm lagði;
ræiþ hann niðr þaþan
Niflhæliar til,
mætti hann hvælpi
þæim ær or Hæliu kom.

3.Sa var bloðvgr
vm briost framan
ok Galldrs Fꝺðvr
gol vm længi.
Framm ræið Oðinn,
folldvægr dvndi,
hann kom at Háfv
Hæliar Ranni.

4.Þa ræið Oðinn
fyrir ꜹstan dyrr,
þar ær hann vissi
vꝺlv læiði.
Nam hann vittvgri
valgalldr kveða,
vnz naꝺðig ræis,
nas orð vm kvað:

5.„Hvat ær manna þat
mer okvnnra,
ær mer hæfir ꜹkit
ærfit sinni?
var ec snivin sniofi
ok slægin rægni
ok drifin daꝺggv,
daꝺð var æk længi."

6. Óðinn said:
"Way-Wont is my name,
I am the son of Death-
Wont,
tell me tidings from Hel
I will tell you tidings from
the world;
For whom are the benches
strewn with rings,
and the floor so fairly with
gold?"

7. The Wand-Witch said:
"Here stands for Balder
the mead brewed
the bright Power-drink
is covered with a shield,
and the mighty Aesir are
dreading this;
reluctantly I spoke,
now I want to be silent."

8. Óðinn said:
"Do not be silent, Wand-
Witch,
I want to ask you
until I know everything,
I still want to know:
Who shall be the Bane of
Balder,
and destroy the age
of Óðinn's son?"

9. The Wand-Witch said:
"Strife [Höðr] shall carry
the high descendant [Bald-
er] here;
He shall be the Bane of
Balder
and for Óðinn's son de-
stroy the age;
Reluctantly I spoke
now I wish to be silent."

6.Oðinn kvað:
„Vægtamr ec heiti,
sonr æm æk Valtams;
sægþv mer or Hæliu,
æc man or hæimi:
hvæim eru bekkir
baugum sánir,
flæt fagrlig floþ gvlli?"

7.Vǫlva kvað:
„Her stændr Baldri
of brygginn Miǫðr,
skírar Væigar,
liggr skiǫlldr yfir,
ænn asmægir i ofvæni;
naðvg sagðak,
nv mvn æk þægia."

8.Oðinn kvað:
„Þægiattv, vǫlva!
þik vil ek fregna,
vnz alkvnna, vil ec ænn
vita:
hverr man Balldri
at bana verða
ok Oðins son aldri ræna?"

9.Vǫlva kvað:
„Höðr berr hafan
hroðrbarm þinig,
hann man Balldri at bana
verða
ok Oðins son alldri ræna;
naðvg sagðak, nv mvn æk
þegia."

10. Óðinn said:
"Do not be silent, Wand-
Witch,
I want to ask you
until I know everything,
I still want to know:
Who shall be the avenger?
Who wins vengeance
against Strife
and carries the Bane of
Balder
to the pyre?"

11. The Wand-Witch said:
"Rejecter [Rindr][378]
births The Choice [Vali][379]
in the western halls,
One night old
he washes not his hands
combs not his hair
before he carries to the
pyre
Balder´s enemy.
I spoke reluctantly,
now I wish to be silent."

12. Óðinn said:
"Do not be silent, Wand-
Witch,
I want to ask you
until I know everything,
I still want to know:
"Who are those maidens
who are bound to weep
and to high heaven hurl
the veils from their
necks?"

10.Oðinn kvað:
„Þægiattv, vǫlva!
þik vil ec fregna,
vnz alkvnna,
vil ec enn vita:
hverr man hæipt Hæði
hæfnt of vinna
æða Balldrs bana
a bal væga?"

11.Vǫlva kvað:
„Rindr berr Vala
i væstrsǫlvm,
sa man Oðins sonr
æinnættr væga:
hǫnd vm þvær
næ hǫfvð kæmbir,
aðr a bal vm berr
Balldrs andskota;
naˊðvg sagðak,
nv mvn ec þegia."

12.Oðinn kvað:
„Þegiattv, vǫlva!
þik vil ek fregna,
vnz alkvnna,
vil ec enn vita:
hveriar 'ro þær mæyiar,
ær at mvni gráta
ok a himin verpa
halsa skáˊtvm?"

13. The Wand-Witch said:
"You are not Way-Wont
as I intended,
you are Óðinn,
that age-old man."

Óðinn said;
"You are not the Wand-
Witch
not a wise woman,
You are rather
the mother of three thurses."[380]

14. The Wand Witch said:
"Ride home, Óðinn,
and be proud of yourself!
Few men will come
back here to visit
until Loki manages to
break free from his bonds
and Ragnarök
comes to tear all asunder."

13. Vǫlva kvað:
„Ertattv Vægtamr,
sæm æk hvgða,
hælldr ærtv Oðinn,
alldinn gautr."

Oðinn kvað:
„Ertattv vǫlva
næ vis kona,
hælldr ærtv
þriggia þvrsa moðir."

14. Vǫlva kvað:
„Hæim rið þv, Oðinn!
ok ver hroðigr!
sva komir manna
mæirr aptr a vit,
ær lavss Loki
liðr or bǫndvm
ok ragnarǫk
rivfændr koma."

DAUÐI BALDRS INS GÓÐA-THE DEATH OF BALDER THE GOOD
[GYLFAGINNING, 49 PROSE EDDA]

49: Wandering Learner said: «Do you have any further tidings
about the Aesir? All-mighty fame won Thor on this journey.[381]"

The High One replied: "It could be possible to speak about the
tidings which commenced when Balder the Good dreamed great
dreams that prophesied danger to his life.[382] And when he told the
Aesir of his dreams, then they all came together for council, and
they agreed to ask for salvation against all dangers for Balder.

Frigg[383] demanded oaths from fire and water, iron and all sorts
of metal, the rocks, the Earth, the trees, the illnesses, the animals,
the birds, the poisons and the serpents, that they should not harm
Balder.

When this was fulfilled and declared, Balder and the Aesir had this pleasure that he should stand in the middle of the Parliament court, and that they should shoot at him, cut him, stone him; and whatever they did to him, it could not hurt him. And the Aesir thought this was a great sport.

But when Loki Leaf Island's Son saw this, then he disliked it greatly, and he was angered that nothing could harm Balder. He took the likeness of a woman[384] and went to Frigg in the Moist Halls[385].

Then Frigg asked if this woman knew what the Aesir were doing at Parliament. She [Loki] said that everybody was shooting at Balder and that he was never harmed.

Then Frigg said: "No weapon or tree will harm Balder. I have extracted oaths from them all."

Then the woman [Loki] asked: "Have all things really sworn not to harm Balder?"

Then Frigg replied: "A tree-shoot grows to the west of Valhalla, it is called the mistletoe. It seemed to me too young to extract oaths from."

Then the woman [Loki] left on her way. Loki took the mistletoe and pulled it up and went to the Parliament. And Strife [Hǫðr] stood in the man-ring[386] without participating, for he was blind.

Then Loki spoke to him: "Why do you not shoot at Balder?

Strife replied; "Firstly because I cannot see where Balder is, and secondly because I am unarmed."

Then Loki said: "You should be allowed to do as the others, and show Balder the same honor as they do. I shall direct your aim. Shoot at him with this twig."

Strife took the mistletoe and shot at Balder, just as Loki directed him. The shot went through Balder, and he fell dead to Earth, and this was the greatest misfortune of gods and of men.

When Balder had fallen, then the Aesir could not even speak, and their arms hung passively down their sides. They just exchanged glances, and everybody thought the same about the one who had committed the deed. But they could not commit vengeance here; this was a very sacred Place of Truces.[387]

And when the Aesir tried to speak, they just began to weep, so that none could say just how sorrowful they were. And Óðinn was the one most badly hurt by this injury; for he saw most clearly what sort of loss and harm the Aesir would suffer because of Balder's death.

When the Aesir had calmed down somewhat, Frigg spoke and asked which among the Aesir would want to win all her love and good intentions by riding the Hel-path[388] and try to find Balder, and offer ransom to Hel if she would let Balder go home to Ásgarð. A man was named Hermóðr [Army's Courage] the Brave, son of Óðinn, and he would undertake the journey. Then Glider [Sleipnir], Óðinn's horse, was brought out and led forth, and Hermóðr got up on that horse and began to ride the path.

Wolf-riding giantess with serpents for reins, detail from a Viking Age picture stone, Scania, Sweden

The Aesir took Balder's corpse and moved it to the ocean. Balder's ship was called the Ring-Horn.[389] He was the best of all ships. The gods wanted to set it out and make it a pyre for Balder, but the ship would not move at all.

Then they carried out onto the ship the body of Balder, and when Nanna Ring's Daughter[390], his wife, saw him, then she broke out of grief and died. She was carried to the pyre and tossed into the fire.

Then Thor stood up to wed the fire with the Grinder.[391] And before his feet a certain dwarf ran, who is named Hue [Lítr]. Thor let his foot out and kicked Hue into the fire, and he burned.

To this funeral pyre came many kinds of people, firstly there is to tell about Óðinn, and that with him came Frigg and the valkyriur and his ravens. Freyr traveled in his chariot pulled by the boar that is called Golden Bristles or Horrible Teeth.[392]

Heimdall rode the horse which is called Golden Top,[393] and Freyia drove her cats.

There came also a lot of frost thurses and mountain giants.

Óðinn laid on the pyre a golden ring, the one called Dripper.[394] He [the ring] had this nature that every nine nights, eight equally heavy gold rings would drip from him.

Balder's horse was led to the pyre with full equipment.

****

It is said about Hermóðr that he rode nine nights through dark and deep valleys, so that he could not see before he came to the river Bellower and traversed the Bellowing Bridge.[395] She [the bridge] was covered with bright gold.

Divine Rage[396] is she called, the woman who guards the bridge. She asked him his name and lineage and told him that the previous day, the bridge had been ridden by five armies of dead men, - "and the bridge did not tremble less beneath you alone, and you do not wear the hue of dead men.[397] Why are you riding the Hel-path?"

He replied that – "I shall ride to Hel in order to seek out Balder, or have you perhaps seen Balder on the Hel-path?"

Detail from 8th century picture stone from Lärbro, Gotland, Sweden, showing a riding man about to cross a bridge, being met by a giantess with a drinking horn, twice his size.

And she said that Balder had ridden the Bellowing Bridge; - "and down and north lies the Hel-path."[398]

Detail from 8th century picture stone from Lärbro, Gotland, Sweden, showing a riding man about to cross a bridge, being met by a giantess with a drinking horn, twice his size.

Then Hermóðr rode until he came to the Hel-gate.[399] He got off the horse and fastened his saddle, then got back up and spurred him hard, and the horse ran so hard and jumped across the gate without touching it.[400]

Then Hermóðr rode all the way to the hall and got off his horse, entered the hall, and there in the high seat he saw Balder, his brother, seated with all honors. Hermóðr stayed the night there. And in the morning, he begged of Hel that Balder may ride back home with him from there, and told her what a great grief had come to the Aesir.

Hel replied that she wanted proof that Balder was really that highly loved as she was being told, "and if all things in the world, living and dead, will weep for Balder, then he shall be returned to the Aesir, but he shall be kept with Hel if even just one person speak against him and will not weep."

Then Hermóðr got up, and Balder accompanied him out of the hall, and took the ring Dripper and sent it to Óðinn as a memory, and Nanna sent to Frigg thanks and many gifts, and to the Fulfilled One[401] she sent a finger-ring of gold.

Then Hermóðr rode back the path he had come, and returned to Ásgarð and told them the tidings, everything he had seen and heard. Then the Aesir sent out all their errand boys into all the worlds to ask them to help weep Balder out of Hel.

And all did that; people and cattle and Earth and stone and tree and all metals – as you may see these things weep when they come out of cold and into the heat.

When the errand men returned home and had counted up their errands, they found in a certain shallow cave a giantess.

Her name has been mentioned as Thanks.[402] They asked her to weep Balder out of Hel. She said;

"Thanks may weep dry tears
for Balder's fire-voyage
Neither alive nor dead
did I enjoy the sons of men;
Let Hel keep what she owns."

> "Þökk mun gráta
> þurrum tárum
> Baldrs bálfarar;
> kyks né dauðs
> nautk-a ek Karls sonar,
> haldi Hel því, er hefir."

And it is said among men that this [giantess] was really Loki Leaf-Island's Son, the one who had harmed the Aesir the most.

Metaphors for Gold and the Banquet in Aegir's Hall
[Skaldskaparmál 40-41, Prose Edda]

Metaphors for Gold

Gullskenningar

40: Aegir said: "How shall we know gold?"
Bragi said: "By calling it the Fire of Aegir[403]
- and the Leaves of Glasir,[404]
- the Hair of Síf,[405]
- the Veil of the Fulfilled One,[406]
- the Weeping of Freyia,[407]
- the Mouth-Listing or the Voice or the Words of Giants,[408]
- the Drops of the Dripper and the Rain or the Shower of the Dripper,[409]
- or the Eyes of Freyia,[410]
- Otter's Compensation,[411]
- the Need-Debt of the Aesir,[412]
- The Seed of the Ebbing Plains,[413]
- Holgir's Tomb-Roof,[414]
- the Fire of all sorts of water, and the Fire of the Arm,[415]
- or the Stones or Rock or Gleam of the Arm.[416]

When Aegir invited the Aesir for a Banquet-Æsir þágu veizlu at Ægis.

41: Aegir said: "Why is gold called the Fire of Aegir?"
Bragi said: "This is the saga that explains it, and it has been told earlier, that Aegir sought to visit Ásgarð,[417] and when he was ready to embark on the home-journey, he invited Óðinn and all the Aesir to come visit him in three month's time.[418]

To this voyage came Óðinn and Njǫrðr, Freyr, Týr, Bragi, Víðarr, Loki, and of the goddesses came Frigg, Freyja, Gefjun, Skaði, Iðunn, Síf. Thor was not there. He had traveled the Eastern Paths in order to beat trolls.[419]

And when the gods were seated, then Aegir let carry into the floor of the hall glowing gold,[420] which shone brightly like hearthfire, and lit up the entire hall, and this was the light they had for this banquet, just as there in Valhalla had been light from swords.[421]

Then Loki mocked all the gods and killed Aegir's slave,[422] the one who was called Clever Catch. Another slave is called Fire Maker.

Rán[423] [Robbery] was the name of his wife, and they had nine daughters, as before has been told. At this banquet, everything carried itself, both the food and ale and everything else that was needed for the banquet.

This was when the Aesir became aware that Rán owned a net in which she hunted/caught all men who drown in the ocean. Now this saga explains why gold is called the Fire or the Light or the Shine of Aegir, or of Ran or of the Daughters of Aegir.[424] And from these kennings, it is known that gold is called the Fire of the Sea and of any of the sea's nicknames [heiti] and it is known that Aegir or Rán are nicknames for the ocean,[425] and from this we know that gold is also called the Fire of the Waters or the Rivers, or of any heiti for river.[426]

And these nicknames [heiti] have also been used for waves and in metaphors [kenningar] that the younger poets have learned from the old poets, as it had been composed their poems, and then they applied these to other themes that they considered similar to what had been used in earlier poetry, such as a lake being a nickname for sea, and river for a lake, and a stream for a river. These are all called "new allegories" [nýgervingar], when the heiti aquire further meanings than what the older poets applied, and this is all considered appropriate when it makes sense and is in accordance with the nature of things.

Thus spoke Bragi Skáld:[427]

102: From the prince I received
the Fire of the Seat of the Mackerel [Sea][=gold][428]
for the Mountain-Fiölnir's [Giant's] Draught
[the Mead of Poetry][=poem];[429]
in a cup the ruler served it to me.[430]

> 102: Eld of þák af jöfri
> ölna bekks við drykkju;
> þat gaf Fjölnis fjalla,
> með fulli mér stillir.

Lokasenna-Loki´s Quarrel
[Poetic Edda]

About Aegir and the gods.

Aegir,[431] who by another name was called Gýmir,[432] he had invited the Aesir for an ale-banquet if they could only only fetch the Great Kettle,[433] as we have told about before.

To this banquet came Óðinn and Frigg his wife. Thor did not come, for he was on the eastern paths. Síf [Kinswoman] his wife was there. Bragi and Iðunn his wife. Týr was there, he was one-armed; the Greed-wolf tore off his arm when he bound him. There was Njǫrðr and Skaði his wife. Freyr and Freyia. Viðarr, Óðinn´s son. Loki was there. And so were Freyr´s servants, Barley-Man[434] and Little Bee.[435]

Many Aesir and elves were there.

Aegir had two servants; Fast Catch[436] and Fire Maker.[437]

The place had bright gold for their fire-lights; the ale carried itself, and the place was strictly peace-bound/a place of Truce.[438]

Aegir´s servants received a lot of praise for being so skilled. Loki could not bear to hear about this, and he killed Fast Catch. Then the Aesir shook their shields and cried out against Loki and drove him out to the forests, and then they began drinking.

Loki turned around and found Fire Maker, and Loki said to him: "Tell met his, Fire Maker, before you take another step forwards; What are they having in here, of ale-speech, the sons of the victorious gods?"	1.Segðv þat, Eldir! sva at þv einvgi feti gangir framarr: hvat her inni hafa at almálom sigtifa synir. "

Fire Maker said:
"Of their weapons they are
judging
and about their war-deeds,
the sons of the victorious
gods;
the Aesir and the Elves
who are in here;
none are your friend in
words."

Loki said:
"I shall walk
into Aegir's hall
to look at their drinking
party;
Quarrel and taunting
I shall bring to the sons of
the Aesir
and blend their mead
with malice.

Fire Maker said:
"Do you know, if you walk
into Aegirs hall
to look at their drinking
party;
If you pour taunting
words
on the sacred rulers,
they will use you to dry it
off."

Loki said:
"Do you know, Fire Maker,
if you and I were to meet¨
in single combat,
then with hard words we
shall contend
your master I shall be in
replies
if you dare too much."

2.Eldir qvaþ:
„Of vapn sín dǫma
oc vm vigrisni sina
sigtifa synir;
Asa oc Alfa,
er her inni ero,
mangi er þer i orði vinr."

3.Loci qvaþ:
„Inn scal ganga
Aegiss hallir i
a þat svmbl at siá;
ioll oc áfo
fœri ec asa sonom
oc blend ec þeim sva meini
mioþ."

4.Eldir qvaþ:
„Veiztv, ef þv inn gengr
Aegis hallir í
á þat svmbl at sia,
hropi oc rógi
ef þv eýss a holl regin,
a þer mvno þar þerra þat."

5.Loci qvaþ:
„Veiztv þat, Eldir!
ef við einir scolom
sáryrdom sacaz,
aþigr verþa mvn ec
i andsvorom,
ef þv mǫlir til mart."

Then Loki went into the hall. But when they saw who he was, who had come inside, they all went silent.

Loki said:
«Thirsty I have
arrived into this hall,
Air[439] has traveled a long
way,
to ask the Aesir
that you grant me a drink
of the Precious Mead.[440]

You are so quiet,
you arrogant gods,
can you not speak?
A seat and a place
at the drinking you must
give me,
or else send me out on the
heath!"

Bragi said;
"A seat and a place for
you
at this drinking,
the Aesir will never give;
For the Aesir know who
they should have as guests
at this splendid drinking
party."

Loki said:
"Do you remember, Óðinn,
that we two in the
beginning time
blended our blood
together;
Never should you drink
ale,
unless we were both
invited."

6.Loci qvaþ:
„Þyrstr ec com
þessar hallar til
Loptr vm langan veg,
aso at biþia,
at mer einn gefi
Męran drycc Miaðar.

7.Hvi þęgit er sva,
þrvngin goð!
at þer męla ne megoð?
sessa oc staþi
velið mer svmbli at,
ęda heitiþ mic heþan!"

8.Bragi qvaþ:
„Sessa oc staði
velia þer svmbli at
Aesir aldregi;
þviat Aesir vito,
hveim þeir alda scolo
gambansvmbl vm geta."

9.Loci qvaþ:
„Mantv þat, Oðinn!
er við i ardaga
blendom bloþi saman:
ǫlvi bergia leztv eigi
mvndo,
nema ocr vęri baþom
borit?"

Óðinn said:
"Rise now, Viðarr,
and let the wolf´s father
[Loki]
sit by the drinking table
Lest Loki shall sing
reproachful runes against
us
in the hall of Aegir."

10.Óðinn qvaþ:
„Ristv þa, Viðarr!
oc lat vlfs faþur
sitia svmbli at,
siþr oss Loci
qveþi lastastafom
Aegis hallo í."

Then Viðarr stood and served Loki, and as soon as he had drunk, he said to the Aesir:

"Hail the Aesir!
Hail the Ásynior![441]
And all the sacrosanct
gods![442]
Except the one Áss
who is sitting inside,
Bragi, on the benches."

11.„Heilir æsir,
heilar asynior
oc all ginnheilog goð!
nema sa einn áss,
er innar sitr,
Bragi, becciom a."

Bragi said:
"Sword and steed
I give you from my estate
thus Bragi compensates
for a ring;
so that, to the Aesir,
you do not display your
resentment;
Do not anger the gods
against you."

12.Bragi qvaþ:
„Mar oc mæki
gef ec þer mins fiar
oc bøtir þer sva baugi
Bragi:
siþr þv Asom
øfvnd vm gialdir;
gremþv eigi goð at þer!"

Loki said:
"Steeds and arm-rings
you shall never again
hope to have, Bragi!
Of all the Aesir and the
elves
who are inside here,
you are the most cautious
in war,
and the most wary of
shootings."

13.Loki qvaþ:
„Iós oc armbauga
mvndv æ vera
beggia vanr, Bragi!
Asa oc alfa,
er her inni ero,
þv ert viþ víg varastr
oc sciarrastr viþ scot."

Bragi said:
"I know, if we were
outside now,
and not inside, as we are,
come into the hall of
Aegir;
I would have carried your
head
in my hands;
my reward for your lies."

Loki said:
"Clever you are in speech,
seated,
but little you will do for
real,
Bragi Bench-Decoration!
Grasp you weapons
if you are so angry,
the brave is never
anxious."

Iðunn said:
"I beg you, Bragi, think
about
the children of the
kinswomen!
And of all the desired
sons!
So that you hurl at Loki
no reproachful runes,
in the hall of Aegir."

Loki said:
"Shut up, Iðunn!
I name you, of all women,
the one most desperate for
lovers,
since you placed
your light-bright pure
arms
around your own brother's
bane."443

14.Bragi qvaþ:
„Veit ec, ef fyr vtan værac,
sva sem fyr innan emc,
Aegis ha/ll vm kominn:
ha/fvþ þitt bæra ec
i hendi mer;
litt [qveþ] ec þer þat fyr
lygi."

15.Loki qvaþ:
„Sniallr ertv i sessi,
scalatv sva gora,
Bragi Beccscratuþr!
væga þv gacc,
ef þv reiþr sér!
hyggz vætr hvatr fyrir."

16.Iðunn qvaþ:
„Biþ ec, Bragi!
barna sifiar dvga
oc allra oscmaga,
at þv Loca qveþira
lastasta/fom
Aegis hallo í."

17.Loki qvaþ:
„Þegi þv, Iðunn !
þic qveþ ec allra qvenna
vergiarnasta vera,
sitztv arma þina
lagdir itrþvegna
vm þinn broþvrbana."

Iðunn said:
"At Loki I shall not hurl
reproachful
words in the hall of Aegir;
Only I can stall Bragi
when he is beer-eloquent
I do not wish for you two
to fight in anger.»

Gefion said:
"Why should you two
Aesir
fight in here with
wounding words?
We all know that Loki is
playful
and that he is loved by
all."

Loki said:
"Shut up, Gefion,
this I shall always
remember,
that you let yourself be
swayed
by the boy so radiant
that he gave you a sigil
and that you spread
your thighs over him."[444]

Óðinn said:
"You are mad, Loki, and
out of your mind
when you make out of
Gefion an enemy;
For, of the destiny of the
ages,
I think that she knows
everything,
just as well as I do."

18. Iðunn qvaþ:
„Loca ec qveþca
lastastarfom
Aegis hallo í;
Braga ec kyrri biórreifan;
vilcat ec, at iþ reiðir ve-
giz."

19. Gefion qvaþ:
„Hvi iþ Aesir tvæir
scoloþ inni her saryrþom
sacaz?
Loptci þat veit,
at hann leikinn er
oc hann fiorg avll fiá."

20. Loki qvaþ:
„Þegi þv, Gefion!
þess mvn ec nv geta,
er þic glapþi at geði
sveinn inn hvíti,
er þer sigli gaf
oc þv lagdir lær yfir."

21. Óðinn qvaþ:
„Ǫrr ertv, Loci! oc arviti,
er þv fǫr þer Gefion at
gremi;
þviat aldar orlag
hygg ec at hon all vm viti
iafngorla sem ec."

Loki said:
"Shut up, Óðinn!
You could never
shift victory in war
between men;
Often you gave to those
who never deserved it,
victory to the dullest."

Óðinn said:
"Do you know, if I gave to
those
whom I owed nothing
and victory to the dull;
You were eight winters
beneath the Earth,
milking cows,
and you were a woman,
and you gave birth to
children there,
I call this the shameful
mark of a wimp."⁴⁴⁵

Loki said:
"But you let yourself go at
Sáms-island
And you beat the drum
like wand-witches do;
In the likeness of a witch
you moved across the
world
I call this the shameful
mark of a wimp."⁴⁴⁶

Frigg said:
"Your deeds in the early
days
ought never be spoken of;
what you two Aesir were
doing together
in the days of origin;
Let the past be forgotten
and hidden."

22.Loki qvaþ:
„Þegi þu, Óðinn!
þu kunnir aldregi
deila vig meþ verom;
opt þu gaft þeim,
er þu gefa scyldira,
enom slævorom sigr."

23.Óðinn qvaþ:
„Veiztv, ef ec gaf þeim,
er ec gefa ne scylda,
enom slævorom sigr:
atta vetr vartu
fyr iorþ neþan kýr mól-
candi
oc cona,
oc hefir þu þar [born of]
borit,
oc hugða ec þat args aþal."

24.Loki qvaþ:
„Enn þic síþa koþo Sám-
seyio í
oc draptu a vétt sem
va'lor;
vitca líci
fórtu verþioþ yfir,
oc hugða ec þat args aþal."

25.Frigg qvaþ:
„Avrlaugom ycrom scylit
aldregi segia seggiom fra,
hvat iþ Aesir tveir
drygdvt i ardaga;
firriz æ forn rauc firar!"

Loki said:
"Shut up, Frigg!
You are Life Struggle's
maiden
and always been desperate
for men,
both Víli and Vé
did you let, Víðris[447]
woman,
bathe in your bosom, take
you."

27.Frigg said:
"Do you know, if I had
here in Aegir's hall,
a son in the likeness of
Balder;
You would never escape
from the sons of the Aesir
and they would have
fought you
in a state of fury."

Loki said:
"You still want, Frigg, that
I count up more of my
malice-runes;
I made it so,
that you shall never see
Balder ride here to this
hall."

Freyia said:
"You are mad, Loki,
When you count up
your vicious harm-runes;
Of Destiny, Frigg, I think,
knows everything
even though she says
little."

26.Loki qvaþ:
„Þegi þu, Frigg!
þv ert Fiorgyns mær
oc hefir æ vergiorn veriþ,
er þa Vea oc Vilia
leztv þer, Viþris qvæn!
bada i baðm vm tekit.“

27.Frigg qvaþ:
„Veiztu, ef ec inni ettac
Egis höllom i
Baldri lican bur:
ut þu ne qvǫmir
fra Asa sonom,
oc væri þa at þer reiþom
vegit.“

28.Loki qvaþ:
„Enn vill þu, Frigg!
at ec fleiri telia mina mein-
stafi:
ec þvi ræd,
er þv riþa serat
siþan Baldr at sǫlom.“

29.Freyia qvaþ:
„Ǫrr ertu, Loci!
er þu ydra telr
liota leiþstafi;
örlög Frigg
hygg ec at öll viti,
þott hon sialfgi segi.“

Loki said:
"Shut up, Freyia!
You, I can fully reveal
about,
you are not lacking in
vices;
Of the Aesir and elves
seated in this hall
each one has been your
secret lover."

Freyia said:
"False is your tongue,
I think that it will cause
more misfortune for
yourself soon;
Raging are the Aesir
and the goddesses;
unsafe shall your home-
journey be."

Loki said:
"Shut up, Freyia!
You are a sorceress
and you are blended with
much malice;
They found you with your
own brother,[448]
the gods were amused,
and then, Freyia, you
farted."

Njǫrðr said:
"It is of little consequence
if a woman plays
with her own man or a
lover;
But that a shamed god
has come in here is worse;
A man who has birthed
children."

30.Loki qvaþ:
„Þegi þv, Freyia!
þic cann ec fvllgerva,
era þer vamma vant:
asa oc alfa, er her inni ero,
hverr hefir þinn hór
veriþ."

31.Freyia qvaþ:
„Flá er þer tvnga,
hygg ec at þer fremr
myni ogott vm gala;
reiþir 'ro þer Aesir
oc asynior;
hryggr mvntv heim fara."

32.Loki qvaþ:
„Þegi þv, Freyia!
þv ert fordǫþa
oc meíni blandin mioc,
sitz þic at brǫþr þinom
stóþo bliþ regin,
oc mvndir þv þa, Freyia!
frata."

33.Niorþr qvaþ:
„Þat er válitit,
þótt ser varþer
vers fái hóss eþa hvars;
hitt er vndr, er áss ragr
er her inn of kominn,
oc hefir sa born of borit."

Loki said:
"Shut up, Njörðr! You were
far eastwards,
a hostage sent by the gods;
The maidens of Hymir had
you
as a pissing pot
and they pissed into your
mouth."[449]

Njǫrðr said:
"I had compensation for
this,
that I was sent far across
the heath
as a hostage sent by the
gods;
That I begot a son
who is hated by no one,
and who is thought the
most
excellent among Aesir."[450]

Loki said:
"Stall now, Njǫrðr,
do not get ahead of
yourself,
I cannot hide this
anymore;
By your own sister did you
beget such a son;[451]
He turned out no worse
than expected."

Tyr said:
"Freyr is the best among
all the chiefs
who are in the world of
the Aesir;
He never makes a maiden
cry,
nor a man´s wife,
and he frees anyone from
their bonds."

34. Loki qvaþ:
„Þegi þv, Niorþr!
þu vart austr heþan
gisl vm sendr at goðom;
Hymis meyiar hafðo
þic at hlandtrogi
oc þer i munn migo."

35. Niorþr qvaþ:
„Sv eromc licn,
er ec varc langt heþan
gisl vm sendr at goþom:
þa ec mag gat,
þann er mangi fiár,
oc þiccir sa asa iadarr."

36. Loki qvaþ:
„Hettv nv, Niorþr!
hafþv a hófi þic,
mvnca ec þvi leyna lengr:
við systor þinni gaztv
slican
mag, oc era þo vóno verr."

37. Tyr qvaþ:
„Freyr er beztr allra ball-
riþa
asa gordom í;
mey hann ne grætir
ne mannz kono,
oc leysir or haptom
hvern."

Loki said:
"Shut up, Tyr,
you who could never
carry the burden of two;
Your right hand,
I want to mention,
was torn off by Greed.[452]"

Tyr said:
"The hand I am missing,
and you are missing Rage
Witness[453]
the grief is great for us
both;
the wolf is wretched
and will be bound
all until Ragnarök.[454]"

Loki said:
"Shut up, Tyr!
It so happened that your
wife
had a son by me;
Never a penny
did you get for this
dishonoring,
you pathetic little man."[455]

Freyr said:
"Wolf I see lying,
by the river mouth,
all until the rulers are torn
apart;[456]
You will be bound next,
unless you keep silent,
malice-smith!"

38. Loki qvaþ:
„Þegi þv, Tyr!
þv kvnnir aldregi
bera tilt meþ tveim;
handar ennar hǫgri
mvn ec hinnar geta,
er þer sleít Fenrir fra."

39. Tyr qvaþ:
„Handar em ec vanr,
enn þv Hroðrs-vitniss,
baⸯl er beggia þrá;
vlfgi hefir oc vel,
er i bondom scal
bíþa ragnaraⸯcrs."

40. Loki qvaþ:
„Þegi þv, Týr!
þat varþ þinni cono,
at hon atti maⸯg viþ mer;
aⸯln ne penning
hafþir þv þess aldregi
vanréttiss, vesall!"

41. Freyr qvaþ:
„Vlf se ec liggia
arósi fyr,
vnz rivfaz regin;
þvi mvndv næst,
nema þv nv þegir,
bvndinn, baⸯlvasmiþr!"

Loki said:
"With gold you bought
the daughter of Gymir,[457]
and you sold your good
sword;
For when the sons of
Muspell
ride the dark forest
then you will miss that
sword,
you pathetic little man."

Barley Man said:
"Do you know, if I had
relatives
the sort of Ingunar-
Freyr´s,
and held such an honored
seat,
marrow and bone I would
have crushed
on the wounding-crow
[Loki]
and struck him into small
pieces."

Loki said:
"What is that tiny thing
that I see waving his tail
here,
and who is sniffing
hungrily;
around the ears of Freyr
you are always fleeting
and clucking around the
mill."

42. Loki qvaþ:
„Gvlli keypta
leztv Gymis dottvr
oc seldir þitt sva sverþ;
enn er Mvspellz synir
ríða Myrcviþ yfir,
veizta þv þa, vesall! hve
þv vegr."

43. Byggvir qvaþ:
„Veiztv, ef ec øþli ættac
sem Ingvnar-Freyr
oc sva sælict setr,
mergi smæra maⁱlþa ec
þa mæíncráco
oc lemþa alla i liþo."

44. Loki qvaþ:
„Hvat er þat iþ litla,
er ec þat laⁱggra sec
oc snapvist snapir;
at eyrom Freys
mvnðv æ vera
oc vnd kvernom klaca."

Barley Man said:
"Barley Man is my name
and I have been called
impulsive
by the gods and by all
men;
for I am righteously proud
that
all the sons of the
Shattered One [Óðinn]
are drinking the ale
together."[458]

Loki said:
"Shut up, Barley Man!
Never did you know
how to shift food among
men;
and you, hiding in the
straws,
are bound to be detected
when men are fighting."

Heimdallr [Great World]
said:
"You are mad, Loki!
You are intoxicated,
let it now be, Loki;
For too much drink
will cause, for all men
that they cannot rein in
their tongues."

Loki said:
«Shut up, Heimdallr!
For you, in the times of
origin,
a lowly fate was made;
with gravel[459] on your
back
you must always be alert
waking, a watchman for
the gods."

45.Beyggvir qvaþ:
„Beyggvir ec heíti,
enn mic braþan qveþa
goð aˈll oc gvmar:
þvi em ec her hroðvgr,
at drecca Hroptz megir
allir aˈl saman."

46.Loki qvaþ:
„Þegi þv, Byggvir!
þv kvnnir aldregi
deila meþ monnom mat;
oc þic i fletz strá
finna ne mattv,
þa er vago verar."

47.Heimdallr qvaþ:
„Avlr ertv, Loci!
sva at þv ert orviti,
hvi ne lezcaþv, Loci?
þviat ofdryccia
veldr alda hveim,
er sina mælgi
ne manaþ."

48.Loki qvaþ:
„Þegi þv, Heimdallr!
þer var i árdaga
iþ lióta lif vm lagit;
aˈrgo baci
þv mvnt æ vera
oc vaca vorþr goða."

Skaði said:
"Amused you are, Loki,
but you will not be so for
long
playing with the loose tail;
For with a rope made of
entrails
from your frost-cold son
the gods will bind you
on the sword's edge."

Loki said:
"Do you know, if I am to
be bound
by my frost-cold son's
entrails
on a sword's edge, by the
gods;
First and foremost
I was in that battle
when we got Slave-Binder
slayed."[460]

Skaði said:
"Do you know, if firstly
and foremostly
you were at the battle
where you got Slave-
Binder slayed;
Then, from my shrines
and my sacred groves
cold counsel shall always
come."

Loki said:
"Milder speech did you
grant
to the son of Leaf Island
[Loki]
when you let me
to your bed, invited me;
Such things must be
mentioned
if we are to count
all our wiles and vices."

49.Scaþi qvaþ:
„Lætt er þer, Loci!
mvnattv lengi sva
leica lᴀsom hala;
þviat þic a hiorvi scolo
ins hrimcalda magar
gornom binda goð."

50.Loki qvaþ:
„Veiztv, ef mic a hiorvi
scolo
ens hrímcalda magar
gornom binda goð:
fyrstr oc ǫfstr
var ec at fiorlagi,
þars ver a Þiaza þrifom."

51.Scaþi qvaþ:
„Veiztv, ef fyrstr oc ǫfstr
vartv at fiorlagi,
þa er ér a Þiaza þrifvð:
fra minom veom
oc vᴀngom scolo
þer æ kᴀld ráþ coma."

52.Loki qvaþ:
„Léttari í malom
vartv viþ Lᴀfeyiar son,
þa er þv letz mer
a beð þinn boþit;
getiþ verþr oss slics,
ef ver gorva scolom
telia vommin vár."

Then Síf went forth and offered to Loki the frosty cup full of mead,[461] and spoke;

«Be you whole, now, Loki,
and take the frosty cup
full of ancient mead!
Let at least one
among the Aesir
be spared your taunts."
He took the horn and
drank;

"The only one you may be,
if you had been so,
who was never tempted;
But I know one
and I know it very
certainly -
who tempted the wife of
the Loud Rider,
and that was the malice-
wise Loki."

Little Bee said:
"The mountains are
trembling
I think he is traveling
homewards, the Loud
Rider;
He will stop
these slandering words
about all the gods and
men."

Loki said:
"Shut up, Little Bee!
You are Barley Man's
woman
And much blended with
malice;
A worse beast never came
to the sons of the Aesir
than you, dirty shepherd
girl!"

53.„Heill ver þv nv, Loci!
oc tac við hrímcalci
fvllom forns miaðar!
heldr þv hana eina
latir með asa sonom
vammalvsom vera."
Hann toc við horni oc
dracc af:

54.„Eín þv værir,
ef þv sva værir,
vvr oc gravm at veri;
einn ec veít,
sva at ec uita þicciomc,
hór oc af Hlorriða,
oc var þat sa inn lævisi
Loci."

55.Beyla qvaþ:
„Fioll avll scialfa,
hygg ec a for vera
heiman Hlorriþa;
hann ræþr ró
þeim er rǫgir her
goð avll oc gvma."

56.Loki qvaþ:
„Þegi þv, Beyla!
þv ert Byggviss qvæn
oc meini blandin mioc;
okynian meira
coma með asa sonom,
avll ertv, deigia! dritin."

Then came Thor back and said:
"Shut up, you perverted spirit![462]
My hammer of Power, the Grinder,
shall silence your words,
your bones I shall break from your neck,
and then your life shall be forfeit."

Loki said:
"The Son of Earth has now arrived here,
why are you raging so, Thor?
You shall not be so daring when you must fight the wolf
and he swallows the Victory Father[463] whole."

Thor said:
"Shut up, you perverted spirit!
My hammer of Power, the Grinder,
shall silence your words;
I shall hurl you high up and on the eastern paths,[464]
nobody shall see you then."

Loki said:
"Your travels to the east you should never mention
since you hid in the thumb of a glove[465]
The Sole Ruler[466]
crouching and cowering
You did not seem much of a Thor then."

57. Þa com Þorr at oc qvaþ:
„Þegi þv, ra‿g vettr!
þer scal minn þrv́ðhamarr
Miollnir mal fyr nema;
herþaklett drep ec þer
halsi af,
oc verþr þa þino fiorvi vm
farit."

58. Loki qvaþ:
„Iarðar bvrr er her nv
inn kominn, hvi þrasir þv
sva,
Þorr? enn þa þorir þv ecci,
er þv scalt viþ vlfinn vega,
oc svelgr hann allan Sig-
fa‿ðvr."

59. Þorr qvaþ:
„Þegi þv, ra‿g vettr!
þer scal minn þrv́ðhamarr
Miollnir mal fyr nema;
vpp ec þer verp oc a aus-
trvega,
siþan þic mangi sér."

60. Loki qvaþ:
„Avstrfǫrvm þinom scaltv
aldregi segia seggiom fra,
sizt i hansca þvmlvngi
hnvcþir þv, æinhæri!
oc þóttisca þv þa Þorr
vera."

Thor said:
"Shut up, you perverted
spirit!
My hammer of Power, the
Grinder,
shall silence your words;
With this right hand
I shall strike you with the
Bane of Hrungnir
so that all your bones
break."

Loki said:
"To live, I have planned
for
a long time still, even if
you
threaten to strike me with
the hammer;
Strong ropes, you thought,
were those bound by
Skrýmir,
and you could not reach
your food
and almost starved to
death."[467]

Thor said:
"Shut up, you perverted
spirit!
My hammer of Power, the
Grinder,
shall silence your words;
The Bane of Hrungnir
[Miöllnir]
shall send you to Hel
beneath and before the
Corpse Gate."

61.Þorr qvaþ:
„Þegi þv, ra‿g vettr!
þer scal minn þrv́ðhamarr
Miollnir mal fyr nema;
hendi inni hǫgri
drep ec þic Hrvngnis bana,
sva at þer brotnar beina
hvat. "

62.Loki qvaþ:
„Lifa ætla ec mer langan
aldr, þottv hætir hamri
mer;
scarpar alar
þottv þer Scrymiss vera,
oc mattira þv þa nesti na
oc svaltz þv þa hvngri
heill. "

63.Þorr qvaþ:
„Þegi þv, ra‿g vettr!
þer scal minn þrv́ðhamarr
Miollnir mal fyr nema;
Hrvngnis bani
mun þer i hel coma
fyr Nágrindr neþan. "

Loki said:
"I sang for the Aesir
I sang for the sons of the
Aesir
whatever came to my
mind;
For you (Thor) alone
I shall leave now,
for I know this, that you
strike.

Ale you brewed, Aegir,
but never again
shall you make such a
banquet;
All your belongings that
are inside here,
flames shall be playing
around
and burn your back!"

64.Loki qvaþ:
„Kvað ec fyr asom,
qvaþ ec fyr asa sonom
þaz mic hvatti hvgr;
enn fyr þer einom
mvn ec vt ganga,
þviat ec veit, at þv vegr.

65.Avl gorðir þv, Ægir!
enn þv aldri mvnt
siþan svmbl vm gora;
eiga þín ɑll,
er her inni er, leici yfir logi,
oc brenni þer a baki!"

After this, Loki hid in the Foaming Rage[468] waterfall in the likeness of a salmon[469], and there the Aesir took him. He was bound with the entrails of his son, Nári [Corpse], while his other son Narfi [Corpse] turned into a wolf. Skaði took a poison viper and fastened him above Loki´s face, and he dripped poison down on him. Sígyn Loki´s wife sat there and held a vessel beneath the viper. When the vessel was full, she had to empty it for poison. Meanwhile, the poison dripped on Loki. Then he would bolt so hard that the whole Earth trembled. This is called an Earthquake.

The Binding of Loki
Loki bundin-(Gylfaginning 50, Prose Edda)

50: Then said Wandering Learner: "Great things did Loki bring about, when he was, firstly, the cause behind the murder of Balder, and then behind the fact that he was not freed from Hel. Was this in some way avenged?"

The High One said: "He got a great retribution for this, so that he will feel it for a long time. When the gods had become as angry with him as one could expect, he bolted away and hid on a mountain, and built for himself there a house with four doors so that he could look out of the house in all directions. But often, in the days, he would assume the likeness of a salmon and hid there, where it is called the Waterfall of Foaming Rage [Fránangrsfoss]. Then he imagined to himself what sort of tools the Aesir would surely apply in order to find him and take him in the waterfall. And as he sat in his house, he picked up a yarn of linen and started to tie knots in it, and he did this in the way that people have been making fishing nets ever since,[470] and a fire burned in front of him.

Then he saw that the Aesir were close, approaching him, for Óðinn had sat in the Opening Shelf [Hliðskjálf][471] and discovered his whereabouts. He threw the net onto the fire, got up and ran out into the river. And when the Aesir came into the house, he went first inside, the one among them who was the wisest, the one who was called Kvasir,[472] and he saw the ashes in the fireplace where the net had burned, and he understood that the marks were from a device for catching fish, and he told the Aesir. Then they sat down and made for themselves another net based on how they saw the patterns in the ashes after the net that Loki had made.

And as they finished making the net, then the Aesir went to the river and threw it into the waterfall. Thor held one end of the net, and all the other Aesir held the other end,[473] and they pulled the net, and Loki was hurled forward and fell down between two stones. They threw the net over him and noticed that there was something alive in there. Then they went another time to the waterfall and threw out the net, and tied such heavy weights to it that nothing would be able to escape from beneath it. Then Loki went along with the front of the net, and when he saw that the way to the sea was short, he jumped over the top of the net, slipping back into the waterfall.

Now the Aesir saw where he went, and they went yet another time to the waterfall and divided their group into two parts, and Thor waded through the middle of the river, so that they approached the sea. And when Loki saw that there were two options, the mortally dangerous jump into the sea, or the other option of jumping above the net, he did the latter, and jumped as quickly as he could over the net. Thor grabbed him and held him, but the fish was so slippery, he ended up being held hard by his tail. And this is why the salmon's tail narrows in the end.

Now Loki was taken truce-less [griðalauss][474] and he was taken to a certain cave. There they took three cave-stones and placed them on an edge, and beat a hole into each one of them. Then they took the sons of Loki, Váli [Choice/Chosen Dead] and Nári [Corpse] or Nárfi.[475] They turned Váli into the likeness of a wolf,[476] and he tore apart Nárfi his brother.

Then the Aesir took his entrails and used them to tie Loki up above the three sharp stones; one stands beneath his shoulders, the other beneath his loins, and the third beneath his knee sockets; and the rope (the entrails) turned into iron. Then Skaði took a poison viper and fastened it above him, so that the poison of the viper dripped into his face, and Sígyn his wife stands with him and holds and small mouth-bath[477] beneath the poison drops. And when that cup is full, she goes to pour out the poison, and meanwhile the poison drips into his face. Then he bolts so hard that the whole Earth trembles. And this is called earthquakes.

There he lies bound until Ragnarök.

Loki bound – Viking Age standing stone, Kirkby, Sweden -Engraving by Julius Magnus Petersen (4 Sep 1827–1 Feb 1917)-Public Domain

13: ON RAGNARÖK

Hví er gull kallat barr eða
lauf Glasis? Í Ásgarði fyrir
durum Valhallar sten-
dr lundr, sá er Glasir er
kallaðr, en lauf hans allt er
gull rautt, svá sem hér er
kveðit, at

103. Glasir stendr
með gullnu laufi
fyrir Sigtýs sölum.

Sá er viðr fegrstr með
goðum ok mönnum.

Frá lundinum Glasi.
(Skáldskaparmál 42, Prose
Edda)

"Why is gold called the
pines or the leaves of the
Crystal?"
"In Ásgarð, before the
door of Valhalla, stands
a grove which is called
Crystal, and his foliage
is completely made out
of red gold, as it is here
composed;
103: Crystal stands
with golden leaves
before the halls of the
Victory God.

This wood is the fairest of
all among men and gods."

About the Grove of
Crystal
Frá lundinum Glasi.
(Skáldskaparmál 42, Prose
Edda)

ABOUT THE SHATTERING OF THE RULERS-FRÁ RAGNARÖKUM.
(GYLFAGINNING 51, PROSE EDDA)

51: Then spoke Wandering Learner: «What tidings are there to say
about Ragnarök?[478] I have never heard about this before."

The High One said: "Great tidings may be spoken and there are
many of them. The first is that there comes a winter which is called
the Great Winter [Fimbulvetr][479]. Then snow will drift from all
directions, and there is a strong cold and sharp winds, and nothing
may benefit from the Sun. There are three such winters without
summer in between.[480] But before this happens, there are three
years with un-peace all over the worlds. Then brothers will kill
each other out of greed, and nobody spares neither father nor son
from murder and the abuse of family relations. As it is said in the
Völuspá:[481]

Brothers will fight their own brothers and be their kin's slayers Children of sisters will betray their relations; Hardness is in the world, prostitution abounds, Axe age, sword age, shields are cleft asunder Wind age, Wolf age, Before the world plunges no man will spare another.	Bræðr munu berjask ok at bönum verðask, munu systrungar sifjum spilla; hart er með hölðum, hórdómr mikill, skeggjöld, skalmöld, skildir klofnir, vindöld, vargöld, áðr veröld steypisk.

Then it shall happen, what most people would regard as a great tiding, that the wolf swallows the Sun, and people will consider this a great harm. Then another wolf takes the Moon, and by this also makes a lot of mischief. The stars will whirl away from heaven. And there is this other tiding, that the Earth shall tremble all over, and even the mountains shall quake so much that trees shall loosen from the ground, and the mountains shall fall down, and all bonds are broken apart.

Then the wolf Fenrir is free. And then the ocean floods in across the lands, because the Middle World Serpent shall be twisting in giant rage[482] and is seeking up to land. And in this great surge of the ocean, Naglfar [Nail Traveler][483] shall be floating, a ship that is called thus. It is made by the nails of corpses, and this is why one will do well to remember that a man who dies with uncut nails will help increase the mass of this ship that both Aesir and men would wish was finished late. But Naglfar shall be loose in this great ocean-flood.

Weakener [Hrymr][484] is that giant named who steers the Naglfar, and the Greed Wolf [Fenrisúlfr] shall run free with a gaping mouth. The lower part of his jaws is down on the Earth, and the upper part is up by heaven. And he would have gaped even higher if there had been enough space for it. Fire burns out of his eyes and his nostrils.

 The Middle World Serpent blows his poison, so much that it is spread across all the land and the sea, and he is all-terrifying, and he moves side by side with the wolf. In this turmoil, the heaven is torn apart, and there shall ride the sons of Múspell.[485]

Sooty [Surtr][486] rides first, with burning fire both before him and after him. His sword is very good, from it, a light shines more brightly than the Sun. But when he rides the Shivering Voice [Bifröst][487], she will break, as has before been told. The Muspell-sons shall advance across a field which is called Vígríðr [Battle Ride]. There also comes the Greed wolf and the Middle World Serpent now. There has also Loki arrived, and Weakener, and with him all the frost thurses; and with Loki shall follow the residents of Hel (= the walking dead).

The Muspell-sons shall also bring an army for themselves, and she (the army) is particularly shiny. The field, Battle Ride, is a hundred miles broad in both directions. And when these tidings shall happen, then shall Heimdall [Great World] stand up and blow mightily into the Bellowing Horn [Gjallarhorn] and wake up all the gods, and then they shall gather for Parlioament. Then Óðinn [Spirit] shall ride to the Well of Memory [Mímisbrunnr] and ask the advice of Memory-Murmurer [Mímir] for himself and for his companions. Then shivers the ash Yggdrasill, and nothing is then without fear – in heaven or on Earth.

The Aesir make ready for battle and all the Sole Rulers [Einherjar] advance towards the fields. Óðinn rides first with his golden helmet and his fair armor and his spear, which is called the Swaying [Gungnir]. He advances against the Greed wolf, and Thor walks beside him, but cannot help him, for he himself has more than enough to contend with the Middle World Serpent.

Freyr fights with Sooty, and it shall be a hard battle[488] before Freyr falls. That shall be his bane, that he gave up his good sword, because he gave it to Skírnir.[489] Then has also the dog Garm[490] arrived, he who lies bound before the Protruding Rock,[491] he is the worst among monsters. He owns the battle against Týr, and they shall be the banes of one another. Thor shall carry the bane-words of (=be victorious against)[492] the Middle World Serpent, and he shall walk nine steps away from him.[493]

Then he shall fall dead to the Earth because of the poison that the serpent spewed at him. The wolf shall swallow Óðinn, that shall be his bane.[494] But just then, Víðarr[495] hurls forth and places one of his feet inside the mouth of the wolf. On that foot, he shall wear a shoe, and the material for that shoe has been collected through all the ages; they are the triangles that people cut out of the shoe leather in order to make space around the heel and the toes of the shoe.

This is why every person who wants to helpt the Aesir should always throw these pieces away. With one hand he shall grab the upper jaw of the wolf and tear asunder his mouth, and that shall be his bane. Loki shall now attack Heimdall, and both of them shall fall. Thereafter, Sooty hurls fire out on all the Earth and burns up all the world (...)

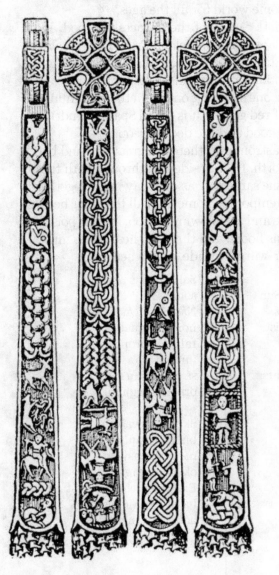

Gosforth Cross, depicting various mythological scenes. The images have been identified as:

Loki bound with his wife Sigyn protecting him.

The god Heimdallr holding his horn.

The god Víðarr [son of Odin] tearing the jaws of Fenrir.

Thor's failed attempt to catch Jörmungandr, the Midgard Serpent.[514]

-Public Domain-

The World after Ragnarökr–Vistarverur eftir ragnarökr.
(Gylfaginning 52, Prose Edda)

52: Then said Wandering Learner: "What happens afterwards then, when burnt is all the world and dead all the gods and all the Sole Rulers and all of humankind? You have told me that every human shall be living in some world for all the ages."[496]

Then said the Third [Þriði]: "Many of these places are good, and many are bad. The best place to be is Shielded From Fire [Gimlé],[497] and it has plenty of good drink[498] in that hall which is called High Tide Wave[Brímir],[499] he stands on Un-Cold [Ókólnir].[500]

Another great hall is the one standing on the Nether Mountains [Niðafjöllum], made out of red gold.[501] It is called Sparks [Sindri].[502] In this hall shall build the good and the decent people.

At the Corpse Shores [Náströndum] there is a great hall and bad, and it has a door facing north. He is braided all through with the skins of viper backs, just the same way as one may braid together twigs and branches for a temporary home; and all the viper heads face inwards to that house and are blowing poison, so that poison rivers are running down his floors; and through these rivers must oath-breakers and murder-wargs[503] wade, as it is here said;

I know a hall
standing far from the Sun
on the Shore of Corpses
to the north that door is
facing;
Poisonous drops fall
in through the roof-vents;
That hall is woven
from the spines of
serpents.

There shall wade
the heavy streams;
Oath-breakers
and murder-wargs.
And in Cauldron-
Bellower[504] it is worst:
there Shame Biter[505]
strangles
the forthcoming corpses.
[506]

Sal veit ek standa
sólu fjarri
Náströndu á,
norðr horfa dyrr;
falla eitrdropar
inn um ljóra;
sá er undinn salr
orma hryggjum.

Skulu þar vaða
þunga strauma
menn meinsvara
ok morðvargar.
En í Hvergelmi er verst:
Þar kvelr Níðhöggr
nái framgengna."

Who Shall Live after Ragnarök-Hverir lifa af ragnarökr
(Gylfaginning 53, Prose Edda)

53: Then said Wandering Learner: "What sort of life do the gods
have then, and shall there be earth and heaven of some sort?

The High One said: "The Earth shall shoot up from the ocean, and
shall be green and fair, fields shall grown unsown. Víðarr and Váli[507]
shall live, neither the sea nor the Flame of Sooty [Surtalogi] shall
harm them, and they shall build on the Fields Returning to Source
[Iðavelli] in the same place as Ásgarð used to be, and there come the
sons of Thor, Móði and Magni, and they have Miöllnir. Next come
Balder and Höðr from Hel, and they sit there all together and talk
and memorize their runes, and they speak of what happened before,
about the Middle World Serpent and the Greed Wolf. There in the
grass they shall find the golden chequers that the Aesir had owned.
As it is said:[508]

Wood/Expanding Warrior and Choice
shall live in the shrines of the gods
when the Flame of Sooty is quenched
Rage and Greatness
shall own the Grinder
when Weapon-Quaker's strife is over.

> Víðarr ok Váli
> byggva vé goða,
> þá er sortnar Surtalogi;
> Móði ok Magni
> skulu Mjöllni hafa
> Vingnis at vígþroti.

And there where it is called the Treasure Memory's Holt [Hoddmímisholt], two people are going to hide from the Flames of Sooty, and they are called Life [Líf] and Heritage Seeker [Leifþrasir], and they have the morning dew for food, and from these people shall come such a great lineage that it shall settle all over the world, as it is here[509] said;

Life and Heritage Seeker
hidden they shall stay
in Treasure memory's Holt;
Morning dew they shall have for food
from them shall great lineages come.

    Líf ok Leifþrasir,
    en þau leynask munu
    í holti Hoddmímis;
    morgindöggvar þau at mat hafa,
    en þaðan af aldir alask.

And it may amaze you also, that the Sun has given birth to a daughter who is no less fair than she is. She shall travel the path of her mother, as it is here[510] said;

A daughter shall be born
to Elfin Splendor [the Sun goddess]
before Greed quenches her;
She shall ride when the rulers die,
the maiden on her mother's path.

    Eina dóttur
    berr alfröðull,
    áðr hana fenrir fari;
    sú skal ríða, er regin deyja,
    móður brautir mær.

But if you were to ask me even further into the future, then I cannot imagine how you could have heard about it,[511] for I have never heard anyone report of tidings about the fate of the world any further than this. Be you satisfied with what you have learned."

A depiction of Líf and Lífþrasir (1895) by Lorenz Frølich.-Public Domain

ABOUT WANDERING LEARNER
FRÁ GANGLERA.
(GYLFAGINNING 54, PROSE EDDA)

54: After this, Wandering Learner heard a loud sound from all directions around him, and he peered sideways. And as he kept looking around, he realized that he was standing out on an empty plain, and he saw no hall and no wall.[512]

He began to walk away from there, and returned home to his realm, and told people about what he had seen and heard. And after him, one after the other kept telling these stories.[513]

But the Aesir sat down together and spoke and held council. And they remembered all the stories that they had told him. And to the peoples and the places that where there, they gave the names that they had given them in their stories, so that people, when many ages had passed – should not doubt that they were the same Aesir that they had just talked about, and who just now gave themselves the same names as they had in the stories.

As such, this was in fact when Thor first was given a name; he is Divine Thor the Old [Ása-Þórr inn gamli].

Þórr qvaþ:
„I eino briosti
ec sác aldregi
fleiri forna stafi;
miclom talom
ec qveð teldan þic:
vppi ertv, dvergr! vm dagaþr,
nv scinn Sól i sali. "
Allvísmál st. 35, Eddukvæði
　　Thor said:
　　«In one single chest
　　I never saw
　　more ancient runes.
　　With much talk
　　I spoke beguilements for you;
　　you are up, dwarf, it is dawn,
　　now Sun is shining in the hall!"
　　(The Song of All-Knowing, 35, The Poetic Edda)

BIBLIOGRAPHY

PRIMARY SOURCES IN OLD NORSE:

Bugge, Sophus, ed. (1867/1965): Sæmundar Edda hins Froda – Norrøn fornkvædi – Islandsk samling av Folkelige Oldtidsdigte om Nordens Guder og Heroer – Universitetsforlaget, Oslo (Online resource: https://etext.old.no/).

Jónsson, Finnur, ed. (1907): Edda Snorra Sturlusonar, Reykjavik

Jónsson, Finnur, ed. (1912): Den norsk-islandske skjaldedigtning (800-1200), udgiven af Kommisjonen for det Arnamagnæisk legat B: rettet tekst, 1.bind, Gyldendalske Boghandel – Nordisk forlag, København og Kristiania. Online resource: http://www.heimskringla.no/wiki/Den_norsk-islandske_skjaldedigtning

Jónsson, Guðni: Edda (Online resource: http://heimskringla.no/wiki/Edda_Snorra_Sturlusonar).

Linder, N. and Haggson, H.A. (1869-1872) Snorri Sturluson: Ynglinga saga, Heimskringla (Online resource: http://www.heimskringla.no/wiki/Ynglinga_saga)

PRIMARY SOURCES IN TRANSLATION:

Björnsson, Eysteinn: Þórsdrápa (Online resource: https://notendur.hi.is/eybjorn/ugm/thorsd00.html)

Eggen, Erik (1978): Snorre Sturluson Den Yngre Edda, Det Norske Samlaget, Oslo.

Faulkes, Anthony (1987): Snorri Sturluson EDDA - University of Birmingham Everyman, London.

Førde, Stein and Aase, Sigurd, Leif Høegh Stiftelse (2014-2016): Flatøybok bind 1-3, Norsk faglitterær forfatter- og oversetterforening, SAGA BOK AS, Stavanger

Holm-Olsen, Ludvig (1985): Eddadikt, Cappelen, Trondheim.

Hødnebø, Finn og Magerøy, Hallvard (1944): Snorre Sturluson: Norges kongesagaer, Gyldendal Norsk Forlag, Oslo.

Larrington, Carolyne (1996): The Poetic Edda, Oxford University Press, Oxford, New York

Mortensson-Egnund, Ivar (1993): Edda-Kvede, Det Norske Samlaget, Oslo

DICTIONARIES:

Caprona, Yann de (2013): Norsk etymologisk ordbok, Kagge forlag AS, Oslo.

Den Arnamagnæanske Kommisjon (1989): Ordbog over det norrøne prosasprog/ A Dictionary of the Norse Prose – Vol.I-XII, København.

Fritzner, Johan (1886): Ordbog over det gamle norske sprog – Det Norske Forlags Forening.

Fritzner, Johan (1972): Ordbog over det gamle norske sprog – rettelser og tillegg – Universitetsforlaget, Oslo.

Heggestad/Hødnebø/Simensen (1975): Norrøn ordbok – Det Norske Samlaget.

Iversen, Ragnvald (1972-1994): Norrøn grammatikk – Tano.

Simek, Rudolf (1996): Dictionary of Northern Mythology, translated by Angela Hall, D.S. Brewer, Cambridge.

SECONDARY SOURCES ABOUT OLD NORSE MYTHS AND PRE-CHRISTIAN
RELIGION:

• Acker, Paul/ Larrington,Carolyne (red.) (2002): The Poetic
Edda: essays on Old Norse mythology - Routledge Medieval
Casebooks, New York
• Bartha, Antal (1992): Myth and Reality in the Ancient Culture
of the Northern Peoples (in Hoppál, Pentikäinen,1992)
• Bessason, Haraldur / Glendinning, Robert J. (red.)(1983):
Edda: a collection of essays- University of Manitoba Icelandic
studies; 4 Winnipeg: University of Manitoba Press
• Clover, Carol J. /Lindow, John (red.)(1985):Old Norse-Icelandic
literature: a critical guide -Islandica; 45, Cornell University Press
• Clunies-Ross, Margaret (1987). Skáldskaparmál –Snorri
Sturlusson's Ars Poetica and Medieval Theories of Language
Odense University Press
• Clunies-Ross, Margaret (1994): Prolongued Echoes -Old Norse
Myths in Medieval Northern Society, Volume I: The Myths -
Odense University Press
• Davidson, Hilda Ellis (Hilda Roderick Ellis) (1968): The Road
to Hel – A Study of the Conceptions of the Dead in Old Norse
Literature
• Diószegi, Vilmos (1968):Tracing Shamans in Siberia. The
story of an ethnographical research expedition Oosterhout cap.
Anthropological publications
• Eliade, Mircea (2004): Shamanism – Archaic Techniques of
Ecstasy - Princeton University Press, Princeton and Oxford
• Enright, Michael J. (1996): Lady with a Mead Cup -Ritual,
Prophecy and Lordship in the European Warband from La Tène
to the Viking Age Four Courts Press, Dublin
• Flint, Valerie I. J. (1991): The Rise of Magic in Early Medieval
Europe. Princeton
• Flood, Jan Peder (1999): Volver, Seidmenn og Sjamaner:
en komparativ analyse av norrøn seid- Hovedoppgave i
religionshistorie, Universitetet i Oslo
• Halvorsen, Eyvind (et. al) (1992): Eyvindarbók: Festskrift til
Eyvind Fjeld Halvorsen 4.mai - Universitetet i Oslo
• Hansen, Jan Ingar (et.al) (1994): Fra hammer til kors –
brytningstid i Viken, Schibsted, Oslo

• Harris, Joseph (1983): Eddic Poetry as Oral Poetry: the Evidence of Parallel Passages is the Helgi Poems for Questions of Composition and Performance (in Bessason H./Glendinning R.J. Editors, 1983)
• Haugen, Einar (1983):The Edda as Ritual: Odin and His Masks (in: Bessason / Glendinning, eds., 1983)
• Kvilhaug, Maria Christine (2004): The Maiden with the Mead – A Goddess of Initiation in Norse Mythology? – Thesis - University of Oslo, History of Religion – Available online at: http://www.duo.uio.no/sok/work. html?WORKID=18497&lang=en
• Kvilhaug, Maria Christine (2009): The Maiden with the Mead – a Goddess of Initiation Rituals in Old Norse Mythology? – VDM Verlag Dr. Müller, Deutschland
• Kvilhaug, Maria Christine (2013): The Seed of Yggdrasill – Deciphering the Hidden Messages in Ols Norse Mythology – Whyte Tracks Publishers.
• Kvilhaug, Maria Christine (2017): The Poetic Edda – Six Cosmology Poems, Createspace.
• Mitchell, Stephen (2011): Witchraft and Magic in the Nordic Middle Ages University of Pensylvania Press
• Näsström, Britt-Mari (2001): BLOT –Tro og offer i det førkristne Norden Oversatt av Kåre A. Lie Pax Forlag A/S, Oslo
• Solli, Brit (2002): SEID Myter, sjamanisme og kjønn i vikingenes tid Pax Forlag A/S, Oslo
• Stafford, Pauline (1983): Queens, Concubines and Dowagers: The Kings Wife in the Early Middle Ages London
• Schjødt, Jens Peter(red.) (1994): Myte og ritual i det førkristne Norden – et symposium -Odense Universitetsforlag, Odense
• Steinsland, Gro (1986): Giants as recipients of cult in the Viking Age (i Steinsland, ed, 1986)
• Steinsland, Gro (ed.) (1986): Words and Objects Towards a Dialogue Between Archaeology and History of Religion Norwegian University Press, Oslo
• Steinsland, Gro (1991): Det Hellige Bryllup og Norrøn Kongeideologi En Analyse av Hierogami-Myten i Skírnismál, Ynglingatal, Háleygjatal og Hyndluljód Solum Forlag, Larvik
• Steinsland, Gro (1992):Døden som erotisk lystreise (i Hødnebø, Fjeld Halvorsen, 1992)
• Steinsland, Gro (1997): Eros og død i norrøne myter Universitetsforlaget, Oslo

• Steinsland, Gro (1998):Hedendom mot kristendom i norrøne myter(i Hjelde/Ruud (ed.)
• Steinsland, Gro/Meulengracht Sørensen, Preben (1999):Voluspå Pax forlag A/
• Strömbäck, Dag (2000): SEJD och andra studier i nordisk själsuppfatning Kungl. Gustav Adolfs Akademien för svensk folkkultur, Gidlunds förlag, Uppsala
• Tacitus, Cornelius (A.D. 98): Germania – Available in English translation online at http://www.ourcivilisation.com/smartboard/shop/tacitusc/germany/chap1.htm

SECONDARY SOURCES ON COMPARATIVE RELIGION AND HISTORY:

• Allentoft, Morten E. ; et al. (2015). "Population genomics of Bronze Age Eurasia". Nature. 522: 167–172. doi:10.1038/nature14507
• Brockington, J.L (1996): The Sacred Thread – Hinduism in its Continuity and Diversity, University Press, Edinburgh
• Cohen, Signe / Reinvang, Rasmus (ed./transl.)(2003): Vediske skrifter. Utvalg og innledende essay av Signe Cohen. Verdens Hellige Skrifter, Bokklubben, Oslo.
• Doniger O´ Flaherty, Wendy (1981): The Rig Veda – an Anthology Penguin London
• Eppie R. Jones; et al. (2017). "The Neolithic Transition in the Baltic Was Not Driven by Admixture with Early European Farmers". Current Biology. 27 (4): 576–582. doi:10.1016/j.cub.2016.12.060
• Fari, Camilla Helene (2003): Hieros-gamos : en sammenligning mellom symbolets uttrykk i den nordiske bronsealderens helleristningstradisjon og myteverdenen i det østlige middelhavsområdet / Hovedoppgave i nordisk arkeologi, Universitetet i Oslo
• Fari, Camilla Helene / Prescott, Christopher / Melheim, Anne Lene (2006): Myter og religion i bronsealderen : studier med utgangspunkt i helleristninger, graver og depoter i Sør-Norge og Bohuslän / Christopher Prescott (red.)
• Flood, Gavin (1996): An Introduction to Hinduism, University Press, Cambridge
• Flint, Valerie I. J. (1991): The Rise of Magic in Early Medieval Europe. Princeton

• Fortson, Benjamin W. (2004): Indo-European Language and Culture: An Introduction, Blackwell Publishing
• Gelling, Peter / Davidson, Hilda Ellis (1969): The Chariot of the Sun - and Other Rites and Symbols of the Northern Bronze age Frederick A. Praeger, Publishers, New York, Washington
• Gibbons, Ann (2015): http://www.sciencemag.org/news/2015/06/nomadic-herders-left-strong-genetic-mark-europeans-and-asians
• Gimbutas, Marija (1991) The Civilization of the Goddess – The World of Old Europe, Harper, San Francisco
• Haak, et.al (2015): New Results: Massive migration from the steppe is a source for Indo-European languages in Europe, https://www.biorxiv.org/content/early/2015/02/10/013433
• Hooke, S. H. (1963): Middle Eastern Mythology from the Assyrians to the Hebrews, Penguin Books, London
• Van Voorst, Robert E. (2007): Anthology of World Scriptures: Eastern Religions
• Kinsley, David R. (1975): The Sword and the Flute – Dark Visions of the Terrible and the Sublime in Hindu Mythology, University of California Press, Berkely and Los Angeles
• Larson, Gerald James/ Littleton, Scott/ Puhvel, Jan (1974): Myth in Indo-European Antiquity Berkeley
• Lazaridis, Iosif (2014). "Ancient human genomes suggest three ancestral populations for present-day Europeans". Nature. 513: 409–413. doi:10.1038/nature13673. PMC 4170574 Freely accessible. PMID 25230663
• Mallory, J. P. (1997): «Yamna Culture» i: Encyclopedia of Indo-European Culture, Fitzroy Dearborn.
• Manco, Jean (2015 revised and updated edition): Ancestral Journeys – The peopling of Europe from the First Venturers to the Vikings, Thames and Hudson Ltd., London
• Mithen, Steven (2004): After the Ice – A Global Human History 20.000-5.000 BC, Phoenix, London
• Olson, Steve (2002): Mapping Human History, Bloomsbury, London
• Oppenheimer, Stephen (2004): Out of Eden – The peopling of the world, Robinson, London.
• Pakkanen, Petra (1995): Interpreting early Hellenistic religion: a study based on the cult of Isis and the mystery cult of Demeter Avhandling - Faculty of Arts at the University of Helsinki

• Rodenborg, Erik (1991): Marija Gimbutas teori om "Gamla Europa"s samhälle, kultur och religion – Uppsats i fordjupningskurs i arkeologi – Stockholms Universitet. A summary in English is available online at: http://potnia. theladyofthelabyrinth.com/the-critique-and-defense-of-marija-gimbutas%c2%b4-old-europe-thesis/

CITATIONS & ENDNOTES

1 These are the Latinized forms of Thunar/Thor and his son Magni.

2 In the tradition known as Interpretatio Romana, the Romans believed that the gods of other peoples were but different names for their own gods, hence the Germanic thunder god was often identified both as Jupiter [in his capacity as lord of all gods], and as Hercules [in his capacity as a semi-divine human hero]. This tradition of identifying foreign gods with their own gods was also common among the Greeks [Interpretatio Graeca] and among the Germanic tribes [Interpretatio Germanii], and is even detected in Norse literature, as when Snorri explains that Freyia took upon herself different names as she was known among different people. In the Edda poem Grimnismál (see The Poetic Edda [Volume 1] – Six Cosmology Poems), the god Óðinn declares that he "never had just one name" as he "moved among people."

3 Singular masculine; Áss. Singular feminine: Ásynia. Plural masculine; Aesir. Plural Feminine: Ásyniur. The masculine plural may also denote both genders. Plural genitive; Ása.

4 He refers to this river as Tanais, Tanakvisl or Vanakvisl, but it is the Don and is, as he says, the border between Europe and Asia.

5 Edda literally means "great grandmother" in the Norse language. The name was applied at some point to describe the lore of past generations, the lore told by the great grandmothers.

6 Kvina – literally meaning "the woman" – is a river in Kvinedal (Kvina valley) in Agder. At the time, Agder was an independent kingdom of the tribe of the Egdir in south Norway. His nickname could just as likely refer to a county by the Hardanger fjord, Kvinnherad (the Reign of Women), apparently the name was a result of a failed summer expedition where all the men were lost at sea.

7 How historically accurate that counting of a royal lineage actually is, we shall never know. The interesting part about this poem as an historical source is that it shows how pagans of the 9th centuries viewed their own history, and how one king, at least, believed that each of his ancestors had lived and died ever since their lineage's beginning, and how they were descended from the gods. This belief was true for many Scandinavian dynasties. It is said that Sæmund the Wise wrote a prose explanation of this poem during the 12th century, and that Snorri Sturlusson preserved a copied or else a another, later version of the Ynglingatál in his prose take on this poem; the Ynglinga saga.

8 Rendered in full in chapter 7

9 Skáldskaparmál 65: Kristskenningar, Prose Edda

10 Anatolia became Turkey [«Turk-land»] after the invasion of the Turks only a few centuries before Snorri was born.

11 Þessir höfðingjar hafa verit um fram aðra menn, þá er verit hafa í veröldu, um alla manndómliga hluti.

12 Hlóra, as well as Lórikus [Hlórriði] may be associated to the Norse verb hlóa: to glow.

13 Þrúðheimr – incidentally, Thor's daughter is called Þrúðr – "power"

14 In reality, Hloriði, «Loud Rider», was a Thorsheiti – a nickname for Thor himself. It is usually translated as "Loud Rider" [Simek], although it could also be translated as "Glow Rider" [from hlóa – to glow].

15 This was also really another heiti – nickname- for Thor

16 In Norse myths, this was one of Thor's sons by the giantess Iarnsaxa (Iron Scissors). Her name is otherwise listed in Hyndluljóð (See The Poetic Edda – Six Cosmology Poems) as one of the nine mothers of Heimdallr.

17 Skjöldr [Scyld], «shield», a son of Óðinn in other sources, and/or else the father of Danish royal lineages and the clan of the Skjöldungar [Scyldings]

18 Gangleri. The Gylfaginning part of the Prose Edda takes the form of a dialogue between Gylfi (a Swedish sorcerer king who assumes the name Gangleri – Wandering Learner – when he visits Ásgarðr) and a trinity representing Óðinn in three aspects; as Hárr [High], Jafnhárr [Equally High] and Þríði [Third]. All three names are heiti [nicknames] for the god Óðinn, as testified in the Þulur [recitals] of Skáldskaparmál as well as in the Edda poem Grimnismál (see The Poetic Edda [Volume 1] – Six Cosmology Poems), and Skaldic poetry.

19 The High One: Hárr [=Óðinn]. See previous footnote 17

20 Sliding/Driving Thor: Öku- Þórr

21 The Power Fields: Þrúðvangar (Þrúðr, "Power", is also the name of Thor's daughter). See footnote 12.

22 Or «Diminishing Shine», «Moment's Shine» - Bilskirnir. Perhaps an allusion to lightning.

23 Grímnismál stanza 33, Poetic Edda. In his Gylfaginning, which is basically a treatise on Edda poetry, Snorri frequently quotes from the Poetic Edda.

24 Tanngnjóstr ok Tanngrisnir

25 Frost thurses and mountain giants: hrímþursar ok bergrisar

26 The Power Belt: Megingjarðar

27 Divine Power/Might: Ásmegin

28 Iron gloves: járnglófar

29 Son of Óðinn and Earth: Sonr Óðins ok Jarðar (or by applying any other nickname for Óðin and for Earth).

30 Father of Greatness and Rage and Power: Magna ok Móða ok Þrúðar

31 Verr Sifjar -The name of Thor's wife, Síf, means "Kinswoman".

32 Stjúpfaðir Ullar: Ullr – meaning of name uncertain, a very old god associated with hunting and bowmanship whose myths are largely forgotten, but he is said to be Síf's son.

33 Stýrandi ok Eigandi Mjöllnis ok Megingjarða, Bilskirrnis

34 Verjandi Ásgarðs, Miðgarðs. Ásgarðr = the Realm of the Aesir/ Miðgarðr = "Middle World" – the realm of human beings. Verjandi means "protector".

35 Enemy and Bane of Giants and Troll Women: Dólgr ok Bani Jötna ok Trollkvinna

36 Bane of (or "one who fights") Hrungnir, Red-Spear and Rules-Three: Vegandi Hrungnis, Geirröðar, Þrívalda

37 The Lord of Binding Together and Maturing: Dróttinn Þjálfa ok Rösku

38 Enemy of the Middle World Serpent: Dólgr Miðgarðsorms

39 Fosterling of Friend-Maker and Listener/Heat: Fóstri Vingnis [Óðinn] ok Hlóra [Listener/Heat=Earth]

40 Here follows numerous quotes of verses from different, once famous Skaldic poems. Snorri frequently refer to and quotes Skaldic poetry in his Prose Edda Skáldskaparmál, which is basically a treatise on Skaldic poetry – and his work is thus one of our main sources to these poems. Many of these verses are only known from Snorri.

41 Þialfi [Binding Together], brother of Röskva [Maturing].

42 Or "penises" – in any case, someone's stone is in Norse poetry often a symbol of internal courage and manliness, referring to the organs that possess these. In this setting, the most common interpretation is "hearts". This particular verse is a version of the Þórsdrápa (see chapter 7).

43 Aegir Öflug-barða: In this kenning, the name Aegir is used as a heiti for Thor, meaning "terrorizer".

44 The hammer Miöllnir is the "bane", the one who destroys; the "mountain whale" is the Middle World Serpent.

45 This line refers to a mythical narrative that has become lost to us.

46 This verse is from Snorri's version of the Þórsdrápa (see chapter 7 for the full poem).

47 Keila = «Gorge», «Narrow Fiord»; a giantess

48 Kjallandi = «Caretaker» - from kjala - to take care of; a giantess

49 Lut=«Bent Back», Leidi –«Disliked One»; two giants

50 Búseyra = «Large Ears»; a giantess

51 Hengjankjöfti = "Hanging, Gaping Mouth", the one who once owned the mill of Destiny in Gröttasöngr (See The Poetic Edda [Volume 1] – Six Cosmology Poems)

52 Hyrokkin – the giantess whose might is greater than all the gods together [see chapter 12]

53 Svívör: According to Simek, this name may mean «Shamed Goddess», made up from the words sví/ svívird: " shameful" and vör – a heiti for "goddess". In this case, it would refer to a giantess.

54 Fárbauti Jötunn :Loki's father

55 Laufey, Nál: Loki's mother

56 Byleistr: Loki's brother, and, incidentally, a heiti for Óðinn.

57 Helblindi – this is, incidentally, a heiti [nickname] for the god Óðinn, and may be the very same.

58 Angrboða, Loki's giantess mistress

59 Gýgr is the Norse word used for «giantess». The etymology and meaning is unknown, but the feminine gýgr matches the masculine Jötunn ("giant").

60 Jötunheim: The world of the giants, also called Utgarðr (Outer World) or the "eastern paths".

61 Fenrisúlfr: "Fenrir's wolf" – Greed's wolf

62 Jörmungandr, þat er Miðgarðsormr: Iörmun means something immensely, formidably large and great. Gandr means magic or spell, associated with witchcraft.

63 Etymologically, Hel means «Hidden», but is used synonymous with «death».

64 Níflheimr – one of the primeval realms of cosmic creation, now serving as an underworld for the dead.

65 Éljúðnir heitir salr hennar, Hungr diskr hennar, Sultr knífr hennar, Ganglati þrællinn, Ganglöt ambátt, Fallandaforað þresköldr hennar, er inn gengr, Kör sæing, Blíkjandaböl ársali hennar.

66 Sonr Fárbauta ok Laufeyjar, Nálar : In these sorts of kenningar, Loki is known through his relations.

67 Bróður Býleists ok Helblinda: Loki known through his relations

68 Ván="Hope", the river by which the Greed Wolf is bound, Vánargandr=Hope Magic/Monsters, (the ones who destroy hope).

69 föður Vánargands, þat er Fenrisúlfr, ok Jörmundgands, þat er Miðgarðsormr, ok Heljar ok Nara ok Ála

70 frænda ok föðurbróður, vársinna ok sessa Óðins ok ása

71 heimsæki ok kistuskrúð Geirröðar: Refers to Loki being stuck to the casket that Geirröd owns (ch. 7)

72 þjóf jötna, hafrs ok Brísingamens ok Iðunnar epla: Loki known by his role as a thief, chapters 4, 5, 8, 9.

73 Kinsman to Sleipnir: Sleipnis frænda (actally, Loki is Sleipnir's mother). See chapter 3.

74 Verr Sigynjar: Loki known through his relations

75 Enemy of the Gods: goða dólgr

76 The Harmer of the Kinswoman's Hair: hárskaði Sifjar. See chapter 8

77 Mischief-Smith: bölvasmiðr

78 The Sly God: inn slægi áss

79 Slanderer and Tricker of the Gods: rægjandi ok vélandi goðanna

80 The Counsel-Bane of Balder: ráðbani Baldrs. See chapter 12.

81 The Bound God: inn bundni áss. See chapter 12.

82 The Great Enemy of...: þrætudólgr Heimdallar ok Skaða. See chapter 4, 9 and 13.

83 Týr literally means «bull» or just «beast», but is also derived from older Indo-European names for "god", related to Tiwaz, Deus, Theos – all words for "god". In Norse myths, he is associated with victory and war.

84 Wind-Shield Council= Læðing – my translation here is controversial as there is no general agreement on what the name of this first fetter means. In "The Seed of Yggdrasill", I explained how I chose this interpretation of the name, by suggesting that it could have been an early, erroneous spelling of Hlé- "wind shield" and Þing – "council". In Norse myths, a "wind shield" refers to immortality, because the winds of the universe derive from the ultimate power of Death [Hræsvelgr – the Corpse Swallower].

85 Drómi – a word that means "fetter". In Norse myths, as Snorri explains in Skáldskaparmál 68, words for "fetter" or "chain" are metaphors for the divine powers who rule [bind together] the world.

86 Skírnir – the same god who is sent to the underworld by Freyr in the Edda poem Skirnismál, a shaman archetype. As payment he receives Freyr's sword which fights by itself against the giants.

87 World of the Black Elves = Svartalfaheimr – here lived the Dökkalfar – the Dark Elves of the underworld, often identifiable with dwarfs, supernatural craftsmen of below.

88 Opening One = Gleipnir – the meaning of Gleipnir refers to something that opens up and frees.

89 Black Darkener = Ámsvartnir

90 Shrine Covered by Heather= Lyngví

91 Wooden Post: Gelgja

92 Bellowing= Gjöll, also the name of one of the cosmic rivers running close to Hel/the Underworld.

93 Batterer= Þviti

94... their sanctuaries and their places of Truce= vé sín ok gríðastaði

95 Miðgarð – the human reality world

96 Valhöll – the Hall of Choice, the Chosen, or the Dead. An alternate afterlife ruled by Óðinn.

97 Harm Traveler: Svaðilfari

98 Giant rage = jötunmóð

99 Misty World = Níflheimr. This is also the World of the Dead where Hel rules, and is one of the three the primordial cosmic realms that created the present universe. According to Snorri, cold streams from Misty World met with the heat from Muspellheimr in the middle of the empty void, Ginnunga gap (The Open Mouth of the Sacred Descendants).

100 "En Loki hafði þá ferð haft til Svaðilfara, at nökkuru síðar bar hann fyl»

101 Vóluspá, Poetic Edda, stanza 25-26

102 Otherwise associated with the ocean, a husband to the sea goddess Rán and their nine daughters.

103 Hlér – Wind-shield. Wind is a metaphor for death in Norse poetry, wind-shield for immortality, hence his name really means "The Immortal One".

104 Hlésey – the Island of immortality

105 Sjónhverfingum: Sight-Warpings: illusions

106 In the Edda poem Völuspá and in Gylfaginning, Hænir ["Chicken"] is the god who offers the gift of thought/mind to the first human beings, alongside Óðinn's gift of inspiration. He represents "thought".

107 ok eigi lítill – a typical Norse understatement. "He is not tiny" actually means that he is enormous, formidable.

108 Slave-Binder the Giant: Þjazi jötunn (From Þiaza= to bind, capture, take as a slave). The fact that he is a giant in eagle's hide seated in the top of a huge tree is an allusion to an eagle mentioned in Gylfaginning 16, a "much knowing" (margs vitandi) eagle who sits in the top of Yggdrasill, the world tree. In the Edda poem VafÞruðnismál, the eagle is identified as another giant in eagle's hide, Hræsvelgr [Corpse Swallower], who by flapping his wings at the end of the universe (top of the tree) is creating all the winds of the universe, and these winds are alluding to mortality.

109 In eagle's hide = í arnarham

110 The World of the Drummer = Þrymheimr – from thruma-«to drum», make repetitive sound.

111 Iðunn was the goddess of rejuvenation and immortality – it is because of her that the Aesir enjoy divine immortality in the sense that their youth and life is regenerated when receiving the fruits of the goddess.

112 In the giant worlds = í Jötunheima

113 Falcon hide = Valshamr. The type of bird hide is a significant reference. In poetry, hawks and falcons are identifiable, the use of the word val for falcon is in itself a metaphor and gives association to the chosen dead, those who will achieve immortality. According to Snorri's Gylfaginning 16, a falcon/hawk called "Wind-Diminisher" (Vedrfölnir)sits between the eyes a large giant in eagle hide whose wings create all the unseen winds of the worlds of the universe. According to the Edda poem Vafthrudnismál, this giant eagle's name is Hræsvelgr, «Corpse Swallower»(see The Poetic Edda – Six Cosmology Poems). As such, the giant in eagle's disguise, who sits in a large tree just like Slave Binder, represents mortality, his wings blowing the winds of death, while the "wind-diminishing" hawk/falcon, owned by Freyia but now worn by Loki, represents a hope for immortality.

114 tekr hann arnarharminn ok flýgr eftir Loka, ok dró arnsúg í flugnum: arnsúg = «eagle-blown». This is, again, a reference to the winds of mortality created by the giant in eagle hide, Hræsvelgr («Corpse Swallower»). As Loki is here rescuing the goddess of immortality from a giant in eagle hide, and there is an additional reference to the blowing of eagle-winds in his wings as he tries to get away with the goddess of regeneration, the entire story is about immortality versus mortality.

115 Wooden splinters = lokarspánir

116 Njörðr ór Nóatúnum – the Vanir god of winds and waves.

117 Ölvaldi: Ale-Ruler – a reference to the precious mead, or Allvaldi = All-Ruler

118 Iði – the same root word that makes up the name Idunn – "Stream Returning to Source"

119 Wanderer= Gangr. The giant trinity is a poetical/mythical formula that repeats itself numerous times in Norse myth, just as it does among the gods, essential to creation. The same characters and trinities may also take different names, riddles for the readers to be solved.

120 Þá mælti Ægir: "Þat þykkir mér vel fólgit í rúnum."

121 A kenning usually consist of one or more subjects who are owned by, related to or in other ways associated to some other subject in the genitive form. In this kenning for the giant Slave Binder, "snótar ulfr", the first subject is the wolf (úlfr), who is "owned" by a snótr in the genitive form: snótr is a word used to describe an eloquent, intelligent woman, as explained by Snorri in his Skáldskaparmál and confirmed by the general use of this word for smart, wise women in Norse poetry and literature. In a kenning, someone's "wolf" always refers to that someone's enemy or abductor or killer, this because your "wolf" is that which chases you, poetically speaking. That the goddess is an "eloquent woman" is known, after all, Iðunn is a goddess who searches for wisdom and knowledge, as testified in the Edda poem Hrafngaldr Óðins, stanza 6, where Iðunn, the goddess of immortality and regeneration, is described as a "knowledge-hungry goddess" (dís forvitin). Her "wolf", her enemy/abductor, is a reference to Þiazi (Slave Binder), the lord of mortality and enemy to knowledge. In my work "The Seed of Yggdrasill", I have offered an extensive explanation of the kenningar (metaphors) used in this poem. I can also provide an online article with similar (shorter) content here: http://freya.theladyoft-helabyrinth.com/?page_id=79 .

122 Tellers of the Stories= Segjǫndum Sagna: the Aesir are the "verse smiths" of the universe.

123 The metaphor indicates that Þiazi is the Giant of "the Mountain of the Giantess", which is a known metaphor for the burial mound, yet another emphasis placed on his role as the representative of death and mortality.

124 Wandering Learner [Gangleri] is engaging in a word-duel, where the one who cannot reply to a question may lose his head.

125 Jafnhárr – Wandering Learner [Gangleri] is actually contesting with three aspects of Óðinn together, a trinity of The High One [Hárr], Just-As-High [Jafnhárr] and Third [Þriði].

126 Þriði: Third – a heiti for Óðinn (see previous footnote). He answers the toughest questions.

127 Thialfi: Þjálfi, from Þjálfa: to connect pieces together, to bind together – a symbol of understanding and the rational mind?

128 Röskva – from röskvast: to grow, to mature, a "sister" to the rational mind?

129 One of several indications that Thor's hammer had the function of ritually sanctifying things.

130 "...and he was not tiny": Ok var sá eigi lítill. This was a typical understatement meant to emphasize that he was formidably, incredibly huge.

131 Skrýmir, a typical giant name associated with sounds and speech; there is Ýmir (murmuring, sound), Hýmir (hymn), Mímir (murmur, memory), and here, Skrýmir, from skryma: to brag, boast, speak loudly, speak out loud.

132 Útgarðr literally translates as "outside world, outside settlement or outer world".

133 In mythical geography, the north is the way towards death and mortality. The east is the path towards dangerous realms of giants, but also illumination.

134 Útgarða-Loki

135 Lógi literally translates as a flame.

136 Hugi – from húgr; meaning something in between thought, intent, desire, love, heart and will.

137 Vítishorn, from víti=correction, punishment

138 Elli – Old Age

139 sjónhverfingar

140 Grésjárni [="iron thread"?]=magical band

141 "þat var hugr minn" – "that was my thought/intent/desire/will/heart"

142 Shivering Voice: Bífröst: from bífa – to tremble, vibrate, shiver, and röstr: voice

143 Muspell is the southern cosmic realm of heat and poison. The realm was one of the three that created the universe, but is also going to destroy it.

144 The World Tree [Universe]

145 Well of Origin: Urðarbrunnr [Urð's Well. Urðr is the oldest norn, representing the past, and the origin].

146 Divine Bridge: Ásbru

147 Protecting and Diverting: Körmt ok Örmt

148 Kettle Baths: Kerlaugar

149 Thor's mother is the Earth goddess.

150 Hildolfr

151 Meili – "lovely", one of Óðinn's sons. Perhaps a heiti for Balder.

152 Magni

153 See chapter 6

154 Great Guardian – or "Much Alert": Fiölvari – from fiöl: much, great and vari: guardian, alert

155 Slave Binder: Þiazi – see chapter 4

156 Allvaldi

157 Myrcridur- riders of darkness=witches, sorceresses, giantesses

158 Hlébarðr – Hlé means wind-shielded and alludes to immortality, since wind is a metaphor for mortality in Norse myths.

159 Valland, another way of saying Valhöll [Valhalla], although, in heroic poetry, it is sometimes used to refer to Frankland.

160 A reference to the story of Thor and Outer World Loki [earlier in this chapter]

161 Fjalarr, either from fela – to hide, or fjela – to spy [The Observer], in other myths, Fjalarr and his brother, Galarr – "The One Who Crows [like a rooster, or like one who makes a spell-song/incantation]", are two dwarfs who kill Kvasir, the divine embodiment of wisdom and knowledge, in order to make the mead of poetry and monopolize it. In this poem, however, Fjalarr is a direct reference to Skrymir/Utgarðsloki [The Loud Speaker/Outer World Loki].

162 The name Svárangr is only mentioned in this source. The meaning is uncertain; according the Simek, it means "The Clumsy One", but that interpretation is left unexplained and inexplicable. However, the name is a combination of two words; svára means a witch or a giantess, while angr is related to English anger [but also means regret and grief]. Svárangr, although presented as masculine, is thus a strong candidate for another name for Angrbóða, the giantess mother of Hel, Jörmungandr and Fenrir, Loki´s mistress. As such, the "sons" would be referring to Fenrir [Greed] and the Middle World Serpent [the border between the worlds]. Other possible meanings could relate to the verb svara: to swear [an oath], to explain, repay, take responsibility.

163 Leynþingr – "secret council/parliament" – usually a metaphor for love-making.

164 Stanza 30-33 refer to a myth otherwise unknown to us [not preserved].

165 Hlésey: Wind shield [Hlér] is a metaphor for immortality in Norse myths. It is also mentioned as the home of Aegir, the ocean giant, and his nine daughters provide the lights there [see chapter 11]. Aegir is also called Hlér, and Heimdall, son of nine mothers, is called Vindhlér [Wind-windshield] [see chapter 9]. Aegir´s divine counterpart is Njördr, god of winds, waves and harbors, who in the Sólarljód 79 [Poetic Edda] is also said to have nine rune-carving daughters.

166 Þialfi – from Þialfa – to connect, bind together [a symbol of the rational mind?] Thor´s servant. Stanza 37-39 refer to a myth otherwise unknown to us [not preserved] where Thor, apparently, fights with the nine daughters of Aegir and Rán, who live at Hlésey.

167 Since Long Beard appears to be a disguise for Óðinn, the reference to him leading an enemy army to the world of the gods is a reference to an otherwise unknown [unpreserved] myth. The only similarity is found in the Völuspá and Gylfaginning, where Loki is the one who leads an army against the gods during Ragnarök [see chapter 13]. This may be one of many myths in which the boundary between the Óðinn and the Loki characters are blurred.

168 Þrymr - from Þruma: to drum, to beat rhythmically, make a repetitive sound.

169 Vár – "alert", "conscious", "aware": the goddess of oaths [such as a marriage oath]

170 The ageing sister of the giant would probably be identical to Eldi, the embodiment of old age, who managed to wrestle Thor to his knees in Skáldskaparmál [see beginning of this chapter]. In this story, Thor wins over old age.

171 Metaphors = Kenningar – «that by which something/someone is known»

172 Giant Worlds: Jötunheima

173 Roarer= Hrungnir, or «Brawler», «Rioter», «Noise-Maker», from hrungna: to roar, riot, shout out in rage.

174 hvat manna sá er með gullhjálminn, er ríðr loft ok lög

175 Golden Mane = Gullfaxi

176 «Preposterous boast»: Ófrmæli – too much speech

177 Giant Rage: jötunmóð

178 Divine Gate: Ásgrindr

179 stór orð – «great words», «large speech» [boastful speech] – an allusion to Skrýmir, the "Boaster" / Loud Speaker

180 The Old Norse language is gendered – everything is either masculine, feminine or neutral, and even objects are referred to as «him» or «her» in the case of being masculine or feminine.

181 Divine Ale: Ásaöl [meaning all the ale that the Aesir owned – but is also a reference to the precious mead of inspiration and immortality].

182 þá nefna þeir Þór – apparently, by just saying his name, the god is invoked and appears.

183 «little honor»: litil frami. There are many Norse words for «honor» (and for «dishonor»), this particular word, frami, means both honor, courage and "benevolent conduct", as well as meaning "help" and "useful".

184 Grjóttúnagörðum – in the Giant Worlds. The homes of giants are always described as rocky in some way.

185 Holmgang – a duel between two warriors within a limited space court [such as a holmr – a type of reefe].

186 «legg ek þér við níðingsskap» - then I accuse of being a níðing – "lowly", "cowardly", "dishonorable", was about the worst thing a Norseman could be accused of.

187 Man-to-man combat = einvígr

188 Dirt Calf: Mökkurkálfi

189 Allhræddr – all frightened, all fear – completely terrified.

190 Reef-contest: Hólmstefnr – the place for holmgang [duel]

191 Binding Together: Þjálfi, from Þjálfa – "to bind together"/"to connect". Thor's young, human servant, brother to Röskva ["Maturing"]. See chapter 9.

192 Divine Rage= Ásmóðr

193 Heinberg: mountain -as in a mine - of stones suitable for whetting/honing blades.

194 Iarnsaxa – a giantess, one of the nine who birthed Heimdallr["Great World"] in Hyndluljód st. [See: The Poetic Edda [volume 1] – Six Cosmology Poems].

195 Gýgjarsónr – son of a Gýgr [giantess]

196 We have no further sources to elaborate this disagreement.

197 Power Fields: Þrúðvangar

198 Gróa – «to grow». A vǫlva was an oracle/witch/priestess – and healer.

199 Aurvandill: The meaning of this name is disputed. It is made up of aurr – "gravel" [often a metaphor for gold], the same word for gravel used to describe what the norn Urdr [Origin] uses to nourish and daily revive the world tree Yggdrasill itself, aurr from the Well of Origin. The –vandill part is the disputed part: it has been suggested that it is related to vöndr – "wand" – a meaning that makes sense seeing as he is married to a Wand-Witch [vǫlva].

200 Hon gól galdra sína yfir Þór. The use of the word gala (gól) for singing galdr indicates that the spell-songs were sung in a high-pitched, hawking tune.

201 Elivágar: In Gylfafinning, Snorri explains that the «Waves of Age» emerged during the cosmic creation, streams from the ice cold northern realm of Misty World [Niflheimr] where Hel rules. As they came into Ginnungagap [Open Mouth of Sacred Descendants], the empty space, they were heated by stream from the southern hot realm Muspell. The hoarfrost that emerged from the streams gathered together to make the giant Ymir ["Murmuring Sound"]. The waves are also mentioned in the Edda poem Vafthrudnismál 31 [see The Poetic Edda [volume 1] – Six Cosmology Poems].

202 Aurvandilstá – a star. In Old Norse, tá means "toe", making sense to a Norse audience of the Viking age and being explained by this myth about the giant's frozen, cut-off toe - but it could also derive from an older word applying the archaic *taho – "beam", what would make sense since we are speaking of a star.

203 Wood: The splinters that were lit in order to burn Slave Binder [see chapter 4]

204 Grasper = Greip, a giantess. Her lover is a giant, his son is Thiazi – Slave Binder.

205 "Mountain-Finn": Giant – any foreign identity could be used in metaphors for giants. In this case, the kenning for "giant" is a part of a larger kenning for "shield": the Giant's Bridge of the Sole.

206 A painted shield – the shield that Thorleif gave to Thióðolf was painted with images from the myth of Iðunn [chapter 4] and the myth of Hrungnir. This provided Thióðolf with the two themes for his poem Haustlöng.

207 Tree is a heiti for "man". Cave of flames is a heiti for "gold". Gold's man; Poetry's or wisdom's man: The poet is here addressing and complimenting his audience, probably Thorleif who gave him the shield.

208 A haugr is a mound, but more precisely, a burial mound (a cairn), its common use in connection to the giants also connects the realm of the giants with the realm of the dead.

209 Meili is mentioned as one of Óðinn's sons in the Þulur and as Thor's brother in Edda and Skaldic poetry, but little else is known about him. His name means "Lovely" and may, as such, be a heiti for Balder.

210 Shrine of the Sacred Descendants: Ginnunga Vé =The air. Ginnunga is otherwise known from the creatios story; Ginnunga gáp = The Open Mouth of the Sacred Descendants, the still, empty void in which creation happened (Völuspá, Poetic Edda). Vé: shrine. Ginnr: sacred (adj.). –unga: descendants (gen.pl.)

211 Dark Bone = Submerged rocks. Haki's Chariots = Ships. Land of Haki's Chariots = Sea. The "Watcher of the Rocks of the Sea = Hrungnir

212 Bellower: Beli is one of the giant adversaries at Ragnarök who fights with Freyr. In Gylfaginning 36, Snorri explains that Freyr had to fight Beli with an antler because he lacked a proper weapon after giving it to Skírnir. Beli's "harmful troops" are the giants, and the "Destroyer of their Lives" is Thor.

213 Öl-gefn/Öl-gefjon= "Ale-Provider" is a common poetical metaphor for a benevolent "woman" or "goddess," in this case the vǫlva/giantess Gróa, who sings the hurt out with her spell-songs.

214 The word for «god» used here is «Týr». In Skáldskaparmál, Snorri explains that all gods could be known by calling them by the name of another god, and then identifying the actual god in question by adding a relevant description, such as "Reðii-Týr" – Wound-Giving Týr, in this story, Thor is the wound-giving god.

215 The poet, Thióðolfr, composed Haustlöng as a way of thanking a certain Thorleif for having gifted him with a beautiful, painted shield with illustrations of the myths of Iðunn and Thiazi (chapter 4) as well as this myth of Thor and Hrungnir.

216 Red Spear: Geirröðr – otherwise a human by the same name appears in Grimnismál, the Poetic Edda (see The Poetic Edda [volume 1] – Six Cosmology Poems). In this story, he is a jötunn – a giant.

217 Megingjarðar eða Járngreipr

218 Frigg's falcon hide: Valsham Friggjar – in chapter 4, we saw that he used Freyia's falcon hide.

219 This is why Loki may be known in kennings as Red Spear's Casket Decoration. See ch. 1. Pg.34.

220 Gýgr: giantess

221 Víðars ins þögla – a son of Óðinn, destined to kill the Greed-Wolf at Ragnarök and take over after his father. His name either means "Wood-Warrior" [the wood is a metaphor for the physical body of the universe or of a person] or "Expanding/Widening Warrior".

222 Hundvíss – cunning, intelligent in a negative way ("wise like a dog").

223 Gríðarvölr -The reference to a völr [wand] is a hint: that Griðr is a vǫlva, a Wand-Witch [oracle, spiritual teacher]. Thor may use her wand like he uses his hammer.

224 Vímur: vibrating, shaking, bubbling. In the skaldic poem Húsdrápa 6, this river appears to represent the border between the worlds of giants and of humans.

225 Howler: Gjálp (or Gjölp), from gjalpa: to bark or howl like a dog. A common name for giantesses in Norse literature generally, also for "seeresses". Gjalp is listed as one of the nine mothers of Heimdallr in the Hyndluljóð 37 (see The Poetic Edda – Six Cosmology Poems).

226 Actually, what Thor "holds on to" is a "rowan tree", but reyna also meant "to experience" – the Norse poets were aware of the double meaning and used it consciously.

227 reynir er björg Þórs - or: "Rowan is Thor's Salvation"

228 Gjálp and Greip: Greip is another of Heimdall's ("Great World"'s) nine mothers, her name indicates someone who grasps or clasps something, or who possesses a strong grip.

229 Ocean Rope: Lögseim = Middle World Serpent

230 Thorn=Þorn: the name means "thorn" or else something sharp which sting, a buckle with a needle, , or else something that is cooling or drying. In this context, it obviously refers to some giant, since all giants may be known by the name of another, or by kinship to another giant. Thorn is otherwise unknown.

231 Iði is the name of a giant, one of Ölvaldi's ["Ale Ruler's"] three sons in Skáldskaparmál 1, brother to Þiazi ["Slave-Binder"] [see chapter 1]. His name may be derived from the same root word as makes the name of Iðunn and the Iðavellir ["The fields of the iðs"], iðr meaning a stream that separates from the main stream and returns towards the water source. However, the name Iði could also be related to the verb iða, to work hard, move towards something. The "settlement" of this hard-working, moving, streaming, contrary, source-returning being is a metaphor for the ocean in Old Norse poetry. "Scots" are here a metaphor for giants, as all foreign competing peoples could be applied in poetry to generally mean adversaries.

232 Þriði «Third» = Óðinnsheiti [a heiti – nickname- for Óðinn]. His realm is Ásgarð/Valhalla.

233 Ymsi is a giant otherwise unknown in the sources. The word is related to modern Norwegian ymse, meaning "varied", "different", "diverse" or "several", from Old Norse ýmiss/ímiss which means "varied", "alternately", "taking turns" more spesifically suggesting that within something/someone, there is an inner, mutual movement of sides taking turn, alternating from one quality to another [from Old Germanic *missa]. It is also possible that it is a variant of the first world giant Ymir from whose physical body the physical universe is shaped. His name is derived from ýmr = "sound", "murmur"and ymta = to suggest, speak carefully, to hint. His "kindred" would be a metaphor for the giant race.

234 Þjálfi [Thialfi]– «binds together», «connects», Thor's boy-servant [see chapter 9] – a metaphor for the thinking mind? That would explain his role as the "Ruler of the Stories" [Sagna Rögnir]. In this poem, he has taken the place of Loki in the myth, the identities of the two are in fact blurred.

235 Þyl ek Granstrauma Grímnis: I recite the Beard/Lip streams of Grimnir [Masked = Óðinn]: I recite poetry

236 Endill is a giant appearing in kenningar for the ocean in skaldic poetry as well as in very old runic inscriptions. The meaning of his name is unknown, but Old Norse endi means "end", "border", "boundary".

237 Nanna is otherwise the name of Balder's wife. The name of any goddess could be used as a heiti for another goddess, or else simply mean "goddess". Giantesses may be referred to as goddesses in kennings, and are recognized as giantesses by the sort of goddess they are presented as; the "Hilt's goddess" would be a giantess. When applying the particular name Nanna, the poet is also indicating that she is a wife, as this goddess' primary function is to be a good wife.

238 Þjálfi benefited from Thor's power belt by hanging onto it while Thor waded through the river.

239 Mörn is an otherwise inexplicable word that in all the sources obviously refer to a giantess, and is speculated to be particularly referring to the giantess Skaði. This is because Skaði is clearly called Mörn in the poem Haustlöngr. Her "children" is a kenning for giants in general. Skaði/Mörn is also mentioned as the recipient of a horse-penis sacrifice in the famous poem Vǫlsa þáttr ["The Song of the Wand/Horse Penis"] preserved in The Saga of Ólaf the Holy and in Flateyiarbók.

240 Þorn here appears to be a heiti for the first giant, Ymir, from whose body and bones and blood the physical world was shaped; his blood is the ocean. See footnote 228, stanza 2.

241 Gleipnir: the bond that bound Fenrir (see chapter 2): The ones who fastened it were the Aesir.

242 Hylridar: the ones who crossed the deep [ocean/river]

243 This is a typical kenning for battle: referring to the legend of Heðinn, the foreign [Serkland] enemy of the Danes in Sörlatáttr. The Bowls of Heðinn's Parting of the Hair is a kenning for "helmet" [the parting of the hair is his head], the "game of enemy helmets" equals battle.

244 Skyld-Breta: This reference to a Briton, like the earlier reference to a Scot (stanza 2), would be a way of referring to contemporary, foreign adversaries/enemies/competitors while poetically and indirectly actually just referring to the giants. Giants are often referred to as the kinsmen of a typical tribal enemy contemporary to the poet and his audience, who in this case were Norwegian Thronds from Trondheim (Trøndelag, Norway).

245 As with the Britons and the Scots, this reference to Svear [Swedes from the realm of Svearíki north of Götaland in Sweden] is also a way of referring metaphorically to giants, that is, to adversaries. Apparently, the poet who made this poem at the time was in a court that regarded the Svear as quite fit to be likened with giants. Any contemporary adversary could be used as a poetical metaphor for giants.

246 Dreig i vé: the vé was a temple or a sanctuary

247 Again, this poet was big on applying foreigners with whom there might have been conflicts going on as metaphors for the giants. Here, even the Danes are filling in, metaphorically speaking!

248 Utvé – a temple lying outside of the settlement, like a grove

249 Jólnir = the name appears as a heiti for the god Óðinn, his kinsmen being a metaphors for gods, and may possibly be related to the word for Yule (jól). The etymology is uncertain but appears to be related to various Indo-European words meaning joy or something joyful and pleasurable. In Skáldskaparmál 68, jólnar is a heiti for "gods".

250 Þorn [Thorn] = Ymir, the original jötunn/giant: His cave [hellir] is the home of the giants.

251 Sound=hlymr – as usual, the giants are associated with various words for sounds.

252 Welsh= Kumra: foes/giants - see footnote 168

253 The «hood» of the giantess is the chair – and refers to how she was rising beneath his chair.

254 Time Counter =Tungl: Otherwise used for heavenly bodies, mainly the Moon, but in this case, for Thor.

255 Konr Iarðar: Son of Earth

256 Aegir, otherwise the name of the ocean giant, means "terrifyer" and is here referring to Red Spear as an archer [the one who "terrifies" -shoots- the bow]

257 The "Southerner" is Suðri, also the name of one of the four dwarfs who forged Freyia's Necklace of Flames [Brisingamen], who represent the four directions; Northern, Southern, Eastern, Western. Here, the giant Red Spear is identified as a descendant of these dwarfs. In the Edda poem Völuspá, the gods too are descended from dwarfs and enter the Earth through their dwarfish forms.

258 Þröngvir is a sexually laden word for "conqueror". One of Freyia´s heiti is Þröng – "narrow", also used as a metaphor for the vagina. The –vir ending is related to "virility", manliness, and verr- "husband". As such, Thor is here "husband to the vagina", or even "Husband to Freyia" – but it means "conqueror".

259 Kveldrunnina kvinna: «the women who run in the night». These are probably giantesses, and their "kinsmen" are the giants that Thor conquers.

260 Þröng is a name for Freyia which means "narrow", particularly as in a narrow gap, possibly referring to the vagina. When Thor is referred to as her old friend, we must probably consider the lines in Völuspá stanza 25-26 where Thor rushes to defend her after she has been promised to the giants, or as one of the many symbolic references to sex in this poem.

261 Red Spear's hand [the grip's chest] is referred to as hostile because it is hurling a weapon

262 Hrimnir: the name could either mean «sooted» or «covered with hoar-frost». He is referred to in the Edda poems Skirnismál 28 and Hyndluljóð 32 and in skaldic poetry as part of kenningar for giants, like here.

263 Power: Þrúðr = the name of Thor's daughter. It has been suggested that this and other kennings about Thor and his daughter, "Power", are referring to an otherwise lost myth about how Thor misses his daughter who has been married off.

264 Þrasir: the name indicates something threathening, or yearning, or seeking - otherwise listed as a dwarf.

265 Heiðrekr : "The One Who Travels the Heath/Bright Open Space" - Here it is used to describe Geirröðr

266 The fishing line may be a reference to the story of Thor fishing the Middle World Serpent, and Red Spear may here be identified with Hymir, who in that story is a "foe" to the "tooth"[bait] of the fishing line, as he sabotages the fishing adventure by cutting off the lie.

267 Glaumr: "Loud Sound", a reference to Ymir, the original giant, whose name means sound, murmur.

268 Actually, the whole point of this story, according to Snorri [see the prose introduction in this chapter] appeared to be how Thor went into the giant world WITHOUT his hammer. Now, he suddenly has it – or the wand that he was given by Griðr has mysteriously become his own hammer. It has been suggested that this myth may originally, forgotten by the time of Snorri, be describing how Thor actually got his hammer, or how he got it back, or how he retrieved his power, symbolized by the hammer and by the reference to his daughter Þrúðr in stanza 16, and that he has turned the iron rod, the weapon that Red Spear hurled at him, into the hammer. Maybe this story originally told the myth of how Thor first got his thunderbolt hammer, while Snorri's tale in chapter 7 is a later or an alternative version where this original theme has been forgotten.

269 This is the only direct use of the word jötunn [giant, devourer] in the entire poem.

270 Apparently, even the people of Rogaland, another county in Norway, were foes enough for this audience of Thronds to be used as metaphors for giants. The "District of the Falcon Lair" refers to rocks, stone and mountain, and the people who reside in rocky realms are always kennings for giants.

271 «Hví er gull kallat Haddr Sifjar?»

272 Black Elves: Svartálfar. «Black» was a way of saying «dark».

273 Ívaldasynir; Ivaldi= «In-Ruler» [Ruler Within?]. In the Edda poem Hrafngaldr Oðins, the goddess of immortality, Iðunn, is also mentioned as a child of Ivaldi, "Frá Yggdrasills" – The Seed of Yggdrasill.

274 Skíðblaðnir = "Assembled from Pieces of Thin Wood": The ship is mentioned in Grímnismál 43 [Poetic Edda]; Gylfaginning 42, and Skáldskaparmál 35

275 From gungna: to sway, vibrate. Mentioned in Skáldskaparmál 9 & 33, Sigrdrífumál 17 [Poetic Edda] as well as in Skaldic poetry; Bragi Skald [9th century] called Óðinn by the kenning "Gungnis Váfaðr": "The Shaker of the Swaying One", Egill Skald called him "Geirs Drottin": "Lord of the Spear", among others.

276 Brokkr: Meaning of name is disputed, maybe from brokka: to run [«The Runner»], but by the time of the Viking Age, his name had also become a word that simply meant "blacksmith".

277 Sindri: «Sparks»/ «Sprays» [«spraying sparks»] = Blacksmith.

278 Draupnir is mentioned in Gylfaginning 48, Skáldskaparmál 33, Skírnismál 5 and 21 [Poetic Edda] and is said to be a ring that drips eight new rings every ninth night. The formula "nine nights" is generally associated with initiation and underworld journeys [as Óðinn hung nine nights on the world tree in order to get access to the runes of fate. The symbol of the red golden ring is also a recurring theme associated with the quest for divine wisdom and eternal rejuvenation/renewal [immortality]. It may be the mythical counterpart of a temple ring often described in sagas; a large ring would reside in a temple to be used for swearing sacred oaths, among other things, and could also be a symbol of kingship/lordship.

279 This would be the tale of how Thor got his hammer, Miöllnir.

280 In this feature, Loki is akin the the Roman god Mercury, the messenger between realms, whose shoes are winged. In Roman times, however, Mercury was likened to Wodan [Óðinn]. This is one of several indications that Óðinn and Loki are two aspects of the same, where Loki had maintained his aspect as divine messenger/servant, while Óðinn, eventually, got the High Seat.

281 Vartari: Meaning unknown. Perhaps related to the adverb vart: Badly, meagerly, too little; varlaunat: to get really bad pay for something of greater worth. This could be a way of saying that Loki got far less gratitude than he had really deserved for the gifts that he had offered to the gods, and may explain why Loki turned against the gods eventually.

282 Temple priests: Hófgóðar

283 Concubine: Frilla

284 Alfrigg/Alfregg – possibly written erroneously, as we see in older sources an "Alfríkr", which is derived from Alfr: elf and ríkr – lord/realm/powerful ["Powerful Elf", "Lord of Elves"].

285 Hibernation: Dvalinn – one of the first dwarfs in cosmos [See Völuspá 11, Poetic Edda]. The norns (fate goddesses) who have a dwarfish rather than elfin or divine nature are called "Daughters of Dvalinn" (dötr Dvalins) according to the Edda poem Fafnismál 13 and Snorris Gylfaginning 15, Prose Edda.

286 Short Beam: Berlingr

287 Bellower: Grérr (from Old English gerar: to bellow, or else from Irish grerr: "short" (Simek).

288 Dvergr – originally, the name meant «mutilated». Elves and dwarves blur together in Norse myths.

289 In Norse myths and folklore, dwarfs and dark elves lived inside "stones", a way of saying a burial mound, indicating that these were beings associated with the underworld and the souls of the dead.

290 The "stone" was a burial mound or any other entry to the underworld and the world of the dead. Being able to enter or communicate with the beings who lived within "stones" was a feat of Seiðr – the shamanic type of Seiðr. In the Ynglinga saga 7, we hear that Óðinn, who had learned the art of Seiðr from Freyia (Ynglinga saga 4) knew how to sing galdr (spell songs) that coule made everything open up for him; earth and mountain and stone and mounds, and he could bind with words their inhabitants and enter and take what he wanted. In this passage, Freyia, who taught him the art, is doing just that.

291 The necklace is called Brisinga Mén: the Gem of Flames, a possible allusion to the Sun goddess.

292 Dangerous Hitter the Giant: Fárbauta Jötunn: Loki´s father (see chapter 1)

293 Leaf Island: Laufey – Loki Laufeysson´s mother (see chapter 1)

294 Nál : Needle, another name for Loki´s mother(see chapter 1)

295 However, in chapter 1, we saw that there was a tradition where Loki had two brothers.

296 Sonr Níu Mæðra: Son of Nine Mothers

297 Vörðr Goða: Guardian of the Gods

298 Hvíta Áss: Bright/Light/White God. The adjective hvítr could mean the color white, but also bright and light. Neihter "white" nor "black" was ever used to refer to skin color; the Norse rather believed that they were "red" or "pink" while dark-skinned people were "blue". As such, a better translation is "bright".

299 Loka Dólg: Loki´s Enemy/ Mensækir Freyju: The Seeker of Freyia´s Gem

300 Sverð: Sword

301 Heimdallargaldr – sadly we have only a few fragments and references to this poem.

302 mjötuðr Heimdallar : Heimdall is a name made out of the words heimr = world, and dallr = great, awesome, splendid. In Norse sources, term mjǫtuðr refers to fate and is sometimes also associated to a name for the world tree, mjǫtviðr: Mead Tree or Fate Tree. This mysterious word is composed of mjöt, which means a target, the right target, indirectly associated with fate [or mead] and uðr: a small wave.

303 Manns mjötuðr – «Man´s Fate» = «Man´s Doom" [that by which he will die]. See previous footnote.

304 Heimdallr er Eigandi Gulltopps. Hann er ok Tilsækir Vágaskers ok Singasteins

305 Vindlér: See chapter 4 where Aegir is called Hlér [wind-shielded]. Wind is a metaphor for death, being shielded against it is a metaphor for immortality. Here, the term is used to describe Heimdall.

306 Ulfr Uggason was a skald who lived during the 10th century, his poem Húsdrápa was composed ca. 965 AD. How and when he composed the poem is described in the Laxdæla saga 29: "The wedding feast was a very crowded one, for the new hall was finished. Ulf Uggason was of the bidden guests, and he had made a poem on Olaf Hoskuldson and of the legends that were painted round the hall, and he gave it forth at the feast. This poem is called the "House Song," and is well made. Olaf rewarded him well for the poem."

307 «þeir váru í selalíkjum" – they were in the likenesses of seals. This is the only known (surviving) reference to their taking the shape of seals, the myth it refers to is otherwise lost to us.

308 The first part of this paragraph about metaphors for Loki in the Skáldskaparmál is quoted in chapter 1

309 Singasteinn: possibly from singirnast – "to desire for oneself" or singirni: stinginess, selfishness

310 "Hér er þess getit, að Heimdallr er son níu mæðra." This assertion from Skaldskaparmal 23 is also confirmed in Gylfaginning 27: Ok enn segir hann sjálfr í Heimdallargaldri: Níu em ek mæðra mögr/níu em ek systra sonr ["And as he himself says in the Spell-Song of Heimdall: Of nine mothers am I child/ of nine sister am I son"], in the Edda poem Hyndluljóð 35-37 and in skaldic kennings like in the Húsdrápa quoted here.

311 Bonds=powers/gods – being a "friend of the gods" is a kenning often used for either Thor or Loki.

MARIA KVILHAUG

312 Men Storðar – the gem/ring/necklace of Earth – is actualy a
kenning for the Middle World Serpent, however in this context it
also alludes to the theme of the previous stanza, the Brisinga-men
[Freyia's "Gem of Flames"].

313 Otter's Compensation (or "Otter-Debt"): Ótrgjöld

314 Aesir traveled in order to know the world: æsir fóru at kanna
heim

315 Rage Ocean: Hreiðmarr.

316 Very cunning/versed in magic: mjök fjölkunnigr. The word
fjölkunnigr literally means "very cunning", so the adjective mjök
(very) appears superfluous, however, the fjöl- together with some
word for knowledge, wisdom or cunning (such as kunnigr) always
indicates that it is a particular form of knowledge that is linked to
magic, as such it means "versed in magic".

317 Fafnir – from ON fafna: "to embrace". Fafnir is a giant who
takes on the shape of a large serpent coiling itself around the treasure of the Red Gold. It is an allusion to the Middle World Serpent.

318 Red gold: rauðu gulli. Often appears a mysterious quality
encountered by gods and heroes on the path of initiation, a symbol
for divine wisdom and power.

319 Black Elf World: Svartalfaheimr. Like "white" refers to a
quality of lightness and brightness and even spiritual illumination,
"black" would refer to darkness and be associated with the underworld and hidden mysteries. When it came to skin color, the Norse
referred to red versus blue rather than white and black.

320 Andvari – from and: "spirit"/"breath" and vari:"alerted",
"guardian": Spirit/Breath Guardian/Alert.

321 A stone could in poetry be a metaphor for a burial mound,
but also for the heart or other vital organs connected to the inner
personality or courage of the person who owns the «stone». The
"red gold", likewise, appears to have a deeper, spiritual meaning
connected to a path towards knowledge and enlightenment.

322 Granahár: whisker – literally "beard/mouth hair": Gran
would otherwise refer to a beard, and indirectly to the mouth/lips.
Hár means "hair".

323 Nú er sagt, af hverju gull er Otrgjöld kallat eða Nauðgjald
Ásanna eða Rógmálmr.

324 Hialprekr – from hial: conversation, chat

325 Rage Ocean: Hreiðmarr

326 Fiölkynnig – "Much Knowing"/"Very Cunning" = Versed in
magic, knowing secret arts

327 The Waterfall of Spirit Alert: Andvarafors

328 Spirit Alert: Andvari

329 In the likeness of a pike: I geddo liki

330 Otter: Otr

331 In the likeness of an otter: i otrs lici

332 "...with the Red Gold": "...Með rauðo gulli"

333 Rán – "Robbery" – was the giantess/goddess of the ocean, married to Aegir and mother to the nine daughters who function as waves, lights in Aegir's hall of immortality, and as the nine mothers of Heimdallr. She was pictured as a woman fishing for drowned men with her net; if she caught them, their souls woud reside in her hall and have a banquet with her and her daughters. To drown at sea was often referred to as making love to Rán or her daughters, or to feast with them.

334 Lindar Logi: The Flame of the Serpent = the Red Gold.

335 Óinn appears as the name of a dwarf or as a serpent in some Norse sources, but the meaning of the name is obscure, although it could mean "The Frightened One".

336 Days Before: árdaga, this is the time of origin, creation.

337 Vaðgelmir: The Noise of Standstill, or more precisely, the Standstill-Roarer. From gelmir: the bellowing, howling, roaring, noisy one, and vað from vaða: to wade – this is a reference to the river of punishment in Hel, where oath-breakers, rapists and murderers, among others, are doomed to wade without getting forward – a standstill (Völuspá st. 36, 39, Poetic Edda). It could also derive from váði (m.sg): accident, danger, misfortune ("Noise of Misfortune").

338 Blowing Breath: Gustr – the name means "gust", a blow of breath, a blow of wind, related to the verb gusta: to blow. It is likely a heiti for Andvari – Alert Spirit.

339 The Ring of Spirit Alert: Andvaranautr

340 The Embracer: Fafnir – possibly a poetic allusion to the Middle World Serpent, who also has two brothers, the Fenrir-wolf and Nári/Narfi (or Sleipnir). Later on in Edda heroic poetry, the poem Fafnismál, this giant in serpent/dragon disguise coils himself around the Red Gold and wears the Helmet of Terror (Aegirhjalmr). When the hero Sigurð slays him, he drinks of his blood and enters a trance where he has a vision of a sleeping goddess. Wearing all the red gold, he enters her abode and wakes her up.

341 Since Loki and Thor have no role to play in the continuing storyline, I have left the rest of this poem (and all the other heroic poems that are dealing with the quest for the "red gold") for another book and concentrated on this part of the story - of how Loki and Óðinn first discovers the "red gold" that is also referred to in the stories of Freyia´s gem (chapter 9), the ring Dripper (chapter 8), and Balder´s death (chapter 12), where it is clearly linked to resurrection from Hel.

342 Here we are back to what happened right after the account of Thor´s trials in the Outer World described in the previous chapters of Gylfaginning (chapter 43-47) – see chapter 5 for these chapters.

343 Hymir – «Hymn» / «Humming», on par with Ymir – «Murmurer»/ «Sound», Skrymir – «Bragging»/ «Speaking Loudly» and even Mimir – «Memory»/ «Murmurer» , all giants of the Outer World.

344 Himinhrjóðr – "the one who tears up Heaven"

345 «Summoned his divine power»: færðist í ásmegin

346 Valtívar; from val: choice, chosen, the ones who die in battle, and tívar: gods. Val may also mean "hawk" or "falcon", often used when the gods assume a falcon/hawk hide, and possibly an allusion to the "wind-diminishing" hawk that sits between the eyes of the eagle who creates the winds of death (see chapter 4).

347 «Carved twigs»: hristo teina =Rune staves.

348 The giant lord of the [cosmic] ocean; "The Terrifying One". This is a reference to the banquet that the Aesir held in honor of Aegir as stated in Skáldskaparmál 1(see chapter 4). Towards the end of the banquet, Aegir is compelled to invite the Aesir for a banquet in his hall at the Wind-Shielded (immortal) Island (see chapter 12, Skáldskaparmál 41), but declares that the Aesir must come with a cauldron large enough to hold all his mead – the ocean itself (or the Cosmic ocean). In this poem, we understand that the challenge is a vengeance of the labor they have caused him, a labor not explained further in other available sources.

349 Miscorblindi – otherwise, Aegir´s father is said to be Fornjótr ["The Previous Owner/Enjoyer"]

350 Yggr is another name for Óðinn, his child being Thor. The name Yggr, like Aegir, means "terrifying" or could else refer to someone/something very ancient. It is also a part of the name Yggdrasill.

351 The word used for «cauldron» here is hverr – the same word used in the name for the well in Hel; Hvergelmir [Bellowing Cauldron]

352 Týr is the god of victory, what may be significant; This is the adventure that finally renders Thor victorious after his encounter with Outer World Loki (see chapter 5) insofar as he is able to fetch the cauldron that may hold all the precious mead.

353 Elivágar; these «waves of the ages» are described in the creation myths as cold streams running from Níflheim [Misty World/ the world of the dead] into Ginnungagap, where they are met with streams from Muspell [the world of heat], which cause them to warm up and create the world giant Ymir [Sound, Murmur], from which the universe is shaped (Gylfaginning 5-6).

354 Egill may, according to Simek, be the father of Thialfi and Röskva, Thor's servants. This because of a hint offered in stanza 38 of this comment, linking Egill to the story in Gylfaginning 43 [chapter 5 in this book] where a farmer has to offer up his children to the god after laming Thor's ram.

355 Grandmother: Amma. If the «Son» is Thor [Thor is usually «the son»], then his grandmother is the terrifying giantess Nött: Night, mother of Earth (see chapter 1).

356 Thor's mother is Earth, so the one who carries ale to "her son" Thor is the Earth mother. The offering of ale is symbolic of the mead of inspiration, poetry and immortality. Recall Long-Beard's [Óðinn's] suggestion that Thor should seek his mother Earth to show him the way to the lands of the gods (Harbardsljóð 56, Poetic Edda, see chapter 5).

357 The gods are descended from the jötnar according to all Norse myths about their descent

358 Hróðr: from hróði: quarrel/conflict/fight, un-peace: identified with the Greed-wolf Fenrir; Týr is known in this kenning by being his enemy. Thus, Tyr is the one who follows Thor to his mother, who live in the giant world (Outer World) as a concubine to this frost giant.

359 Veorr/Veurr: from vé: temple, or arr:warrior or vördr: guardian, a known heiti for Thor.

360 Bergdanir – literally "Mountain-Danes" – but the meaning is "Mountain-Men". Mountain-men is a heiti for giants, their breaker is Thor. This kenning also applies the word Danes for "men": as we saw in the Skaldic poem of chapter 7, Thorsdrápa, poets could apply the names of foreign tribes, particularly competing or hostile ones, to indicate giants. In this case, the Norwegian poet thought that "Danes" was an appropriate, metaphorical way of describing giants.

361 Hlunngotr: Hlunn is a kind of wave (there were many words for different kinds of waves), gotr actually means «Goth», as in a person from Götaland in Sweden. However, for some reason or other, it was also used to mean "steed" or "horse". A "Wave-Goth" means a "Wave Horse", which is a kenning for "boat".

362 Hreingalkn refers here to the Middle World Serpent, but the meaning is uncertain. Galkn means a monster, troll or terrible being. Hrein would either mean "pure", "clean" or else "reindeer". A "Reindeer-troll" would be a good Norse kenning for a wolf [hunting reindeer, the "troll" of reindeer], the wolf again a kenning for a hunter or an enemy, like the Middle World Serpent. Or else it is the "troll" – enemy – of all that is pure. Most scholars believe it is supposed to be a hraungalkn: a rock troll/rock giant.

363 Cauldron: hverr. The kenning is both an allusion to the theme of the cauldron, and part of a kenning for "canyon" – a "cauldron" of the forest-clad (holtriþa) hills.

364 Basically, the cauldron covers Thor from top to toe when he carries it upside down over his head. This is an allusion to the meaning of the precious mead as being the essence of divine wisdom, power and immortality, now completely engulfing the initiate, Thor.

365 This part actually refers to the story rendered in chapter 5, Gylfaginning 43-48, where Thor's ram is damaged as Thialfi, on Loki's suggestion, breaks one of its legs to suck out the marrow. It seems odd that this is mentioned now, a long time after these events, as if it suddenly happened on the way home from Hymir; such contradictions are bound to happen where there is no dogma to the stories, many different oral storytellers over many generations, and no written fasit.

366 Stanza 37-38 appears to be referring to the children, Thialfi and Röskva [Binding Together and Maturing], Thor's servants (see chapter 5).

367 Aegir's place is Hlésey, the Wind-Shielded Island, that is, a state of immortality.

368 Baldr, a name meaning "bold", "courageous", "brave", in a particularly honorable way.

369 Balder's Brow: Baldrs brár, modern Norwegian; Balderbrå, Latin; Tripleurospermum inodorum

370 Bjartr: fair of color, bright, light

371 Liknasamastr: fair in the sense of adhering completely to justice.

372 Breidablikr – a way of symbolizing the broad-mindedness of Balder.

373 Here, Snorri quotes from Grimnismál 12, Poetic Edda

374 Ali eða Vali: Ali is otherwise known as the son of Loki, even appears in a kenning for Loki, "Ali's Father", or as a kenning for Hel, "Ali's sister". The meaning is uncertain, perhaps from áll: eel, or something that grows or sprouts, or else a current in the ocean, or a creak in a rock.

375 Váli means "the choice", "the chosen", or "the dead" [as in the dead chosen for a blessed afterlife]. Váli is also mentioned as a son of Loki with Sígyn, but here he appears as Óðinn's son.

376 Rindr/Hrindr/Rinda: from hrinda: to reject, throw away. Her story is told in Saxo Grammaticus Gesta Danorum, where she was a human princess much set on riches, who rejected Óðinn's advances until he tricked her and fathered Vali on her. Óðinn was exiled for the crime. Rind is also mentioned in Gróagaldr, where she received nine spell-songs from Rán ["Robbery"], the goddess of the ocean, and was told to shake her burdens from her shoulders and lead her own way.

377 Valgaldr: from val: choice, chosen, the chosen dead, death, and galdr:spell-songs

378 Rindr/Hrindr/Rinda: from hrinda: to reject, strike back. Her story is told in Saxo Grammaticus Gesta Danorum, where she was a human princess much set on riches, who rejected Óðinn's advances until he tricked her and fathered Vali on her. Óðinn was exiled for the crime. Rind is also mentioned in Gróagaldr, where she received nine spell-songs from Rán ["Robbery"], the goddess of the ocean, and was told to shake her burdens from her shoulders and lead her own way.

379 May also refer to the chosen dead, the worthy of Valhalla

380 This is an indication that the Wand-Witch is not the one she appears to be, but rather Loki himself, whose gender ambivalence allows for a pun on his being the "mother" of three thurse children; Hel, Fenrir and the Middle World Serpent. Otherwise, the hidden character is their actual mother, Angrbóða.

381 He is referring to the journey to Hymir where Thor fished the Middle World Serpent (chapter 11)

382 See the poem above in this chapter; The Song of Way-Wont or Balder's Dreams

383 "The Beloved": The mother goddess, associated with Venus [Friggjarstjarna – «Frigg's star»], wife to Óðinn and mother to Balder.

384 "Took the likeness of a woman": brá sér í konu líki

385 Frigg's abode is called Fensalar – The Moist Halls.

386 Mannhringr: The circle of men surrounding the target of a game

387 The Place of Truces is here called Griðastaðr, there was also a giantess by the name Griðr – Truce – who helped Thor on his journey to Red Spear (see chapter 7), and who was also the mother of Óðinn's predestined successor, Víðarr the Silent. A place of Truces is a way of saying the parliament, the law court or a religious sanctuary, where no violence may be committed for no reason whatsoever. There are numerous references to "peace-sanctified" places of ritual, the oldest reference is in Latin and was written by the Roman chronicler Tacitus (Germania) as far back as 80 AD, explaining how, in certain groves, or even during a certain festival to the goddess Nerthus, no violence was committed or would be excused no matter the reason. People who broke this sacred truce would be exiled and without protection from the law no matter how justified they might have been in their anger. This was a way of ensuring peaceful gatherings during times of parliament or religious celebrations.

388 «To ride the Hel/Death-Path»: ríða á helveg

389 Hringhorn – Balder's ship (=life journey, fate) is an allusion to the sacred symbols of enlightenment; the red ring or other circular gem like the Brisingamen, representing divine completion and power, as well as the drinking horn from which the mead of memory, knowledge, poetry, wisdom, inspiration and immortality is drunk.

390 Nanna Nepsdóttir. The name Nanna may mean «to understand», but is often used as a heiti for «wife» or «woman». The ring symbolizes completion, wholeness, renewal and immortality.

391 «…to wed the pyre with the Grinder": vígði bálit með Mjöllni . This sentence echoes and old pagan ritual where Thor's hammer is applied to "wed" (sanctify) something during rituals, in this case a funeral pyre.

392 Gullinbursti heitir eða Slíðrugtanni: See chapter 7 where the boar is made by Sindri.

393 Gulltoppr – the name of Heimdall's horse.

394 Dripper: Draupnir – see chapter 7 about the treasures from the Black Elves

395 "…the river Bellower and traversed the Bellowing Bridge": árinnar Gjallar ok reið á Gjallarbrúna. The river Gjöll is the river lying closest to Hel, and the Gjallarbrú is the bridge to Hel. Allusions to the Gjallarhorn (the Bellowing Horn), through which Heimdall will blow and Mímir will drink the Mead of Memory.

396 Divine Rage: Móðguðr – a female guardian of the bridge to Hel.

397 lit dauðra manna [the use of the word litr – hue – to explain that Hermod was still alive may be connected to the earlier anecdote of the dwarf Lítr [Hue] that Thor kicked into the fire.

398 Helvegr – death path. To this day, Norwegians may wish someone "north and down" (nord og ned) if they truly hate them.

399 Helgrindr – death gate

400 Touching the death-gate would be equal to dying.

401 Fulla, Frigg's errand maid.

402 Þökk – gratitude, joy, thanks. The meaning of her name may be intentionally ironic. She appears to be the embodiment of ingratitude and selfishness – since she has never had any joy in Balder, she does not care if the rest of the world weeps.

403 Fire of Aegir: Eld Ægis

404 Barr Glasis [Glasir is the tree which stands outside of Valhalla's door, evergreen and sacred. Its name refers to glass or crystal].

405 Haddr Sifjar (The Kinswoman's Hair)

406 Höfuðband Fullu – Fulla [the Fulfilled One] is otherwise a goddess in service to Frigg, a messenger.

407 The Weeping of Freyia: Grátr Freyju

408 Munntal ok Rödd ok Orð Jötna

409 Dropa Draupnis ok Regn eða Skúr Draupnis [Draupnir – «The Dripper» - was the self-renewing ring that was given to the gods [see chapter 7] and that was placed on Balder's pyre (this chapter, and chapter 10).

410 Augna Freyiu (according to Snorri, Freyia wept tears of red gold – figurines from the Bronze Age depict a goddess with golden eyes, driving the chariot of the Sun with serpentine reins).

411 Otrgjöld (see chapter 10)

412 Nauðgjald Ásanna (see chapter 10)

413 Sáð Fýrisvalla – Fýrisvellir referred geographically to the plains close to the temple of Uppsala, and derives from the word fyrva – to "ebb", this was where people could leave their ships. According to a story about Hrólf Kraki found in many texts, Hrólf spread gold on this plain as he and his men were fleeing the Swedish king Adils. The king's men then dismounted to collect the gold.

414 Haugþak Hölga [A haugr means a burial mound, and here is a reference to a myth about the roof within Hölgir's burial mound. Hölgir may refer to the ancestral father of the Háleygir, the northermost tribe of Norsemen in Norway, who lived in Hálógaland].

415 Eldr allra vatna ok Handar – here, the gold refers to the light that shines in waters [lakes, seas, streams, rivers] or the light that shines from the gems worn on arms and hands.

416 Grjót ok Sker eða Blik Handar- here, the gold refers to the rings and gems worn on the arms by people.

417 See chapter 4, Aegir's visit to the Aesir was described in the beginning of the Skáldskaparmál.

418 See chapter 11; here is a reference to the upcoming banquet and the cauldron-challenge mentioned in the Edda poem Hymiskvíða 2-3.

419 Farinn í Austervég – the eastern paths refer to the giant world, the Outer World.

420 Glowing gold: lysigull. Gold appears to be a metaphor for divine power and spiritual illumination, associated with immortality.

421 "...just as there in Valhalla had been swords for fire": sem í Valhöllu váru sverðin fyrir eld

422 Þræl – in this prose version, Fimafengr is called slave, whereas in the other he is called servant.

423 «Rán er nefnd kona hans, en níu dætr þeira, svá sem fyrr er ritat. At þeiri veizlu vannst allt sjálft, bæði vist ok öl ok öll reiða, er til veizlunnar þurfti.Þá urðu æsir þessir varir, at Rán átti net þat, er hon veiddi í menn alla, þá er á sæ kómu»

424 ...at gull er kallat Eldr eða Ljós eða Birti Ægis, Ránar eða Ægis dætra

425 Ok af þeim kenningum er nú svá sett, at gull er kallat Eldr Sævar ok allra hans heita, svá sem Ægir eða Rán eigu heiti við sæinn

426 ok þaðan af er nú gull kallat Eldr Vatna eða á ok allra árheita

427 Bragi hinn gamli Boddason, a famed poet who lived between ca. 800-850 AD in Norway.

428 Here is an example of what Snorri explained just before; that gold may be called, in kenningar, the "fire of the sea" – or of any other heiti or kenning for the sea, such as "the Seat of the Mackerel". The "Fire" of the "Seat of the Mackerel" is, thus, a kenning for "gold". While gold is in itself symbolic of some spiritual mystery in the mythological poems, everyday life poems could use the same kennings to also describe actual gold: Bragi had evidently received gold from a prince, and was here probably trying to pay the prince back with a gratitude poem, much like we saw Thióðolf making a poem as a way of saying thank you for a painted shield that he had received.

429 The kenning "Giant's Draught" is an allusion to the mead owned by giants such as Mímir or Suttungr, the mead of memory and inspiration and poetry. In this context, the mead of poetry refers to poetry itself, or to the particular poem composed by Bragi; he is saying that he received gold for the poem he is now composing. By using the kenning "Mountain-Fiölnir" for "giant", the poet also alludes to Óðinn, the god of poetry who actually restored the mead (Fiölnir, "the one who is many", is a heiti for Óðinn). A poet could use the name of any god and combine it with the associations of rock, caves or mountains in order to make a kenning for "giant" – just like they could use the name of any goddess and combine her name with words associated with giantesses in order to make a kenning for "giantess".

430 The prince either actually gave Bragi his gold-payment in a cup, a symbolic gesture which was now used to make an allusion to the mead of poetry, and thus to the poem itself, or else, Bragi felt inspired by the gift he had received from the prince, and compliments the prince (or his gift) as being the source of his inspiration, making this compliment or declaration of gratitude to the prince through the language of allegory and metaphor.

431 The name means «terrifying» and refers to an ocean giant, said to be married to the ocean goddess Rán [Robbery] who receives the drowned in her net. Their nine daughters are said to be the waves, although they are also parallels to the nine giantesses who birthed Heimdallr [Great World], our universe. Aegir is also known as Hlér – "wind-shielded", and lives on Hlésey [The Wind Shielded Island], wind being a metaphor for death and mortality. As we saw in the Hymiskviða [chapter 11], Hýmir is also identified as "wind-shielded"- Vindhler. Here, he is also identified with Gýmir.

432 Gýmir is otherwise known as the father of Gerðr ["Yard, Enclosure, Fenced/Walled Settlement"], wife to the god Freyr, whose story of wooing her in the underworld is told in the Edda poem Skírnismál. The name Gýmir is typical of giants [Skrymir, Ymir, Hymir etc] but unusually enough does not refer to any kind of sound; rather it may derive from geyma – "to hide, keep, protect" [he keeps his daughter hidden in the underworld]. This is the only source where Gýmir is identified with Aegir.

433 The Great Kettle: Ketill inn micla – a reference to Hymiskviða (chapter 11)

434 Byggvìr – literally «Barley-Man» although the –vír, like verr, usually refers to a man in the sense of being a husband or lover, related in meaning to the word "virile". Barley was important for brewing ale.

435 Beyla – the meaning of her name has been debated, but a good case has been made for «Little Bee» from Germanic *biulio. Honey was important for brewing mead. Could also be related to baula: "cow".

436 Fimafengr: from fimi: fast, swiftness , hurry, quick, nimble, clever [quick of mind] and fengr: catch, supply, prize [something that has been caught, gathered, fished, hunted, taken in war, won].

437 Eldir – from eld: fire, eldir: the one who lits the fire.

438 Gríðarstaðr: "Place of Truce" – a place where peace/truce is sacred; to break the peace or commit an act of violence/hostility meant that you lost all your cases no matter what, and you could become exiled or lose your life for such sacrilege. This ensured the possibility for enemies to show up at the same place to raise their cases or partake in ritual without danger.

439 Loptr : "Air" – one of Loki´s other names

440 This is not just any mead or drink: the precious mead, mæran mjöðr, is a reference to the sacred mead of poetry, inspiration, wisdom and immortality.

441 The goddesses who are wives to the Aesir are called Ásynior.

442 This formula appears often and may have been a common prayer – one which Loki profanes.

443 This is a reference to an (to us) unknown (unpreserved) myth. However, the heroic Edda poems are crammed with the theme of a valkyria who loves her own brother's enemy.

444 Another reference to an unpreserved myth. Gefion [Provider], a goddess credited with the founding of Zealand in Denmark, is a name often used for any goddess or woman associated with generosity and mead, ölgefion/ölgefn, as we saw in chapters 4 & 6, the name is used for both the elfin goddess Iðunn and for the healing witch-giantess Gróa. Gefiun is a form of Gefn, which Snorri identified as a heiti for Freyia.

445 This is another obscure reference to myths we do not know anymore. However, the reference resonates with the story of how Loki changed into a mare in heat and gave birth to Sleipnir [chapter 3], and to how he changed shape and became a woman before visiting Frigg, as well as his appearance as a wand-witch in Vegtamskvíða [this chapter] and as the selfish giantess Tökk [this chapter], and there is a reference to Loki becoming pregnant from eating the burnt heart of a woman in the Edda poem Hyndlyljóð [see The Poetic Edda [volume one]- Six Cosmology Poems]. The bickering between Óðinn and Loki in this poem, accusing each other for unmanly behavior in the past, is also echoed in an exchange between Sinfiötli and Gudmundr in the Edda poem Helgakvíða Hundingsbani.

446 Yet another reference to myths we do not know because they were not preserved for us; however, it is not the only reference. In the Edda poem Hávamál, Óðinn declares that he can speak truthfully about men and women both, because he has been both. In Saxo Grammaticus Gesta Danorum, Óðinn takes the shape of a wise woman in order to forcefully father Váli on Rinda. In general, gender-bending appears quite often in Norse myths and is associated with the journey into other worlds.

447 Víðrir= Óðinn [Óðinnsheiti], kvæn=woman, wife [relat-
ed to the English word for queen]. This is a reference to a myth
explained by Snorri where Óðinn disappears for such a long time
that his two brothers, Víli [Will] and Vé [Shrine], start to rule the
realm and marry Frigg. As soon as Oðinn returned, he took his wife
(kvæn) back.

448 According to Snorri, marrying one's own sibling had been
common among the Vanir. Otherwise, we do not know what myth
this exact event refers to, as it is one of the unpreserved myths
only hinted at in our sources.

449 Again, a reference to a myth the audience then knew, but
which has been lost to us. Since Hymir appears to be another ocean
giant, identifiable to Aegir, the maidens must refer to the nine
daughter waves.

450 The excellent, unhated son who was begot in compensation
for Njörð's being sent as a hostage to the "maidens of Hymir" is
Freyr, the god of growth, fertility, law, order and kingship.

451 Snorri testifies to this divine incest in the Ynglinga saga 4,
saying; "When Njörðr was among the Vanir, then he had been married to his sister, for it was legal there, their children were Freyr
and Freyia. Among the Aesir it was forbidden to marry such close
relations." (Þá er Njörðr var með Vönum, þá hafði hann átta systur
sína, því at þat váru þar lög; váru þeirra börn Freyr ok Freyja.
En þat var bannat með Ásum at byggja svá náit at frændsemi.)
. Scholars have sometimes tried to figure out who this sister/wife
may have been, and she has often been identified with the Nerthus
of Roman sources – an Iron Age goddess associated with the union
of tribes, with drowning and with water (a lake or small sea). As
the god of winds and waves and harbors, Njörðr and his sister/wife
of death in water appear to echo the older giant couple, Aegir and
Rán, whose nine daughters may be the mothers of Heimdallr – just
as they here appear involved in the conception of Freyr by pissing
into his father's mouth. In chapter 6, we saw the concept of giantesses pissing into water and creating floods. There are no more
sources to detail this very special conception.

452 Fenrir, the wolf of Greed.

453 Hróðvitnir – Rage Witness = Fenrir [Greed], Loki's son. Týr
is pointing out that while he misses his hand because of Loki's son,
Loki misses his son because of him.

454 Ragnarökr – "Shattering of the Rulers" – the apocalyptic
end of the present world order (See ch.13).

455 A reference to another unpreserved myth in which Loki has a son by an otherwise unknown wife of Týr – we do not know anymore about this story. By Norse laws, if a man dishonored another man by sleeping with his wife, he should by law pay a monetary compensation. That Týr never got compensation is a great dishonor to him that Loki now is pointing out, even though he was the culprit.

456 Another way of saying Ragnarökr

457 He is referring to Freyr wooing Gerðr, the daughter of Gymir [Skirnismál, Poetic Edda] and how he sold the sword that could fight by itself and defeat giants. Freyr is doomed to perish because of this.

458 The presence of Barley Man (Byggvir) and his female companion, Little Bee (Beyla) at this party, and the fact that Barley Man feels proud that everybody are drinking ale, probably has something to do with the fact that barley was important to brewing ale, while the bee's honey was important for brewing mead – these two are the spirits of the drink that is served.

459 The gravel [aurr] refers to the mud from the Urðarbrunnr – the Well of Origin. Every day, the oldest norn, Urðr [Origin], takes aurr [gravel, mud] grom this well and waters the world tree, which is replenished and rejuvenated as a result. As a symbol of the living, sentient, listening and all-seeing universe, Heimdallr ["Great World"] is an aspect of the world tree itself. See Völuspá, Poetic Edda.

460 A reference to the killing of Skaði's father [see chapter 4]. Loki is taunting her for having lost her father and that he, the main culprit, is still free.

461 Hrímcalci Mjöðr – the allusion to frost (hrím) is an indication of how this special mead-cup is hidden in the Underworld, Nífl-heimr, the realm of mist, frost and darkness.

462 The words used are ragr vettr: ragr roughly means shamed, perverted, vettr means "spirit" and is always female, meaning that Loki is being called by a feminine term, possibly referring to his gender bending.

463 Sígfaðir: «Victory Father» = Oðinn

464 East is the direction of the giant world in Norse myths.

465 See chapter 5, the story of Thor's visit to Outer World Loki

466 Thor is mockingly called einheri [sole ruler], otherwise a reference to the heroic warriors who have been chosen for Valhalla.

467 [See chapter 5; Thor's journey to Outer World Loki]

468 The waterfall of Foaming Rage: Fránangr

469 In the likeness of a salmon: I lax líki

470 This passage echoes a typical «origin of how something was made/came to be» myth; how fishing nets were invented – and credits Loki with this invention too.

471 Óðinn has a seat called Hliðskjálf, mentioned earlier in the Gylfaginning as well as in Edda poems such as Skírnismál, where the god Freyr uses the seat to watch into all the worlds, as this seat/shelf "of openings" had the quality that whoever sat in it would be able to look into all the worlds and know what was going on.

472 In another story told by Snorri in the Skáldskaparmál, Kvasir was created by the mead that had been brewed by the divine spit of all the Aesir and Vanir gods together, and he was the embodiment of wisdom. When he was killed, his blood became the precious mead of poetry and inspiration.

473 One of many indication that Thor was as strong as all the Aesir together.

474 Being griðalauss – «truce-less» - meant that you would be met without mercy, that there would be no peace for you, that you had no rights and no option to bargain – this was the situation for the outlaw, the already convicted criminal who was without further legal protection and could be treated as others saw fit.

475 The sons here appear to represent two options after death; the Vál of Valhalla, and the Nár of Hel.

476 The likeness of a wolf: vargslíki (Brugðu æsir Vála í vargslíki.)

477 «Mouth-Bath»: Mundlaugr – a vessel, cup.

478 Ragnarök literally translates as "Shattering of the Rulers" – from rök: shattering, and ragna: genitive plural form of reginn: ruler. Usually, the rulers in question are interpreted as the Aesir, who are shattered during Ragnarök, although "ruler" could be used for all the other divine and giant powers of the universe, as well as for human rulers. It is usually translated (or paraphrased) to the more Biblical "apocalypse".

479 There are many words for «great» in the Old Norse language, all with a slightly different meaning. In this case, fimbul means "great" but also "mysterious", "subtle". The word appears in other mythical concepts such as Fimbulþul – the Great/Mysterious/Subtle Reciting Sage.

480 It has been speculated that the prophecy about this three year long winter is based on an actual occurrence which happened in 536 AD, when volcanic eruptions elsewhere led to a volcanic winter and a small ice age – and indeed a winter that lasted for three years. The incident led to great famine and need, was followed by a period of pestilence – the first known case of the Black Death – and the collapse of societies all over Northern Europe. One of the results was that the proto-Norse language changed into the Old Norse that we know. Another was an increase in ritual sacrifice and the building of great burial mounds.

481 Völuspá 45, Poetic Edda (See The Poetic Edda – Six Cosmology Poems)

482 Giant Rage: jötunmóð

483 Naglfar: «Nail traveler», the ship of Muspell.

484 Hrymr: from hrymjast – «to weaken» (from within) or hruma – "to weaken (something else)." In Völuspá 51, Loki is the one who steers the Naglfar, while Hrymr is mentioned in st. 50, fighting the gods. This name is otherwise not known to us, although it could be a heiti for Loki, who has been weakened or who is weakening the gods.

485 Múspellheimr is the primordial, cosmic realm of heat, fire and poison that contributed to the creation of the first life and awareness in the universe according to the beginning of Gylfaginning.

486 Surtr – the name is usually taken to mean "sooted", "burnt" or "black" (as in burnt black), although it also has some allusion to "sour" and "acid". He is the lord of Múspellheimr and the arch enemy/nemesis of the Vanir god Freyr, who is the lord of growth and fertility. In other versions, he fights with Beli.

487 Bifröst, from bífa – to shiver, tremble, and röst: voice. The rainbow bridge to the realm of the gods.

488 Freyr is actually the god of growth, fertility, law, order, and cultivated nature. He must fight the leader of the realm of poisonous gases and heat, a leader symbolic of the ashes and soot that remains after a fire.

489 Skírnir: from skirr: shining, bright, pure, clean. Skírnir plays a major role in the Edda poem Skírnismál, where he is a servant of Freyr and plays the role of a court shaman who travels to the underworld on behalf of his lord in order to woo the a hidden maiden whose arms illuminate the sky and the ocean – the giantess Gerd, daughter of Gýmir (=Aegir, Hymir). For payment, Skírnir receives "the sword which fights by itself against giants and thurses", and this is why Freyr is without a good weapon when Ragnarök comes, and must fight with an antler instead.

490 Garmr (Gluttony?)is otherwise mentioned in the Edda poems Grímnismál 44, and in the Völuspá 44, 49, 58 (see The Poetic Edda – Six Cosmology Poems). Some have assumed that it is the same dog which barks at Óðinn in the Edda poem Vegtamskvíða (see chapter 12), the Hound of Hel. Snorri lets Týr fight this particular wolf/dog, which gives association where I personally think it is due; to the Fenris-wolf (Greed). The nature of heiti, nicknames, means that a character will appear with several different names, and must be recognized through function, attributes, associations and relations.

491 Gnipahelli; The Protruding Cave - this is where Garmr is bound according to the Völuspá.

492 «...carry the bane-words of...»: bera banaorð af – this is a way of saying that he shall conquer, be victorious, be his bane.

493 ok stígr þaðan braut níu fet: That Thor walks "nine steps" before he dies is symbolic is some way, the number nine being associated with the number of worlds ruled by Hel (mortality), with the ninth world in which Freyia rules the further fate of dead souls (and from where you may be sent to Valhalla), with the number of nights it takes to reach the core of the underworld, with the number of nights it takes to know your fate after death, and with the number of nights of initiation, and with the number of previous worlds.

494 Norse myths should often be read as parables, what becomes easy as soon as we consider the meanings of names: When Óðinn – The Spirit – is swallowed by Fenrir – Greed – the sentence should read; "Spirit is swallowed by Greed, that is its bane."

495 Víðarr the Silent (see chapter 7 and Lokasenna, chapter 12) is Óðinn´s son by the giantess called Gríðr – Truce, destined to take over after his father. His name means "Wood Warrior", wood being a symbol of the physical body of the universe and of human beings. It could also bear association to "widening", as in silent expansion (of the spirit). Víðarr is the only mead-serving male god in the lore (Lokasenna).

496 hverr maðr skal lifa í nökkurum heimi um allar aldir. This represents a firm belief in the eternal life of the human soul, that it shall always be living in some world or other.

497 Gimlé: from gimr: glimmer (from fire, flame) and -lé = hlér: shielded, protected place, as in windshield, a place of immortality such as Hlésey, where Aegir lives. Gimlé is mentioned in the Edda poem Völuspá 64, where it is presented as a hall covered with "gold", in which people will survive after Ragnarök. According to Snorri in Gylfaginning 3-5, Gimlé is a heaven where good people will live after their deaths and lies in the third heaven Víðbláinn [Expanding Dead/Wide Death (bláinn - "the blue" is a heiti for a corpse, or for death].

498 This emphasis on good drink in the afterlife is not just because Viking Age Norsemen were alcoholics (although they enjoyed drinking, obviously), but is a reference to the sacred mead of inspiration, memory and immortality.

499 The name Brímir appears to be derived from the masculine noun brími: "fire" – an odd name for a hall standing in the middle of a realm known as "Shielded from Fire". However, it could also be derived from the neutral noun brim, meaning "high sea", "high tide wave" or "wave splashing hard against the shore", the kind of wave that would make it hard to embark ashore. The Norse language, developed among seafarers, had many words for different kinds of waves. Waves were important symbols in poetry as well, playing a part in the very creation of the universe. I have chosen the latter meaning, although the association to fire is also sensible, a sort of enigma of a fire hall within the fire-protected realm – where it is never cold. The realm of the gods and norns was situated in a mythical (not geographical) "south", from where the Sun also derives, and all the good powers. It serves as a divine counterpart/ benevolent alter ego to Múspellheimr. In the Völuspá, Brímir is mentioned twice (9 & 37) as a giant, and in Grímnismál 40, we hear of an ale-hall owned by the giant called Brímir (bjórsal jötuns, en sá Brímir heitir). Here, the hall itself is called Brímir.

500 Ókólnir – literally «un-cold», as in «warm», or "where it is never cold".

501 rauðu gulli : the red gold appears to be symbolic of divine power, spiritual enlightenment, immortality.

502 Sindri is otherwise known as the blacksmith dark elf/dwarf of Skáldskaparmál 33 (see chapter 8) who forges the golden boar Gullinbursti, the ring Draupnir (see ch.12 & 8), the ship Skíðblaðnir and the hammer Miöllnir. Here, he has become another divine hall of the afterlife.

503 In an age and culture that saw a great deal of violence, there was a difference between killing another human for the sake of righteous vengeance (if that person had killed or seriously dishonored (raped or maimed) some of your family, if there had been a lawful man-to-man combat or a war. If a person had killed someone, they would have to publicly declare their deed and explain why if they hoped to be let go with a fine and compensation. But people who killed someone for no convincing reason, and then tried to run away from the responsibility or hide the deed from the public were condemned as lowly murder-wargs (morðvargar) and would lose all legal protection against those who wished to avenge the murder.

504 Cauldron-Bellower: Hvergelmir – the watersource of all the cosmic rivers, situated in Hel, a place where the souls of dead people are disintegrated.

505 Shame Biter: Níðhöggr. Niðr roughly translates as shame, something shameful. Another, more direct meaning is "low", "beneath", "nether", such as in the Niðafjöll, Nether Mountains, and this does not have to bear any negative meaning.

506 Those readers who have seen my translation of the Völuspá 38-39 in The Poetic Edda – Six Cosmology Poems may notice small but significant differences between this translation and that of the other book. In the other version, the vǫlva says "She sees a hall standing…" (Sal sá hon standa). In this version, it says "I know a hall…" (Sal veit ek standa). This is because there are slightly different versions of the same poem, and Snorri's version differs somewhat from the other manuscripts. Stanza 39 is even more different between the two versions, as the other version goes; "There she saw wading/ in heavy currents/ oath-breakers/ greed-murderers (murder wargs)/ and those who by force take the beloveds of others (ok þanns annars glepr eyrarúnu)/ there sucks the Shame Biter/ from their dead rotten bodies/ wolves tear them/Do you understand now, or what?" Snorri simply wrote down a different or altered version of the same.

507 Two of the main divine survivors of Ragnarök are these two sons of Óðinn – the one who "avenged the father" by destroying Greed, and Váli – "The Choice" - the one who "avenged the brother" by bringing Blind Strife to the pyre. Of the divine survivors in general, there are six named male children and two named females – the Sun's daughter and the reborn Earth.

508 This is Snorri's version of the Vafþrúðnismál 51 (see The Poetic Edda – Six Cosmology Poems)

509 Snorri here quotes from the Vafþrúðnismál 45 (see The Poetic Edda – Six Cosmology Poems)

510 Snorri here quotes from the Vafþrúðnismál 45 (see The Poetic Edda – Six Cosmology Poems)

511 The dialogue between Wandering Learner and the three aspects of Óðinn takes the form of a word-duel in which the one who asks questions must know a little about the answers in order to judge whether the one who replies knows the answers or not – if he were to ask the impossible, what happens even further into the future, then he should be able to answer that himself.

512 Gangleri, Wandering Learner, had so far believed that he was standing in the hall of the Aesir.

513 This is an explanation of the origin of the myths; they were told after a vision. As we can also see from what follows, the idea is that the gods actually did not get names for themselves or for anything else until they had told their stories first; the stories made them come alive and gave them identity – the entire world being the result of a story told over and over. Basically, this is in tune with many other spiritual traditions in which the world is, ultimately, an illusion, a theme that repeats itself in Norse mythology.

514 Image description taken from: https://en.wikipedia.org/wiki/ Gosforth_Cross

ABOUT THE AUTHOR

Maria Kvilhaug was born in Oslo, Norway, in 1975. She studied History of Religions and Old Norse Philology at the university of Oslo. She has written several non-fiction and fiction books concerning Old Norse Pre-Christian culture and religion.

http://www.bladehoner.wordpress.com
http://www.youtubecom/user/ladyoft-helabyrinth

NON-FICTION:
The Maiden with the Mead (2004/2009)
The Seed of Yggdrasill (2013/2018/2020)
The Poetic Edda, Six Cosmology Poem (2017/2021)
The Trickster and the Thunder god, Thor and Loki in Old Norse Myths (2018)

FICTION:
Blade Honer Series:
The Hammer of Greatness
My Enemy´s Head
The He Rune´s Claim
A Twisted Mirror

The Three Little Sisters

The Three Little Sisters is an indie publisher that puts authors first. We specalize in the strange and unusual. From titles about pagan and heathen spirituality to traditional fiction we bring books to life.

https://the3littlesisters.com

Printed in the USA
CPSIA information can be obtained
at www.ICGtesting.com
LVHW022018171023
761321LV00015B/486

9 781959 350132